AUTHOR'S PREFACE AND ACKNOWLEDGMENTS

NEARLY FORTY YEARS AGO, as Editor of The *Stanford Alumni Magazine,* it was my privilege to attend the first press conference held by Herbert Hoover as President-elect of the United States. This took place in the basement recreation room of his home on the Stanford University Campus. My mission was to obtain a personal message from our most distinguished alumnus for the Stanford people who had worked for his election. His secretary, George Akerson merely said, "Word it as you wish, and I will get The Chief's okay."

When that short message topped my editorial page I did not dream of the years of research and travel I would devote later to chronicle Herbert Hoover's service to the world. It began in 1949 when a publisher asked me to use my Stanford memories and acquaintances for a book about some of the more personal aspects of Hoover's life. A short time before this Eugene Lyons characterized him in a book entitled "Our *Unknown* Thirty-first President."

Two years later a request came from The Chief's office to postpone publication because of the forthcoming "Hoover Memoirs." This was done, and the publisher withdrew his proposal. Up to then many friends and acquaintances had shared their memories with me and had guided my research. Because I felt obligated to them I let the manuscript grow while I waited for an appropriate time to release it. Now, on the eve of the fortieth anniversary of Herbert Hoover's nomination and election to the Presidency, it is my privilege to present this volume as our gift to one of his lasting memorials, The Boys' Clubs of America.

It comes as a challenge to those who are groping for guidance in this puzzled world; as a hope-filled saga of a steadfast patriot who dedicated all that he was and possessed to his fellowmen and to his ideals for America.

It is my prayer that the story in the following pages may give new meaning to his life for these boys and others of a new generation as they read of the Quaker orphan who became in turn the highest paid and most widely-traveled engineer of his era, the unparalleled humanitarian of pre- and post-World War I years, Food Administrator, Secretary of Commerce, President of the United States, and wise Elder Statesman for more than thirty years.

Many of those who helped me in the early stages are now gone. Herbert Hoover's brother Theodore pulled long on his pipe and reminisced with me by the fireside of his California ranch home. Later this house with all its bookshelves of invaluable papers was destroyed by fire. He read and approved the first part of the manuscript and then said: "Now Herbert Hoover passes out of my ken." Their sister, May Hoover Leavit and Mrs. Hoover's sister, Jean Henry Large, were equally cooperative.

Mrs. David Starr Jordan, my neighbor on the Stanford campus, used her ebbing energy to listen and criticize. Edith Jordan Gardner, last surviving member of the Jordan family, read the first draft and contributed meaningful incidents. I am particularly indebted to Mrs. William H. Shockley who allowed me to read her late husband's letter books during the period when he, as a representative of Bewick-Moreing, had a part in Hoover's first overseas employment.

In his last years of life Edgar Rickard, mining engineer and publisher, Hoover's confidant and friend through most of their adult lives, answered my many questions. Suda Bane, Hoover's secretary during his Department of Commerce years and later curator of the Hoover Institution on War, Revolution and Peace, started my research there.

Charlotte Kellogg, only woman on the official roll of the Commission for the Relief of Belgium, shared her own and her

HERBERT HOOVER

A Challenge for Today

BRADFORD BACHRACH PHOTO
Carol Green Wilson

"Nearly forty years ago, as editor of the *Stanford Alumni Magazine,* it was my privilege to attend the first press conference held by Herbert Hoover as President-elect of the United States . . ." So begins the preface by Carol Green Wilson.

Over the intervening years, she researched deeply into his life, consulting published and unpublished works, letter books of his associates and family, and obscure files of old mining reports. She interviewed those who knew him, and those who worked for and with him.

Mrs. Wilson traveled to the various continents to interview and research wherever he had been. At one time, when the book was ready for publication, a request came from Hoover's office to postpone publication because of the forthcoming "Hoover Memoirs". The request was honored and the book continued to grow as the remarkable career of its subject expanded.

It was finally decided that on the ninety-fourth anniversary of his birth this biography would be published. In these times there is great urgency in its message to youth seeking identity, our legislators searching for solutions, and our statesmen seeking peace.

Mrs. Wilson, who is the author of six published biographies, graduated from Stanford University, Phi Beta Kappa, and was editor of the *Alumni Review* for ten years. She is the national historian of Kappa Alpha Theta. In 1966 she was given an "Award of Merit" by the California Historical Society.

BOOKS BY CAROL GREEN WILSON

CHINATOWN QUEST

CALIFORNIA YANKEE

GUMP'S TREASURE TRADE

ALICE EASTWOOD'S WONDERLAND

WE WHO WEAR KITES

ARTHUR FIEDLER: MUSIC FOR THE MILLIONS

HERBERT HOOVER

A Challenge for Today

BY CAROL (GREEN) WILSON

The Evans Publishing Company

NEW YORK

TO

OUR TWELVE

GRANDCHILDREN

Library of Congress Catalog Card Number 68-29040

Manufactured in the United States of America by
The Colonial Press Inc.

husband's memories. As we sat facing the blue Pacific through the windows of her Carmel home she took me through their experiences of 1914-17 and later of post-war Poland, as well as of their Washington associations with the Hoovers. Her introductions added to the interest of my interviews with eminent Belgians in 1951. At the time we were visiting our son, Lloyd, who was then district manager for Pan American World Airways and president of the American Club in Brussels. His affiliations gave me access to the *Fondation Universitaire* and the guidance of its director, Jacques van der Belen; to le Baron Carton de Wiart, former secretary to King Leopold II, and to Edgar Sengier, both of whom had gone to Hoover in England in 1914 as emissaries from the King to seek aid for their country. Many other Belgians including Firmin von Bree, then known as "King of the Congo," shared personal memories of their days with Hoover and the C.R.B.

Fred I. Kent, former president of the American Bankers Association, wrote me a long letter revealing hitherto unpublished data on the beginnings of American Relief in London in 1914. Adolph Miller of the Federal Reserve Board and a former neighbor of the Hoovers in Washington talked with me far longer than his watchful nurse approved.

In 1963 the late Maurice Pate, director of UNICEF, welcomed me to his office at the UN. I was introduced to him by Gilbert Redfern, a former associate in Hoover's humanitarian world service. Mr. Redfern had read my manuscript and urged me to study that phase of Hoover's life more thoroughly. Through Mr. Pate it was possible to let The Chief know before his own life ended that I had accomplished what I had hoped when I first asked his permission to start this project. Mr. A. Boyd Hinds, then Associate National Director of The Boys' Clubs of America and now National Director, was especially helpful.

My agent, Waldo Mayo, and his associate, Publisher Henry S. Evans, brought the project to fruition with untiring zeal. I thank both of them, as well as their friend, Edward J. Stapleton, Director of Public Information for The Boys' Clubs of America, who obtained permission from Richard M. Nixon to use his eloquent summation of Herbert Hoover's greatness. Both Mr. Stapleton and Mr. Nixon have my sincere appreciation.

Gratitude goes too, to Dr. Franz Lassner, director of the Hoover Presidential Library in West Branch, Iowa, for information and photographs; to Doctors Glenn and Rita Campbell of the Hoover Institution at Stanford for consultation and for pictures selected from their files; to my dear friend, Mrs. Gerrit J. Diekema, who gave me two autographed pictures sent by President Hoover to hang on the walls of the Embassy office when her husband was Minister to The Netherlands. Other illustrations were supplied by The Boys' Clubs of America through Mr. Stapleton in New York, and Mr. E. L. McKenzie, regional director in San Francisco.

Thanks are due also to Elsie Branner Fowler, daughter of Hoover's beloved Geology professor John Casper Branner, for stories of early Stanford years. Our life-long friends, Hugh and the late Eloise Fullerton opened their home in Washington to me and brought in many of Hoover's associates, including Tracy Kittredge; the late Lawrence Sullivan, author of "Prelude to Panic," a study of the depression of the 'thirties; the late William R. Castle, Hoover's neighbor and Undersecretary of State during part of his Presidency. Hugh Fullerton also introduced me to Laurene Anderson Small of Nevada City, once Hoover's secretary. In London I was fortunate to have the help of Alice King Stephen, Hoover's secretary during his early days in the British capital. I also had the understanding assistance of Ruth Fesler Lipman, one of Mrs. Hoover's secretaries and my own longtime friend. All through the years of preparation Bernice ("Bunny") Miller, Mr. Hoover's personal secretary and the daughter of a Stanford associate of mine, has lent a sympathetic ear.

It is not possible to list all the people who supplied first hand information about Hoover. Among them are members of the staffs of the Belgian-American Educational Foundation and the Hoover Commissions; of the many cooperative libraries including those at Stanford, the Bancroft Library at the University of

California, the Huntington Library in Pasadena and the Engineering Library in New York. At the Library of Congress, Miss Katharine Brand of the manuscript room made available the treasured papers of Robert Lansing, General Tasker H. Bliss, William Allen White and Senators Walsh and Norris. In Brussels I was welcomed at the *Bibleotechqué Royale* and in London the American Embassy arranged for access to early files of the *London Times.* Leaders of the Quaker faith from Oregon to Washington, D.C. shared their records; and Dr. David Elton Trueblood, our friend from the time he was the Chaplain of Stanford, graciously gave permission to quote from his graveside tribute to Herbert Hoover. Quotations from Mr. Hoover's books are included by permission of the Hoover Foundation.

The complete list of sources is much too long to include here. I can only say that without the faith of all these friends and the continuing support of my family I would never have had the courage to finish the rewarding task of amalgamating the various viewpoints. May the result reach a new generation with the story of a great American who was still punching the clock of self-imposed public service when death took him—two decades beyond the accepted three-score-years-and-ten.

Carol Green Wilson,
San Francisco

FOREWORD BY RICHARD M. NIXON

I could describe Herbert Hoover as a great statesman. I could describe him as a great businessman. I could describe him as a great humanitarian. But, above all, he will be remembered as a man of great character.

No leader in our history was more viciously vilified. Deserted by his friends, maligned by his enemies, he triumphed over adversity. In the twilight of his life he stood tall above his detractors. His triumph was a triumph of character. We can be thankful that he was one of those rare men who lived to hear the overwhelmingly favorable verdict of history on his career.

Two thousand years ago when these great trees were saplings—the poet Sophocles wrote, "One must wait until the evening to see how splendid the day has been."

Herbert Hoover's life was eloquent of those words.

Excerpt from Mr. Nixon's talk under the redwoods at the Bohemian Grove in California July 29, 1967. Quoted with the permission of the Board of Directors of the Bohemian Club.

PART ONE

IN TRAINING

CHAPTER ONE

FARM CHORES TO OFFICE JOB

SORROW CAME EARLY to Herbert Hoover. When the ring of his father's anvil ceased, he squared sturdy shoulders to bear whatever a six-year-old could of the burdens left to his Quaker mother. No longer would the black-bearded man stoop to pat those shoulders. Nor would his happy smile pierce the reserve of the blue-eyed youngster.

That magnetic smile and the strong practical hands of an Iowa blacksmith were almost the only heritage thirty-three-year-old Jesse Hoover could leave this child. True, Jesse had recently begun to augment the family income by adding a farm machinery agency to the business of shoeing horses. But death came too soon.

Bertie, as family and friends called the chubby boy, and his older brother Tad (Theodore) did their manly best for their mother and the baby sister. For less than three years after their father's death the children had the loving guidance of their mother, except when Huldah Minthorn Hoover heeded an inner call to a preaching mission. At such times, she left the family in the pleasant household of Jesse's uncle, Benijah. He had bought the machinery agency for cash; this money she had put away with the $2,000 realized from Jesse's insurance policy for the children's education.

Simple daily needs were met with returns from her skillfully applied needle. Then, in September, 1883, Huldah returned from a neighborhood meeting in Muscatine, tired and feverish. In a few short days she, too, was gone—like so many pioneers, the victim of typhoid-pneumonia.

Quaker-like the relatives met in solemn conclave. As the stunned children heard their futures debated Bertie walled up his grief in stoic silence. Then a shy smile lighted his blue eyes. He was going to live with Uncle Allan Hoover!

Companionship with cousins Walter and Alice compensated in a way for separation from Tad and May. He shared farm chores with Walter. On good days the boys trudged two miles together to the country school. If winter snow clogged the road, Uncle Allan perched them tandem on one of his big work horses. Recess and lunch time brought boisterous youngsters pell mell into the school yard. Bertie and Walter swapped crullers for cookies, and played mumblety-peg or leap frog.

Back at their desks, the boys absorbed lifetime inspiration from a teacher who interpreted America in terms small boys could understand and remember. Mollie Brown had even offered to adopt the orphaned Bertie, but had yielded to Uncle Allan's prior claim. Her lasting influence, however, left permanent imprint on the nation she was teaching these children to respect.

West Branch was a neighborly Quaker community. Throughout a life of usefulness Herbert Hoover never forgot that his schoolmates came from homes where the parents helped each other at husking bees and barn-raisings. He cherished, too, the memories of fathers teaching boys to trap wild rabbits in cracker boxes held open by a "figure four", and holding their sons tight during terrifying rides down steep Cooks Hill on homemade sleds.

He wrote in the autograph book his playmate Addie Colip treasured:

> "To Addie: Let your days be days of peas. Slip along as slick as greese.
>
> Bert Hoover."

On Uncle Allan's farm he and Walter sometimes made play of their chores. When the new mower cut rhythmic swaths through fragrant timothy the boys wanted a mower of their own. Uncle Allan encouraged them; they were welcome to whatever they could find in the junk pile back of the barn. There were some warped and broken wheels, and a cross-cut saw with several teeth missing. What they put together ran uncertainly. With fraying rope ends they harnessed their pet heifer to the thing.

Their triumph was short-lived. The heifer dragged machine and driver across the vegetable garden to wreck the contraption against a tree on the far side. Allan Hoover was tolerantly amused as the boys turned to a new project. This time they rigged up a sorghum press from a worn-out clothes wringer with the wheels and cams salvaged from the mower. The heifer was harnessed to a long pole. One boy pushed. The other pulled, and some sweet sap was actually ground from the stalks of sorghum.

Childhood, with such simple pleasures, ended abruptly. Bertie was nearing eleven when word came from his mother's older brother, Dr. John Minthorn, in far-off Oregon that he wanted Huldah's second son to come to him. His letter said that he and his Quaker associates were about to open Pacific Academy in Newberg. He was sure that this would offer greater educational opportunities for the boy than he was getting in the country school on the Iowa prairies.

The family recognized the importance of education. Dr. John and his sister, Phoebe, had been pioneer students in the then new University of Iowa. Later he had supported himself through medical college in Philadelphia. Herbert's mother and another sister had not gone to college; but every Minthorn was well grounded in religious literature and the tenets of the faith their ancestors had brought from England in 1725. All of them had preaching instincts and an outreach of spirit toward the less fortunate.

Such missionary zeal had led the doctor to the last frontier among the Indians of the Northwest. He came as a government agent; but soon left the reservation when he was attracted to a nearby Quaker community which could use his services as an educator and physician. The recent death of his own son now spurred him to send for his sister's orphan.

Herbert left West Branch fortified to face a new frontier. Iowa roots had sunk deep. Work, thrift and patriotism were as indigenous as the red, yellow and white corn that waved in prairie wind. Outwardly his life would change conspicuously. Inwardly the basic personality forged in the Quaker home, the pioneer farm and the simple school would endure unchanged.

It was a wrench to part from kind Aunt Millie and Uncle Allan with his whimsical understanding of small boys, and from his companionable cousins. It was almost harder to leave the teacher who would remain his life-long mentor. Guardian Laurie Tatum had kept close watch of the education fund so carefully guarded by Huldah. From its small interest he had doled out barely enough to compensate the relatives for the children's care. Now he produced the munificent sum of $33.13 to buy a ticket to Oregon. Bertie was to travel in care of Quaker neighbors, Mr. and Mrs. O.F. Hammill. Family gifts of well-packed lunch baskets kept the cost of travel low!

Herbert knew the value of money. He brought with him a small account book. In it was recorded all the money he had ever had and exactly what he had done with it. This included what he had received from Uncle Allan—two cents each time he had cleaned the barn and five cents for every hundred thistles he had cut with Walter on hot summer days. During the first winter Laurie Tatum had sent Uncle Allan $1.50 a month; but Herbert's summer help had reduced the stipend to a dollar. Bertie took pride in being partially self-supporting before he was ten years old!

The boy brought other evidence of his inner security. His safeguard against the desperate loneliness that pulled his thoughts back to Aunt Millie and Uncle Allan was inscribed in two mottoes tucked into his bag.

"Leave me not, neither forsake me, Oh God of my salvation" was printed on one card. The other read: "I will never leave thee nor forsake thee."

There was no time for loneliness. The busy Quaker town just coming into being in a clearing carved out of deep Oregon forests demanded all the energy of adult and child. Bertie slipped quietly into the place where he was needed and welcomed. Chores with which he was already acquainted were soon part of his daily existence. He chopped wood, fed and curried the horses, milked the cow. But he had come to be educated. First, he was enrolled in the primitive clapboard house which had been one of the original structures in the town. This was no improvement over the familiar Iowa school; he missed the gentle voice of his teacher Mollie Brown!

A year or two passed before he was ready to register at the Pacific Academy, now changed to Pacific College. A half century later this institution, renamed George Fox College, would display a plaque on the wall of its entrance hall reading:

In Honor
of
Herbert Hoover
Humble Country Boy
Earnest Student
Distinguished Engineer
Effective Administrator
World Philanthropist
Promoter of Peace
Eminent Statesman
President of the United States

A Tribute of
Love and Esteem
from
His Boyhood School
Pacific College.

Uncle John did not lose contact with the nearby Indians, for whom he continued to run a school. His nephew was equally at home among the little redskins. For several months in the summer following Jesse Hoover's death, Bertie stayed with Minthorn relatives in Indian Territory where this uncle was government agent for the Osages. He had fished beside these playmates, using bent pins for hooks. He watched them snare rabbits and ground squirrels. Eagerly he tried his hand on their hickory bows. And through it all he gained lasting respect for these native Americans.

Pioneering had been part of Herbert Hoover's heritage from both sides of his family. Like the Minthorns, the Hoovers had always been in the forefront of advancing civilization. The first of his American line, Andrew Hoover (Andreas Huber), had disembarked from the ship *Two Sisters* in Philadelphia on September 9, 1738, to join two older brothers in Lancaster, Pennsylvania. Their father, a farmer and linen weaver, had left his Swiss village, Oberkulm, to bring up nine children in the German Palatinate. Andreas, youngest of the family, at fifteen had joined a group who were shipping down the Rhine from Mannheim to Rotterdam, enroute to the New World.

In 1745 he married Margaret Pfautz, who as a child had come to America in 1727, also from the Palatinate. For thirty years they farmed in Carroll County, Maryland. Then they emigrated to Randolph County, North Carolina. The grist mill he set up remained long in the Hoover family, although some of the sons, among them Herbert's direct ancestors, moved on to Ohio and eventually to the Iowa prairies.

Herbert had not been long in Oregon when Uncle John, like all those roving ancestors, felt an urge to push on to something new. He would share in the great Northwest land boom. To this end his Quaker Development was merged with the Oregon Land Company with offices in Portland and Salem. Dr. Minthorn moved to Salem as Manager. Fourteen-year-old Herbert, at that point bored with school, went along as office boy.

He helped with the bookkeeping. With the aid of the office stenographer, he learned to use the new typewriter. Then when Salem's first business college opened, he enrolled for night courses concentrating on mathematics. More important to his future, however, were his daily lessons in business techniques as he listened silently to the practical directors discussing plans for promoting a new community. The tract they had purchased was at Scott's Mills, a few miles east of Salem. Here they built a church, a school, a hotel. The Company operated a sawmill, a flour mill and the local railroad, graded the streets and installed a water system.

They were ready for new citizens. The energetic boy was put in charge of finding them. He contracted with an eastern firm to run an ad in a thousand papers. When the tourists came, Herbert Hoover met them at the station, staying with each one until he could leave his customer satisfactorily located.

At fifteen he was an active participant in this thriving community and a member of the Salem Quaker Meeting. His skill as an organizer was already appreciated by his elders, who often included him in the planning of town affairs. Yet the baseball diamond and the secret fishing hole had equal claim on his time once his well-planned chores were finished. For him life was full and interesting.

One day a stranger dropped into the office. His conversation alerted the attention of the office boy. His name was Robert Brown and he spoke a new language. As he talked with Dr. Minthorn the caller saw the querying look in the boy's blue eyes as he edged closer.

"Son," he said turning to the solidly-built 'teen-ager, "you look like a lad who would make a good engineer."

Bert listened spellbound as Brown launched into a description of the profession that took a man into the out-of-doors, a calling that demanded clear-eyed vision, a sturdy body and a mind that must be practical and exacting in attention to detail.

That night he did not race out of the office to the ball field. Instead, he hurried home to confide his ambition to Grandmother Minthorn, who had recently brought his sister May to join the Salem household. This daughter of pioneers sympathized with her grandson's wish to go to college. So did Uncle John. His brother, Theodore, back in Iowa, was preparing for Penn College. The Quakers had other splendid schools. He might earn a scholarship at Earlham in Richmond, Indiana. But when Herbert found that none of these institutions taught engineering, he was not interested.

For a year he collected catalogues and information bulletins. Then another engineer came to "expert" some mines in the Cascades, in which the local Quakers had an interest. Herbert accepted an invitation to join the survey party. He heard the realistic verdict of this man who *knew*, from tests and assays, that the properties were of no value. The authoritative analyses of this well-trained man further stirred the ambitious boy.

The nation's press was blazoning the story of a new, free university to be established in California. Senator Leland Stanford and his wife had determined to dedicate all of their wealth to commemorate their only son's short life by educating worthy young people.

Herbert sent for an announcement of the Leland Stanford Junior University which was to open in the fall of 1891. When it came, he turned quickly to "Entrance Requirements". "Latin, Greek, algebra, plane geometry, physics," he read. In all of these he was deficient. Another section said that, for the present, certificates from high schools accredited or commissioned by the University of California, or those of other States, would be received instead of entrance examinations. But he had not finished his high school course!

He must try the examinations. He re-enrolled in night school, again concentrating on mathematics. That would be his tool, whether or not Stanford accepted him. He had made up his mind that he would be an engineer.

Chapter Two

STANFORD '95

THE STANFORD BULLETIN had announced that Dr. Joseph Swain, newly-appointed head of the Department of Mathematics, would hold entrance examinations at the Esmond Hotel, Portland, August 6 and 7. Herbert Hoover was there. Obviously the youngest, he bent a puzzled face over the printed sheet on his assigned desk without so much as a glance at anyone else in the room.

The kindly professor watched the quiet lad struggling over his answers. Hoover was the last to lay his blue book on the table. Dr. Swain detained him. Suspicious that the boy had been unprepared, he ran his eyes quickly down the page. Then he asked a few questions—not about the subjects in which the professor was sure the applicant had failed, but about the boy's life and ambitions. To Bert's amazement, Dr. Swain offered to go home with him to Salem, to persuade the Minthorns to let him try again at Stanford in September.

"A few week of tutoring and he will pass all right", asserted the tall handsome man, who had quickly identified himself with his fellow Quakers.

Fred Williams, son of the local banker, was equally anxious to go to Stanford. His father offered to buy railroad tickets for both boys if Bert would help Fred in mathematics—the one subject his son had flunked.

The community gathered to bid Godspeed as the boys climbed onto the *Capitol Express.* Mary Minthorn bowed her head as she said good-bye to her daughter's orphan son. He was going, true to his heritage, to pioneer in new surroundings. She would not hold him back.

The trip took about thirty-seven hours, with stops for meals at Ashland, Sisson (Mt. Shasta), and Sacramento. Finally, at Menlo Park, nearest station to the new University, the boys stepped off the train into the heat of a California August day. They dumped their few belongings, including Bert's bicycle, into a hack and told the driver to take them to Stanford.

The road was dusty. Yellow jackets buzzed around the horse's tail. The air was pungent with the strange smell of tar weed. Garrulous Jasper Paulsen, the driver, was full of tales. He rambled on about the vineyards, the prize horses on the Stanford farm, and the slow progress on University buildings. Soon red-tiled roofs loomed against velvet-brown hills. As they approached the picturesque sandstone quadrangle, Paulsen pointed to a stone building some distance from the Quad.

"Over there", he drawled, "is the men's dorm. But you can't live there yet . . . ain't finished inside. Where're you fellows going, anyway?"

"Better take us to the university office," Bert spoke up. "First thing I need is a job."

"That's right here." Paulsen reined his horse in front of one of the many arches rimming the outer quadrangle. He waved his hand toward an open door half-way down the arcade.

The boys clambered over blocks of stone and hastened to the door. Inside, they presented themselves to a slight man. With an encouraging smile he told them that he was Registrar Elliott. Yes, he had just the job for a farm-trained boy from Oregon.

He led Bert into an adjoining room where he presented him to Miss Eleanor Pearson. Indeed she did need someone to look after her horse and other chores in Adelante Villa, an old house across the creek from the Stanford Farm. Here, she told him, she and her partner, Lucy Fletcher, were preparing to start a girls' boarding school as a feeder to the University.

(Girls in an engineering college! That was a shock.)

Miss Pearson explained that President Jordan had brought them west. Now, she said, homeless faculty families were imploring them to turn the place into a temporary boarding house until their residences could be completed. Room and board were available to a student who would sweep out the nuts hoarded by squirrels and carry on the outside chores.

Bert took charge of Jim, the horse, fed and curried him, dusted the surrey, and drove the ladies on their innumerable shopping trips to Mayfield.

The mistresses of Adelante became of further importance to their chore boy. Time was fast approaching for the final attempt at entrance examinations. These teachers became his tutors, paid by him meticulously each week with a gold piece.

Miss Pearson did her best to implant the fundamentals of good English composition on the practical mind of her helper. He was impatient with the complications of grammar and punctuation. Instead, he applied his energy to what seemed more important, geometry and higher algebra. He passed both with good grades. History, too was easy. That had always been his favorite reading.

He was accepted for admission; but there was a "condition" in the required "English I-B". The distinguished head of the English Department, Melville Best Anderson, stipulated that no one should ever be graduated from Stanford University until he could write an essay correctly spelled and expressed in words and phrases consistent with accepted rules of rhetoric.

That failure did not discourage the Oregon Quaker. He would deal with that later. Right now he was too much concerned with the practical side of life. He had been living in Encina Hall two weeks when other students began to pour in. Dr. Jordan had assigned him Room No. 38 on the main floor, conveniently near the dining room. His problem now was to earn the twenty dollars a month for room and board.

Mrs. Stanford's request for working students to clear the classrooms of debris left by workmen partially solved that. Bert was quick to join the janitorial staff assembled by Dr. Jordan's chore boy, Will Doub, who had arrived a month earlier than he had. When he became one of Doub's twelve assistants, Dr. Swain immediately requested that Hoover serve on the mathematics corner.

He did not remain on the Quad cleaning squad. As soon as there was an opportunity to do the same work in Encina he grabbed it. He could save time by working where he lived. He economized on minutes. When the head janitor called him in to say that one of the boys complained of dust under the bed, he replied,

"Well, he doesn't sleep there, does he?"

He was more interested in the second job that came through Dr. Swain. It better befitted his status as a college man to accept Dr. Ellott's offer of temporary employment as a clerk during the rush of gathering statistics on entering students. He remained on call as a part-time assistant. His round boyish handwriting on the earliest University records attests to Uncle John Minthorn's exacting training.

Disappointment came when he made out his own study course. He found that Geology Professor John C. Branner, who had been named as Dr. Jordan's first faculty appointee, was not to arrive until the second semester. Hoover registered temporarily in the Department of Mechanical Engineering.

Dr. Branner, who had been on leave from Indiana University as State Geologist for Arkansas, arrived at Stanford January 1, 1892. Dr. Swain brought his Quaker protégé to the Geology office at once. Droll eyes twinkled above a neatly-clipped beard as Branner bored into the soul of the shy freshman so earnest about commencing his life work.

A relationship, dormant since the smithy fires of Iowa had flickered out, began to surge again in Herbert Hoover's consciousness. Branner's inner warmth brought more than scholastic inspiration as this freshman took his place among the serious graduate students who had come with Branner from Indiana. The professor began to invite him, along with other geology majors, to the Branner home, largest of the faculty houses built across the hayfields from Encina. Inside the spacious rooms the boy found a welcome that melted away any homesickness for Iowa. Mrs. Branner, one of the earliest graduates of Vassar, had intellectual resources as rich as her husband's. Branner was as good a botanist as he was a geologist; a student of Latin and Greek; alert to every phase of modern political science.

Their family, two boys and a girl, reminded Bert of his own home circle. He found himself drawn into that group as though in a second home.

The white house was quickly surrounded by green lawn as neatly clipped as the famous Branner beard. Ivy was trained over its chimney and porches, and two elms planted symmetrically on either side of the front walk. Every morning the professor was up early with trowel and rake. Then, wearing a closely buttoned coat topped by a shining white collar, he put on his black derby and walked briskly to the Quad.

Such was the man who won Hoover allegiance. But his office was not as well kept as his garden. Bert, citing his experience under Uncle John Minthorn and Registrar Elliott, sought and won the position of office assistant.

Branner's mail was filled with scientific papers, reports and periodicals. One of Hoover's first tasks was the care of these. When he was told to see that they were properly bound, he did not pester his superior with questions. The bound volumes soon stood in place on shelves near at hand; the bill for binding and shipping was on Branner's desk.

Through the remaining months of spring, Dr. Branner watched with increasing appreciation. He said nothing; but when he was ready to go back to the Arkansas Survey, he took Hoover with him.

Those long summer days in the hills of Arkansas implanted more than scientific knowledge in the head of the young man who kept the records and held the bag of rock samples. Dr. Branner applied the methods of his profession to every situation. He liked his companion and he offered good advice.

"Keep your capital intact," he admonished. "While you are in college you can earn enough to keep you going. No one pays attention to how you earn it. Once you get out in the world, don't let yourself look like a beggar."

As they became more intimate Hoover found that Branner spoke from experience. He had worked his way through Cornell. He understood self-supporting students.

"Always keep your time your own as much as you can," the professor said another day. "And when you get into the mining game, keep your eyes open for opportunities. Don't get yourself tied to one outfit too long."

As they sat in that Arkansas dusk watching fireflies dart through the dark trees, how little either could guess that the attentive boy would soon become the most widely-traveled and highest paid engineer of his era!

The summer passed swiftly. Hoover returned to Stanford with money to deposit and with sound experience as a foundation for the profession that would take him so far. But he did not return to Encina. A group of sophomores, indignant over a rise in the cost of board, invited him to manage a house they had rented in nearby Palo Alto. That meant free room and board. He left his money in the bank and accepted the job.

The leader of this group was an older man, named Sam Collins. He introduced the young manager of Romero Hall to a new interest—student politics. A fellow geology major, Edward R. Zion, was presidential candidate of the "Barbs"—self-designated cognomen for non-fraternity men. Hoover used his influence among working students who had pre-empted wooden shacks left from housing construction. Seated on the edge of their bunk beds, he persuaded them to cast votes with the "Barbs" against the "privileged Row candidate".

In this endeavor he found a colleague in a lanky freshman, named Ray Lyman Wilbur. They managed to garner enough votes to give Zion a slight lead in the final count. But for the two electioneers the important outcome was the strong friendship thus developed between them as embryo politicians.

President Jordan's succinct adage—"Wisdom is knowing what to do next; virtue is the doing" became the measuring rod of both their lives. When the six-foot, broad-shouldered President boomed out his ideas on "The Value of Higher Education" to a Tuesday evening audience in the overcrowded chapel, these two listened responsively. His terse observation that no one could fasten a $2,000 education on a fifty-cent boy registered firmly.

They walked out into the moonlit arcades, pondering Dr. Jordan's closing words—"The world turns aside to let any man pass who knows whither he is going . . . . a college education is not a scheme to enable a man to live without work . . . . its purpose is to help to live to advantage, to make every stroke count. . . ."

Such purpose dominated young Hoover as he sloshed through winter mud from Palo Alto to the expanding geology department on the Outer Quad. That winter another influential mentor came into his life. J. P. Smith, who had worked under Branner in the Arkansas hills, was appointed to teach Paleontology. This study evoked childhood memories for Bert. What fun he and Tad had once shared as they collected agate and petrified wood along with specimens of crinoid fossils! Whenever he could spare time from his Branner duties, Hoover was at J.P.'s side, fascinated by research involving microscopic analyses of quartz veins.

Ambition, with a substratum of Quaker yearning to be of service, was surging through the veins of this eighteen-year-old student as he walked from class to class along the shaded arcades, his head bent slightly forward as if hurrying to get there faster than his feet would take him. He was near-sighted after a bout with measles and he often passed fellow students without recognizing them.

But he did keep track of what was going on. He even found time for baseball until a grounder tipped the ring finger of his left hand. The result was a swollen joint that ended his athletic career. Thereafter, his participation in extra-curricular activities was confined to keeping books for the football team and selling tickets for games.

Hoover's second year in college passed swiftly. His circle of acquaintance was limited mostly to the engineers, the Romero

Hall household, and the few political leaders he knew through Collins. When vacation came, Dr. Branner recommended him as assistant to Waldemar Lindgren on a trip through the Sierra for the United States Geological Survey.

With long summer mountain evenings to himself, Hoover pondered the chaotic condition of Stanford student body affairs, revealed by his adventure in campus politics. On scrap paper he jotted down some ideas for efficiency in student government, the prelude to a lifetime of such service.

He was late in registering in the fall because he needed to finish his job with Lindgren. But he had substantial savings to add to the growing Palo Alto bank account. He farmed out some of his lesser jobs, such as a newspaper route and the agency for a San Jose laundry, continuing to take his cut as the entrepreneur!

He also concluded that the job of running Romero Hall was too wasteful of time and energy. He moved back to Encina. As soon as he had his personal affairs in order, he hunted up Zion with the proposition to write a constitution for the student body along the lines he had mapped out in the Sierra. Zion did the actual writing; but it was based on Hoover ideas. By now his fellows were aware of his genius with figures, as well as his absolute integrity. He became treasurer of the Junior Class, his first experience in office holding.

The new constitution adopted in the spring provided that all student organizations were to be under the control of the Treasurer of the Student Body. Herbert Hoover was elected to this office in April, 1894. Recalling his Salem office training, he had a set of vouchers printed. Not one cent, even car fare, was paid without a signed voucher!

That college year closed with all affairs in order, his own and those of the student body; but with no definite plans for summer employment. Dr. Branner was finishing a relief map of Arkansas. He asked Hoover to remain on campus until that was completed. He also hired Zion. Hot sun beat relentlessly on unprotected red tile roofs as the two spent weary days bending over tables in the drafting room. They were anxious to wind up the job and get away from the almost deserted campus. Thus they worked continuously, weekends included. On a Saturday afternoon they stopped a bit early and walked across the fields to Encina, thirsty and tired.

"Let's get a drink of pop," suggested Zion as they passed the all-purpose store in a corner of the dormitory basement; but the door was locked. They could see the rows of thirst-quenching bottles lining the shelves.

Hoover, standing with his hands in his trouser pockets, was jingling the bunch of keys he always carried.

"Walk in", he said as he turned one of the keys in the lock. "What will you have?"

"Got your vouchers handy, too?" asked Zion, as they uncorked a bottle of pink strawberry pop.

"Don't need them", answered the treasurer of the student body, "we'll teach him not to shut up shop early when there are thirsty people around!" With that, he filled the empty bottle with water, recapped it, and put it on the shelf.

They were really thirsty, and the game appealed to their sense of humor. They stayed with it until a complete row was colorless. Then they locked the door again and wandered upstairs to their rooms.

Monday morning the two made a point of stopping in the store to sharpen their pencils on the way to work. The storekeeper greeted the treasurer with an apologetic look.

"What do you suppose could have happened over the weekend? The store was locked when I left and just as securely locked this morning, but look at that shelf! Those bottles are all full of water."

Hoover kept a straight face.

"Too bad," he said, "Guess you'll have to stick around a little later on Saturdays. But here's the money."

The map was soon finished; the boys, restless. Then Zion had an idea. They ought to go to the mountains, Yosemite for instance.

"But how?" questioned cautious Bert. He could not afford to spend his hard-earned cash on a vacation.

Zion was secretive until he returned from a trip to San Francisco. Then he announced a great enterprise. He had contracted with the San Francisco *Examiner* to paint fifty fence signs between Palo Alto and the Valley, displaying in bright colors: EXAMINER—MONARCH OF THE DAILIES.

Collins and another Encinaite, a journalist named Archie Rice, had already joined the party. Would Hoover like to go? Of course. In a few days the quartet started out in an old surrey, equipped with gallons of paint, big brushes and camping outfits. At last, they reached Merced and inquired for the quickest road to the Valley. The farmer who gave them directions added that about half way up they would find another farmer who would sell them eggs and milk, as well as feed for their horses. They were off in high spirits.

They finally came to a ranch. This answered the farmer's description. They drove into the yard, unhitched the weary horses and sent Collins and Rice in search of the owner. In a few minutes the scouts came back, crestfallen. The man had refused to sell them anything. He had told them to be on their way.

But the horses refused to budge. The disgruntled pair sank under a shade tree. In the meantime, Hoover had been silently uncoiling the short fish line he wound around his hat. Pulling out the remnants of their lunch, he broke off a small bit of cheese and baited his hook.

"Ever catch a chicken this way?" He turned to Zion, eyes twinkling.

His friend tried to grab his arm in protest, looking anxiously toward the barn. "They'll hear it squawk."

"Oh no," laughed Bert, "it happens too quickly," as he yanked up a startled hen, silencing her with a deft twist of the neck.

With their dinner safely hidden under a piece of canvas, they rehitched the horses and started looking for more friendly ranchers.

The next day they discovered that the High Sierra did not provide fences for any more signs. At Hoover's suggestion, the remaining paint was daubed in one mammoth sign on a fallen tree.

It was the sixth day out from Stanford when they reached the Valley, about five in the afternoon, and pitched camp near Mirror Lake. To celebrate, they dined at the hotel at the foot of Glacier Point. Here Bert found a telegram from Branner, telling him to meet Lindgren at Milton, a railroad terminus in the mining district. A sun-up camp breakfast started an eighty-mile hike for the young geologist, eager to be back at tasks more to his liking than sign painting.

That summer was spent mapping the Mother Lode. Lindgren even let Hoover sign his name to some of the reports. The college senior returned to the Quad in the fall, ready for the last lap before he would be a full-fledged professional geologist.

Busy months loomed ahead. Football season brought much extra work for the Treasurer of the Student Body.

When the games were in San Francisco, he always went along as Team Manager to take charge of the money. Before the first "Big Game" between the University of California and Stanford, an emergency arose. No one had remembered to bring a ball! Players and rooters waited impatiently while Herbert Hoover took a street car down to a Market Street sports shop to buy a ball with part of the gate receipts.

He had inherited a debt of $2,000 when he became Student Body Treasurer. But his first report in late October of 1894 said: "for the first time since its birth, the Associated Students is a solvent body." And on December 12, the Stanford *Daily* commended Treasurer Hoover because he had rendered an itemized account of receipts and expenditures for the football season.

Experience taught him that the responsibilities of Student Manager were too great for an undergraduate. In the future, he recommended that a graduate student should be hired at an adequate salary. At the same time, he refused to be paid for his own long hours of labor, since he had made the suggestion.

Instead, to augment his income, he teamed with a friend to

bring culture to the campus in the form of a concert and lecture series. Sometimes these ventures paid well, but once he was too ambitious. There was a Polish pianist playing in San Jose by the name of Paderewski. He would come for a guarantee of $1,000. When the receipts were all in, they added up to just $800. In embarrassment Hoover explained, almost more ashamed of the vacant seats than the lack of money. The artist was understanding. He agreed to accept whatever was available, saying he would forgive the balance. The boys managed to pay the rest of the overhead, and Herbert Hoover chalked up a debt to Paderewski as one of his future obligations.

One day during this senior year Hoover stepped into Dr. Branner's office on a routine errand. He found the head of the Department talking with a slender girl in brown, their heads bent over some rocks on the table. As Hoover approached, Dr. Branner turned to him.

"Yes, I am sure these are pre-carboniferous. What do you say, Hoover?"

There was a sly twinkle in his eye as he continued:

"Miss Henry, this is my assistant, Herbert Hoover. Hoover, this is Lou Henry, our first woman in the Geology Department."

They acknowledged the introductions, looked at the rocks together for a few minutes, and Hoover returned to his duties. The intrusion of a woman into the sacred masculine precints of the Geology Department was a bit startling, but it was no affair of his. After all, she was a freshman. Let the younger men meet this. He was not socially minded; but a few weeks later the Branners forced the issue.

Hoover and a junior from Montana, Bob McDonnell, were working on a relief map of the San Francisco Peninsula when Dr. Branner interrupted them.

"Boys", he said, "Mrs. Branner would like to have you come over for supper on Saturday night."

They accepted eagerly. Then Branner fished out some slips of paper from his vest pocket.

"She's asked some girls, and these are the ones she would like you to bring."

As soon as the professor left the room, Hoover turned to his companion, "Who'd you draw?"

"Grace Diggles," answered McDonnell, "Who are you taking?"

"Lou Henry," replied Hoover. "I don't go much for her. What do you say we trade?"

"O.K. by me, one's as good as the other," said McDonnell, and they went on with their job.

In a few minutes Hoover spoke again.

"You know, Mac, we've got to pass our exams. Perhaps we better tell Branner what we want to do," and they went into the office together.

"If it's all the same with you, we'd like to trade girls Saturday night," began Hoover.

"That's quite all right. Trade if you like," replied Dr. Branner, "all we want is for you to have a good time."

But it was not long before he came back into the laboratory.

"I've been thinking about what you boys said. Mrs. Branner is rather particular about the way she plans her parties. Suppose you all come together at the same time, and she won't be any the wiser."

That plan involved some unexpected expense. On Saturday night torrential rain deluged the campus. The boys had to rent a two-seated surrey from Paulsen's Livery in Palo Alto. They could not ask their young ladies to walk in the sticky adobe mud from Palo Alto, where Miss Diggles lived, to Roble Hall, the new women's dormitory, for Lou Henry, and across the campus to Alvarado Row.

When they reached the Branner home Lou handed her rain coat and umbrella to Bob, while Hoover took care of Grace Diggles' togs. Mrs. Branner's eyebrows raised a bit, but she said nothing as she introduced the two couples to the other guests waiting in the little side parlor. When it was time to go into the dining room, she smiled at Bob. "Mr. McDonnell, will you please take Miss Diggles in to supper?"

As they passed their hosts in the entrance hall, McDonnell caught the professor's soothing undertone.

"Now, Susan, what's the odds? I never can get all those details. Anyway, they're having a good time," and he winked a smile at McDonnell.

From time to time, during the evening McDonnell sought Hoover's eye, expecting him to flash him a commiserating look. But Bert did not see his friend. He was absorbed in listening to Lou Henry. They had no sooner heaped their plates with good fried chicken and corn pudding than she had smiled away his bashful diffidence. She had begun with her enthusiasm for the Branners. It had been, in fact, she told him, Dr. Branner's whimsical yet scholarly talk before her graduating class at San Jose State Normal the year before that had made her decide to come to Stanford to study geology instead of acceding to her mother's wish that she become an artist.

Hoover's interest deepened when she told him that she had stayed out a year to work with her father in the bank at Monterey. Her family, old friends and admirers of David Starr Jordan, had agreed with his theory that it was best for young people to wait awhile to be sure of their leanings before coming to college. She had even taught school a few weeks at the end of the term when the local teacher became ill.

They had not talked very long before they discovered that they were both born in Iowa, really within a few miles of each other. Her family, too, had been Quakers, although now they were Episcopalians. They found, also, that they had both come West at about the same age, she to Whittier in Southern California while he went to Oregon. After she had finished the Academy, she told him laughingly, her mother had insisted that she go to Los Angeles Normal because, "that school had the best gymnasium west of the Mississippi."

Two years later her father had been asked to help establish a bank in Monterey. When she spoke of her father, Lou Henry's voice was vibrant. Her listening dinner companion sensed her love of the out-of-doors, her knowledge of camping, her understanding of horses. He began to comprehend why she had dedicated her inquiring mind to study of the world in its making.

By the time the evening was over and the boys had delivered

their young ladies to Roble Hall and Palo Alto, Hoover turned to McDonnell.

"Say," he said, as they drove the surrey back to the Palo Alto stable, "Lou Henry's all right. She's not a bit snooty like I thought she was."

Springtime took the geology classes into the hills on field trips. Hoover watched admiringly as Lou Henry vaulted fences unassisted. He saw that she went about her investigations so unobtrusively that she was accepted into the circle without comment. Here was a girl who could share the life of a geologist, no matter where the job should take them.

His college habits began to change. He even joined the callers waiting in the conspicuous Roble reception hall for their girls to answer the bells in the upstairs corridors. But most of their recreational hours were spent outside the traditional campus social orbit—not at dances, but on picnics, walks in the hills, and an occasional moonlight stroll through the cactus garden in the Arboretum adjacent to the Quad.

Commencement time was approaching; but Herbert Hoover was not sure of graduating with the Pioneer Class. The old "condition" in English I-B was still staring him in the face. Try as he would, he had never satisfied the exacting Dr. Anderson. The Geology Department was up in arms. Here was their prize student, one who had great promise of future success in his profession, a man who had won the respect of Waldemar Lindgren, still unable to meet the University's most rigid rule.

Then J.P. Smith took matters in hand. He asked Hoover to bring him one of his paleontology reports. Together they went over every phrase and comma.

"Now take this home and re-write it as you know it should be written," admonished the professor.

Seven times Hoover brought the paper back and repeated the process. At last J.P. was satisfied. He walked diagonally across the Quad to the English Department offices,

"What do you mean," he asked, waving the report before his friend, Melville Best Anderson, "by refusing to pass a student who can write a paper like this?"

The renowned scholar took the paper.

"Let me have this a while," he said.

His answer was duly credited in the Registrar's office. Herbert Hoover received his sheepskin from David Starr Jordan on May 29, 1895. He was ready to face the world with "A.B. Stanford" to write after his name.

Chapter Three

ON THE PAYROLL

THAT DIPLOMA WAS not much of an asset when the young college graduate trudged up the brush-covered hill to the office of the mine superintendent at "The Reward" in Nevada City. But Herbert Hoover was smart enough not to say anything about it to the gruff Cornishman. He had not worked under Waldemar Lindgren all of two summers without understanding the tradition of the Mother Lode where men were judged by brawny hands, not book learning. The son of the Iowa blacksmith had toil-toughened hands; and his Quaker reserve kept him tightlipped about what he knew.

The job he got required little brain work. Even a mucker could learn if he kept eyes and ears alert and mouth shut. Fellow laborers found the youth made of the stuff they respected. Foreman Tommy Ninnis boasted in later years that he "learned Bert Hoover all he knew about mining." And he always recalled the cautious smile that lighted his protégé's face when a whimsical "Cousin Jack" story went the rounds over lunch pails.

Aside from these noon hours, however, Hoover did not mix much in what social life there was in the town. He could not afford to room at The National Hotel, where Lindgren had always made his headquarters. The Union and the New York House were likewise beyond his budget. Up on Boulder Street near Pioneer Park, he found a plain white frame house that reminded him of Iowa. There was a window above the front door that indicated a garret room under the steep roof. Mr. and Mrs. Fleming seemed pleased to have a quiet young man for a roomer. There he spent his evenings under the kerosene lamp reading his favorite history books, scanning world-wide mining news in the columns of the *Mining and Scientific Press*, or studying Lindgren's survey in the light of his own rapidly accumulating knowledge of the gold ores of the Sierra.

This area was in the midst of a new gold boom. About two miles away over the dusty hill the North Star Mine, one of the oldest in the country, had been re-opened in 1883 after having been shut down for nine years as worked-out. Then W.B. Bourn, recently graduated from Oxford, had returned with John Hayes Hammond as consulting engineer to pump out the old mine discovered by Bourn's father in 1851. They had built a thirty-stamp mill and the following year Bourn had sold a controlling interest to James D. Hague, one of the leading mining men of the day, who brought his brother-in-law, A.D. Foote, from Boston to supervise opening up a group of adjacent mines.

As Hoover read of Lindgren's survey of the increasing productivity of the North Star Mine, he craved an opportunity to work there. Nevertheless, in 1895 there was greater mining activity in Nevada City than in Grass Valley. Hoover read an editorial comment in the *Mining and Scientific Press* which said: "Probably never before in its history . . . . has this district possessed such magnetic force in attracting men of technical knowledge and capitalists of such influence and means." The young man decided that he was just as well off where he was.

In August the Harmony Mine, a gravel pit mine a mile or two up the hill from where he was working, made the largest cleanup in its history. The company paid off its mortgage and prepared to enlarge the crew. Ed Gassoway, one of the few associates Hoover had cultivated during his months in town, persuaded his friend to join him on that crew. But only for a short time.

The community was watching with pride what was going on in another old mine, the Mayflower. Until the summer of 1895 only seven men had been employed there underground. Now as work was rushed on the expanding plant with modern appliances such as a new hoist and large pump, it was spoken of as "one of the most promising and productive mines of the district." When it opened in late September, Herbert Hoover was on the enlarged force drawing the wages of a full miner.

He was learning fast and applying what he had been taught at Stanford, especially by J.P. Smith. As he sampled veins he tried out microscopic examinations mastered in his laboratory days and stored in his mind knowledge useful for the future.

Nights in the mountains turned cold suddenly even though the October days stayed warm. By the time November rains turned dust into mud, the hard-working miner took a severe cold. Since early childhood, when his family told him they had nearly lost him with croup, his one weakness had been his bronchial tubes, which had been further affected by measles in his freshman year. He was really a sick young man. Waking after a night of feverish tossing, he heard a stranger at the foot of the stairs.

"Prepare yourself, young man," called a deep friendly voice. "You don't know me. I'm Mrs. Stansfield, and I live across the street. I've heard you coughing all night. Now I'm coming up to put a tar plaster on your chest or we'll be losing you with pneumonia."

Herbert Hoover thought of kind Aunt Millie back in Iowa. He understood folks who knew how to be neighborly, and he accepted the ministrations with lasting gratitude.

Ambition to make better use of his Stanford education soon convinced him that he should look for more remunerative occupation, especially if his dream of making a home for the girl, who constantly drew his thoughts back to the campus, was ever to be realized. He had found another Stanford geologist, E.B. Kimball, working in the mines. The two often ate together, generally in the miners' boarding houses that lined the narrow street: but occasionally at the Union or the National Hotel.

The town was small; an outsider was conspicuous. One of the important visitors who always stayed at the National when he came up to consult with Foote at the North Star Mine, was Louis Janin, a mining expert who had settled in San Francisco in the early sixties. Kimball and Hoover overheard bits of conversation about the far-reaching interests of this man.

Hoover made up his mind that a position in Janin's San Francisco office was what he wanted. George Hoffman, a rising young mining engineer from Nevada City, arranged an introduction.

Theodore Hoover was now living in Berkeley, working as a linotypist on the *Oakland Tribune*. Their sister, May, and a cousin, Harriet Miles from Indian Territory, were with him, The lure of home, added to his desire for a better job, was too much for young Herbert.

He checked out at the Mayflower, collected his wages, packed his belongings, and said goodbye to the Flemings and Mrs. Stansfield. Then he took the train for the Bay region, joining his family in time to celebrate Christmas.

When Stanford re-opened after the holidays, he made frequent trips down the Peninsula. Lou Henry was not living in Roble that semester. Instead, she had a room in Mrs. Babcock's boarding house on Lasuen Street, opposite the campus post office. Her twelve-year-old sister, Jean, had come up from Monterey with her to attend Castilleja School, now established in Palo Alto instead of in Adelante Villa. Jean was studying violin; they had to live where she could practice. Lou introduced the former geology assistant to her young sister, as well as to her close friend, Evelyn Wight, an alumna of an Eastern university, who was also living at the Babcock's while doing graduate work at Stanford. Evelyn was a member of Kappa Kappa Gamma. Soon Lou Henry, too, was wearing the pledge ribbons; but she did not drag her Quaker friend into the social obligations that new affiliation involved.

Hoover was too busy up in the city, anyway. He had found Janin skeptical when he applied for a job. A few months underground in the Mother Lode plus a college diploma did not make a mining engineer. Moreover, he had no opening for anyone in his office at the time, except, he said in passing, that he needed a typist. Hoover was quick to volunteer. He would be glad to help out, just to be around the office. He had had some experience in that line in his uncle's Salem office.

Rather grudgingly, Janin admitted the young assistant, trying him out on routine jobs. Then a rush letter came from Hague. It contained the report of an expert he had hired to examine the North Star Mine in connection with a suit brought by the Carson City Gold and Silver Mining Company against the North Star Company for trespassing on veins claimed by the former. Hague's lawyer, Curtis J. Lindley, had submitted a draft of his brief. Janin took the penciled sheets to his volunteer assistant. Before Hoover had typed many pages he stood by Janin's desk.

"This is all wrong," he stated with assurance.

"How do you know?" queried Janin.

"I've worked underground up there and I have also made microscopic examinations of specimens from just such 'crossings' as those from the North Star."

The older man was impressed as Hoover described in detail the peculiar dislocations in the rock formation at the North Star, which, he said, according to Lindgren's survey, showed a geologic condition quite different from that of other parts of the Mother Lode. He proceeded to explain the significance of such examinations in determining the extent of the pay chute. Janin's invariable instruction to any assistant was to "get the facts". He was pleased with the thoroughness with which Hoover had studied this situation.

He called in Curtis Lindley, and the two listened to Hoover's further technical criticism of their expert's report. Then Janin turned to Hoover:

"Take this letter to Hague. I am sending you to Grass Valley at once to verify what you have told us."

Hoover's carefully documented report provided convincing data. On March 9, 1896, Judge Beatty of the United States Circuit Court announced a decision in favor of the defendant.

In the meantime, Janin took him on as a regular assistant, sending him to examine mines in various parts of the country. His mastery of facts and his clear presentation of them brought his name before the mining public. Even before the court decision was announced, his first published article appeared in the columns of the *Mining and Scientific Press* for February 29, 1896. He illustrated it with cuts from a report of the U.S.G.S. prepared under Lindgren, explaining the involved nature of crossings, as well as the importance to miners of an understanding of the petrography of the Sierra.

There was much to learn in Janin's office, too. His interests stretched around the world. As the young assistant came to know more about them, his own imagination conjured up dreams of far places. Although American-born, Janin received his university education at Freiburg. He gained his first practical training in mining in that part of the Ruhr which had for centuries been a center of productivity. During Janin's student days, it was the scene of the greatest mining activity in the world.

Although still a young man, he with his brother Alexis had been called to Japan in the early seventies, to assist in remaking their mining industry. The reigning Shogun was attempting to acquire the best knowledge and skill available from other lands. Janin's stories about the "toy people" of Japan, with their friendly smiles and "natural civilized attitude" were intriguing to young Hoover. Brought up as he had been by conservative Middle Westerners, he had heard and thought little about people beyond the seas. His mental horizon was gradually widening.

In the fall of 1896 word came from Louis, Jr., a world traveler like his father, that he had been able to interest a London firm in some Australian mining prospects. Then, on the first of December, Janin, Sr., had a call from William H. Shockley, a graduate of Massachusetts Institute of Technology, who was enroute to China for this same British firm, Bewick-Moreing. In the course of a dinner conversation, Shockley mentioned that he was also seeking a competent engineer to go to West Australia to examine the large mineral fields about which Louis, Jr., had written.

That night Shockley wrote to C.A. Moreing: "You can safely engage any man endorsed by Mr. Charles Goodale of Butte, Montana, or by Louis Janin of San Francisco. I have just had a long talk with Janin, who stands as well as any Pacific Coast expert with regard to getting men. He takes a high view of his duties and responsibilities. . . . Should you write, bear in mind that he does not give his endorsement to a man unless he has fully examined the man's testimonials or his full personal knowledge of his capabilities. . . . He thinks that if his opinion is of enough importance to be considered at all, it is enough to be final. . . . As he gives you the benefit of his long experience and knowledge of mining men and affairs (and I know this to be second to no one in San Francisco) . . . . he expects you to pay attention to that opinion."

Janin said nothing to Shockley about the very young assistant he had been trying out on mine examinations in difficult parts of the still Wild West. At Steeple Rock, New Mexico, Hoover had proved that even a Quaker could wear a six-shooter on his hip and carry a rifle on his saddle as he went about duties as temporary assistant to the mine manager. And his reports were lucidly written, showing attention to details far beyond that expected from a young man of twenty two. One of these, the geology of a four-mile placer mining district in Routt County, Colorado, was informative enough to merit publication.

Before this article appeared in *The Engineering and Mining Journal*, however, Herbert Hoover was starting on his first overseas journey. Janin had called him in one morning to tell him that Bewick-Moreing had requested him to nominate a competent man to examine their holdings in West Australia. If he would like to go, Janin would be glad to recommend him. The salary would be $600 a month.

Hoover stood speechless before his employer; but his quick mind raced with eagerness. He had heard and read plenty about the potentialities of this far-off desert. He was ready for all the adventure it represented. He remembered one of Dr. Jordan's favorite axioms: "Opportunity knocks at every man's door. Open yours and let her in. Success will come. If you do not open, she will keep on knocking; but pretty soon, you will not hear her."

Of course, he would go. But Janin cautioned him that he must appear older than his twenty-two years. Bewick-Moreing had stipulated a "man of thirty-five!" Perhaps, too, it would be just as well if he had a few more sponsors. The Britishers were very exacting. Hoover called on Frederick Bradley, another of the West's leading mining engineers. He was glad to give his endorsement, as was J.F. Halloran, publisher of the *Mining and Scientific Press*. Then he went to some of San Francisco's best known bankers. I.W. Hellman and Frank Anderson were equally willing to vouch for the serious young man they had first known when the treasurer of the Stanford student body had requested audiences with the bank presidents before he was willing to deposit the funds entrusted to his care.

Janin wrote his London correspondents that his nominee was not quite thirty-five, but that he was a young man of courage and integrity, well-informed and careful in his reports. On March 27, 1897, the *Mining and Scientific Press* carried a note under "Personals". It read: "Herbert Hoover, M.E., left last Wednesday for London enroute to Australia to examine some large mineral fields controlled by a London syndicate. For some time he had been assistant to Louis Janin, at whose recommendation he obtained the place. Salary is understood to be $5,000 a year."

The stubble, which was already covering his face when "Huldah's boy" stopped off in West Branch, distressed his truth-loving Quaker relatives; but they, too, were practical people. They understood why he must raise a beard before he crossed the Atlantic to meet his new employers for the first time.

Chapter Four

INTERNATIONAL ENGINEER

Herbert Hoover's hirsute adornment was hardly comparable to Dr. Branner's neat beard by the time he reached London. But it covered part of the round boyishness of his face. Mr. Moreing expressed surprise over the way Americans held their youth; but he asked no personal questions. The young man had a convincing manner. His fund of essential information seemed to prove fitness for the position.

Moreing entertained his Western visitor at his country estate over the weekend. Then he started him on the long journey by way of France, Italy, Egypt, Suez, India, and finally across the three-hundred-mile West Australian desert by narrow gauge railway to Coolgardie.

Nothing in his past experience had prepared him for the desolate country over which he must now travel, partly by horse, some of the time on a swaying camel. It was winter in the Land Down Under, yet the heat was beyond anything he had ever felt in August in the Sierra or summer in New Mexico. A stranger to everyone, he faced the task with the same determination that had brought him thus far in his profession.

He had not been long in the country, however, when he met a fellow Californian, whose name had become familiar through the pages of the *Mining and Scientific Press*. T.A. Rickard had left Oakland to become State Geologist of Colorado before Herbert Hoover was a resident of the Bay Area; but his frequent and informative articles had dealt with many phases of California mining lore. His recent series on "Milling Operations in

Grass Valley" had been of great significance. The two men from California were immediately attracted to each other. Although Rickard was nine years Hoover's senior, he welcomed the keen young American. His thoroughness and integrity set him apart from the pseudo-experts and mining engineers in disrepute who had flocked into the Australian gold fields. At once the men agreed to exchange reports on wild-cat propositions so as to avoid useless examinations of properties turned down by either.

Rickard was a scholar as well as an engineer. The knowledge he shared was invaluable to an understanding of the country. He described to the newcomer the geology of what he termed "the basal wreck of the oldest land surface on the globe". And he explained why, in a continent without mountains to compel rain-clouds to distribute their burden, thunderstorms broke with destructive force. Old waterways were choked with sand. Lakes had become alkali plains. Water, once sweet, was now evaporated to a condition more brackish than the sea.

In fact, every drop of water consumed by man or beast had to be distilled. Government and private companies had erected condensers along lines of travel. These installations were essential to all exploration of this desert land, as were also camel trains led by turbanned Afghans. Water sold for fifty cents a gallon in Coolgardie, although in the mines it could be obtained for about eight.

From Coolgardie to the site of the Leonora Mine, the first of Hoover's objectives, there was a painfully straight road—ninety-one miles long with a difference in elevation of only four-and-one-half feet. At rare intervals the view was bounded by scrub trees, distributed with park-like regularity over the iron-stained sand. There was no undergrowth, except dry spear grass. Everywhere across the desert, quartz was scattered with a profuseness that made the ground seem a jeweled pattern glittering in the blazing sun.

Bewick-Moreing had engaged the young engineer only to examine their properties; but they also knew that they must be looking for a competent manager, in case he reported favorably on the possibilities. Correspondence concerning this search was sailing slowly from continent to continent, even as Herbert Hoover was starting his work. He had scarcely reached Australia when Janin received a letter from James D. Hague, a prominent mining engineer. It was dated, "New York, June 23, 1897," and read: "I have received your letter setting forth the substance of a communication made to you by a prominent mining syndicate now seeking a qualified manager for certain large interests in West Australia and asking me to name any engineer whom I may know as competent to fill and available for the position. . . ." The letter continued with the suggestion that Janin's son, Louis, Jr., might be considered for the position.

Hague did not know that, because of ill-health young Janin was about to retire from active participation in his father's far-flung profession. It was, instead, Herbert Hoover who was in charge of the mine when the Governor-General of Australia paid an official visit a few months later. With no idea that he was thanking the manager, that dignitary offered the khaki-clad young man a five shilling tip in appreciation of his courteous guidance down the shaft!

Bewick-Moreing's interests covered a large expanse of desert. As was the custom in West Australia in 1898, the new manager bought himself a good riding camel on which to make inspection trips. On one of his early jolting jaunts he stopped to rest and to pass the time of day with a group of Welshmen slaving over a small claim. These Sons of Gwalia reminded him of the Cousin Jacks he had known in Nevada City. He listened to their stories with appreciative chuckles and thus won their confidence. Other experts had scoffed at the prospects of this mine. Hoover knew the reputation of the canny Welsh, men with generations of mining sense bred in their bones. This oasis, with plentiful water and feed, became a favorite stopping place for Hoover and his mount.

In fact, it was difficult to guide the animal away from that trail. One day, riding to look at a mine to the east of the Gwalia, there was an impasse. The stubborn beast refused to take the eastern trail. Hoover could pull the camel's head around until it faced the east. But the animal continued to the west. He tried the whip. The stinging lashes had no effect. He dismounted and attempted to lead the animal. Even with the rope pulling through a ring in its nose the camel stuck obdurately to the western trail.

Hoover ripped off his black shirt and blindfolded his mount. Then he permitted him to continue a short way on the familiar route, but gently and gradually swung him to the east. The victorious manager finally reached his destination. To avoid future altercations he had a leather blindfold made as soon as he returned to Coolgardie!

Treks to the Gwalia became more frequent. Hoover took samples. Finally, he negotiated an option and wrote his London backers. It would take a half million dollars to develop this mine. $250,000 would buy a two-thirds interest in the property. That much more would be needed for working capital.

Bewick-Moreing took his advice. Moreover, they voted Hoover a small interest in the enterprise as a commission. Now his letters to the girl geologist entering her senior year at Stanford began to sound a more serious note. He also instructed Lester Hinsdale, a Stanford lawyer who held his power of attorney, to send more money to his relatives, as well as to increase the student-help fund he had started at the University.

He wrote to Theodore, urging him to give up his job and enroll at Stanford. He hoped his brother would study geology and mining, so that they could enjoy the companionship in business they had missed in childhood. He was now able to lift the entire burden of helping their sister and other relatives from his elder brother's shoulders.

Herbert Hoover was gaining an international reputation among mining men. Articles appeared under his by-line in various professional periodicals in Australia, England, and America revealing his efficient handling of difficult Australian mining problems. Frustrating as were the geological and physical difficulties, he found political interference almost beyond endurance.

"Although this is a country of unparalleled democracy," he concluded in one article, "it sometimes seems to the manager that the sole object of Government is to hamper him in relation to his labors."

When he greeted George Starr, a former Grass Valley associate who was returning from South Africa by way of Coolgardie, he poured out more of his annoyances. The inefficiency of his men baffled him. Starr agreed that Australians seemed to accomplish little more than the Kaffirs of the Rand, certainly not more than two-thirds as much as the men they both knew in the mines of the California Mother Lode.

Hoover accompanied Starr to his port of embarkation, probing the experienced older mind for guidance as to his own future. Was he right in devoting his life to a profession so full of chance, so senselessly entangled in government red tape everywhere? Homesickness brought a lump to his throat when Starr spoke of his family. His wife and children had been with him in Africa, but had gone directly home via London. Secretly, Hoover questioned—was he ever to be free to carry out his own longing for a wife, home and children?

"Well," warned his departing friend, "the decision is yours to make. But whatever you decide, stick to it!"

While young Hoover was gaining this practical experience in Australia, possibilities of a more challenging assignment for him were evolving as letters sailed slowly from Shockley in Peking to Moreing in London. About the time when Hoover was leaving San Francisco, Shockley had written his chief about meeting a Member of the British Parliament in the Chinese capital. W. Pritchard Morgan had come to Cathay in response to a cable from Viceroy Li Hung Chang. The Britisher's help had been sought in planning a mining administration for the Empire. He had also been negotiating for the use of foreign capital and methods in their ancient mines.

Shockley's letters expressed concern over greedy grabbing of slices of China by the Great Powers following the Sino-Japanese War. He was particularly indignant over Russia's interference in post-war territorial settlement. He prophesied that if democratic nations did not intervene, Russia would control all of China in less than a hundred years. On the business side, he told his employer that the Chinese Engineering and Mining company of Tientsin was seeking a loan from England, France, Belgium and Germany. The purpose for which this money was needed was to build a coal loading port at Chingwantao on the Gulf of Pechli.

The significance of this news had brought Moreing to the Far East. When he arrived he met the president of this Chinese company. Chang Yen-Mao was also head of the newly-established Ministry of Mines. Although Chang held the rank of Mandarin, he was a man who had come from humble beginnings. As former stable boy he had won this reward from the Dowager Empress by scaling the Great Wall with the baby Emperor strapped to his back during an insurrection. He was fully aware of his lack of technical knowledge for the new position.

Moreing found it easy to convince the Minister of Mines that, with scheming Europeans competing for China's undeveloped resources, he would do well to name a neutral American as Court Advisor. He described the progressive young manager of Bewick-Moreing's West Australian properties. This man, he said, had an engineering degree from a University in California, that Land of the Gold Mountain, which had attracted so many Chinese to cross the Pacific. Not only Chang, but his superior, the Viceroy, agreed. Moreing cabled Hoover.

Sweltering in his hut at the Sons of Gwalia, where the thermometer registered 100 degrees at midnight, the young Stanford engineer stared at Moreing's message electrified. Would he accept an appointment as Manager of the Chinese Engineering and Mining Company, as well as Director of Celestial Mines, salary, $20,000 a year?

The answer was "yes"—with one proviso. He must have leave to return to America on vacation first. With that permission granted, Hoover sent another cable. This one went to Monterey, California, where Lou Henry was living with her parents. Would she return to China with him as his wife?

Her cable said "Yes." The young engineer sailed for home by way of London, arriving in San Francisco late in January.

He hastened to Stanford for a few important hours with Dr. Branner. Then he took the train for Monterey.

The Henrys welcomed their future son-in-law with confidence born of their daughter's trust. There was no Quaker Meeting in Monterey. Lou took her fiancé to call on a loved friend, Father Ramon Mestres, pastor of San Carlos Mission in Monterey, as well as of the historic one at Carmel. Their acquaintance dated from the short time she had taught school before entering Stanford. When the Monterey public school building had burned, her classes had been assigned to the social hall used for parties in the Catholic parish. Most of her pupils were of that faith. At the close of school each day, Father Mestres would arrive to give them religious instruction. She began to see more of the kindly priest, too, in the home of her father's associate in the bank, Thomas Field.

Thus, Father Mestres had been one of her first confidants when she knew that she was going to marry. He had told her, however, that much as he would like to officiate, he could not unite in matrimony two people not of his own faith. Herbert Hoover asked the Padre if there were not some way of securing special permission. Father Mestres replied that it might be possible if the Bishop would give him the right to act in the capacity of chaplain, to which Archbishop Reardon of San Francisco had appointed him during the recent Spanish-American War.

The young people were invited to a reception honoring Bishop Reardon in the same hall were Lou Henry had once taught. When the program was over, they came to greet the guest of honor. Hoover posed his question bluntly:

"Father Mestres has refused to marry us without special permission from you. May we have it?"

The local priest was standing beside the Bishop. His superior turned to him.

"Is that correct?" he asked.

"Yes," answered the Padre, looking with almost fatherly pride at the serious hopeful blue eyes searching the Bishop's face.

"Then you have it," said the church dignitary.

Thus it was on February 10, 1899, Charles Henry gave his elder daughter, Lou, in marriage to Herbert Hoover in a simple ceremony performed at home by their family friend. The next day, the two sailed from San Francisco bound for China.

Chapter Five

THE CHINA YEARS

THE FOREIGN COMPOUND in Tientsin, where Lou Henry Hoover set up her first home, was a good proving ground for international understanding. Representatives of all the important nations were there, pitting wit and capital against greed in the attempt to control the resources of the vast empire. German and French, Belgian and English, Russian and Japanese were all struggling for spheres of influence. Concessions for railroad building and mining development were objects of intrigue.

The young American engineer found much to study. If he had expected relief from frustrating Australian problems he had a rude awakening. Governmental red tape in an English-speaking country may have been exasperating. But in this ancient land, where all business had to be transacted through interpreters, there were complications almost unfathomable to the Occidental mind.

His dual role multiplied the perplexities. As Chief Engineer for the Chinese Engineering and Mining Company he undertook his first assignment with assurance. This took him to the Kaiping Coal Mines near the Gulf of Chihli in Hopei Province, twenty-three miles inland along the Tientsin-Newchang Railroad. With a staff of engineers recruited from his associates in Australia, England and the United States, he undertook building an ice-free port for exporting coal. They built up the sea wall, installed modern machinery for handling coal, and began to dredge the harbor to allow deeper-draught colliers to enter. Such work was straight-forward, a task suitable for an engineer.

The other role, Advisor to the Imperial Minister of Mines, was intangible and confusing. He found Chinese procedure overlaid with traditions dating back to the time of King Solomon and earlier. Commissioners appointed in the reign of Emperor Yu, 2200 B.C., had reported on the resources of the country in gold, silver and cinnabar. During the intervening 4,000 years there had been almost continuous small-scale efforts to exploit these resources. Chang Yen-Mao, scheming to advance his prestige with the Dowager Empress, who had recently de-throned and imprisoned her son, tried to use Hoover for his own ends.

The wily Minister was not satisfied to mine and export prosaic coal and iron. He wanted to find the legendary gold. He would add to the magnificence of the Court and to his own political preferment by discovering new treasure. He knew what this man Hoover had done in Australia. He must produce gold for China as well.

The Hoovers were scarcely settled when Chang insisted upon a journey of exploration into Jehol in Inner Mongolia, one-hundred and fifty-six miles from a railroad. The expedition traveled with all the pomp and ceremony that the tradition-filled Chinese mind could conjure up. Although advance publicity had described the "foreign mandarin who had green eyes that penetrated solid rock to see hidden gold," practical Herbert Hoover only reported that the best veins had long ago been worked out. What was left would not justify the importation of expensive foreign machinery.

Chang was insistent on more exploration. Prospecting journeys were commanded into the provinces of Shantung, Shansi, Shensi, and across The Gobi. Each involved organizing great cavalcades of servants, grooms and hundreds of animals laden with tons of baggage. Occasionally Hoover would take his bride along. Lou Henry had been brought up to know and understand horses. She could camp like any good Californian.

She had already started to study the Chinese language. Her

gracious acceptance of the hospitality offered by local overlords made her welcome in this strange land. Genuine appreciation of beauty reflected in her response to the bold cliffs and precipes, as well as to ancient wares. She began to collect rare blue and white porcelains.

In their tent at night she would collaborate on reports that became bases for articles that began to appear in the *Engineering and Mining Journal.* In one of these Hoover enumerated the difficulties of his profession in China.

He explained that because the government had found itself financially embarrassed after the recent war, they had begun to open the Empire to foreign capital. Direct benefit to the imperial exchequer from their great mineral resources had been their expectation. Theoretically, all such rights belonged to the Emperor. Europeans not only had to obtain imperial consent, they also had to deal with the vested rights of native miners and with holders of surface rights. North of the Great Wall they also dealt with feudal princes, all of whom had direct mining privileges. More than that, there was a maze of governing officials everywhere who demanded their share of deference and "squeeze." Coal mines apparently were operated by natives without imperial notice; but metal mining was always carefully checked and sometimes had imperial supervision. Many doors opened after the Sino-Japanese war (1894-95) were gradually swinging shut, due to rising anti-foreign feeling.

Regulations of foreign participation in 1899 were extremely complicated. Every company had to be at least one-half Chinese, with the administration entirely in Chinese hands. Foreigners were only technical advisors. Each concession covered only one mine, and officials of the district must report favorably on both the mine and the company before granting a charter. While the foreigners were to furnish all capital, the Government claimed twenty-three per cent of the profits.

Hoover considered it part of his task as Court Advisor to attempt to codify mining law to insure government protection from foreign concession hunters. With the thoroughness he had applied to Stanford student affairs, he prepared a decree outlining methods whereby mineral rights could be leased with proper safeguards to investors, workers and government. While Chang smiled approval of its intent, the Minister was too involved with his own schemes to implement such reform.

The Hoovers had been in China only a year when it began to appear that all foreign capital invested in the Celestial Empire would be lost. In the early months of 1900 a society calling itself I Ho Tan—The Mailed Fist—burst in violent attack on all foreigners and any Chinese tainted with western ideas. By late spring these Boxers, as the foreign population dubbed them, had become so vicious that Hoover called in his geologists from their interior explorations. He and Lou were in Peking in June for a conference with Chang when she developed a serious sinus condition. Hastening to Tientsin's medical center, they arrived only a few days before the alarm bell on the town hall warned of impending Boxer attack.

Throughout the month-long siege of Tientsin that followed, the Hoovers became leaders of emergency relief, first of the many such experiences that would fill their later life. The first-aid she had mastered early in her China days made her invaluable to the medical staff. His engineering skills and his inherited Quaker response to need, helped to keep the fear-stricken International Settlement functioning.

Because their home was exposed to gunfire on the edge of the settlement, they accepted the invitation of Edward B. Drew, American Commissioner of Chinese Customs, to move with the other American families into his stoutly-walled home in the center of the settlement. Faithful Hoover servants came with them to aid in the work of this establishment. The house was soon converted into a dormitory. Women slept on the floor in one large room, men in another.

At times during the tense weeks stray bullets from outside whizzed into the area. Hysterical foreign civilians blamed the Chinese who had taken refuge among them. Hoover's personal interpreter, Lon Etong, was arrested and sentenced to death by an officious British Officer, Captain Bailey, who had refused to join with other military personnel commanded by Colonel

Wogack, the Russian who outranked all local officers. With an American flag as protection, Hoover intervened in time to stop the planned execution of Lon and a group of other Chinese. He gave his personal pledge that these men were innocent and would remain under his direct supervision.

He was not so immediately successful with his next plea. Chang Yen-Mao and the president of the Shanghai-Tientsin Railroad, Tong Shao-Yi, were among the leading Chinese who had thus come under his protection. Tong, a graduate of Columbia University and the largest stockholder in the Kaiping Coal Company, had become Hoover's strongest Chinese ally. When word came that these men were under arrest, Hoover leaped onto his bicycle to speed to the place on the river bank where Captain Bailey was holding a drumhead trial under flickering torch lights. Bailey preemptorily ordered the American out of his way. Cycling as fast as he could pedal, Hoover made for the Russian headquarters. He returned with Colonel Wogack and a platoon of Russian soldiers just in time to save the heads of his important Chinese associates.

This was not the only time that Hoover befriended Tong Shao-Yi. Later in the siege, after bullets had narrowly missed the Drew house, the Hoovers had returned to their original dwelling. One evening shells from The Dowager Empress, a powerful gun used by the Boxers, struck the house across the street. This was the home of Tong Shao-Yi, crowded with refugees to whom he had given haven. Horror-struck, the Hoovers watched as panic-stricken men, women, and children clambered out of the debris. The master himself came out, carrying the body of his wife. A servant followed with that of their baby.

Hoover dashed across the narrow street and forced his way through moaning survivors. Flames were bursting through shattered walls as he lifted Tong's four-year-old daughter to safety. (This brought unexpected thanks many years later when the wife of the Chinese Ambassador in Washington, Mrs. Wellington Koo, introduced herself to the United States Food Administrator as the child he had rescued!)

By early July respite came to the besieged Settlement with

the bugles of American Marines sounding across the plains. The first force was not large, but their machine guns symbolized security. Finally adequate reinforcements arrived. The wounded, women and children were evacuated under the guard and sent to Shanghai; but the Hoovers stayed until the siege was finally over. Then this item appeared in the *Engineering and Mining Press* in San Francisco on July 21, 1900: "H. C. Hoover, a California mining engineer, in charge of Chinese mines, cables from Shanghai that he has escaped from Tientsin and is safe."

The Chief Engineer of the Chinese Engineering and Mining Company found his enterprise dismembered. The assets of the company had been seized by competing foreign powers. The British Navy controlled the harbor and coal stocks at Chingwantao. The German Army held the coal yards at Taku and Tientsin. Japanese Army officers sat in the company offices at Tientsin. The American Army seized the coal steamers.

The Hoovers were preparing to return to America when Chang Yen-Mao sent for his Court Advisor. With the still nominal Minister of Mines, Hoover found Gustav Detring, a retired German customs official, who had long been one of Chang's many advisors. Detring had been, in fact, the original negotiator who had brought the Moreing interests to China. He was now distressed over threatened losses to European bondholders in the Chinese Engineering and Mining Company. The two suggested that the bondholders intervene to save the property. A cable consultation with Moreing in London paved the way for Hoover to accept a deed of trust as Moreing's agent, register it with the British Consul in Shanghai and bring it to London. There a new company would be reorganized as a British Corporation.

The Hoovers did some reorganizing of their own. Their travel schedule was changed from a Pacific cruise to a ship taking them to Genoa. On a quick trip through European capitals Hoover consulted the principal bondholders. With consent from all of them, Hoover laid the proposal on Moreing's desk. By December the Chinese Engineering and Mining Company,

Ltd., was registered in London and additional capital of several million dollars was authorized for the purpose of meeting obligations to creditors and restoring the property.

Hoover left London with a new title. He was now General Manager, at an increased salary plus a minor stock interest. Their stop enroute in California was shortened by the challenge to carry on the work the Boxers had interrupted in China.

Mrs. Hoover was in need of rest and left the ship in Japan while her husband proceeded to Tientsin. There he met a Belgian diplomat, Chevalier de Wouters, who had been assigned to carry out the delicate negotiations that would enable the new company to operate under Chinese law. Hoover left such complications to de Wouters. He had plenty to do in the technical field. Coal mining rights extended to the English company were expanded to cover the whole northern territory. Accordingly, he established headquarters at Tong Shan, one-hundred and ten miles from Tientsin.

As soon as he felt that it was safe for her to come, he sent for Lou. The only Caucasian woman in the settlement, she made her home a gathering place for the many young American engineers who came to assist in the undertaking. There was coal to be mined, cement to be made. The conversion of the strategic harbor at Chingwantao into an all-year, ice-free port must be completed. Hoover had 25,000 men under him. Most of them were ignorant, low-paid coolies.

He was appalled at the universal dishonesty, at their slowness and low average intelligence. He was convinced that profitable production rests on efficient labor. Recognizing that his coolies were not earning enough to buy adequate food, he raised wages. This in turn resulted in complications due to padded payrolls.

By the middle of the summer of 1901 Hoover was shocked to learn that Belgians had been quietly buying up a controlling interest in the Chinese Company, capitalizing on a 500 percent rise in the price of its stock in the international market. Soon the representative of the Belgian Syndicate, Emile Francqui, arrived from Hankow, where he had been serving as Belgian Consul. His instructions were to direct the business in China. Francqui had a brilliant mind, a strong will. He asked advice from no one. He immediately repudiated an agreement between de Wouters and Chang, made in February, whereby the Chinese stock-holders were to receive 275,000 shares and have some part in the management.

Hoover stood by his Chinese associates, maintaining that the agreement to which he had given approval was just and fair to all concerned; but Francqui insisted that Chang had committed fraud in assigning the property to the British Company. Bitter words passed between the American manager and the Belgian representative. Hoover resigned, despite Francqui's protests. The latter knew full well that the profits of the mine resulted from Hoover's efficiency. All that mattered to Hoover was justice. He was through with intrigue.

But Bewick-Moreing was not to lose the services of this competent and experienced young man. Hoover's cable to Moreing explaining why he was leaving for America was answered by a request that he accept a junior partnership in the firm. He was still "not quite thirty-five"! In fact, he was only twenty-seven.

Again, there was one condition in the acceptance. He must have home leave for a visit to California. They left via Nagasaki. It was September when they arrived in Monterey. The blue bay never looked more enticing. Those hills with their rim of wind-blown cypress seemed the one place in the world for their permanent home.

They realized that the new assignment meant constant travel; but that would not interfere with having a home base. They purchased a lot and began to draw plans. Once built, they would deed the house to the Henrys. But some day—in what they hoped would not be a too-distant future—there should be little Hoovers. Here would be the place where they could come to ride over the dunes and to acquire from their grandfather the same rapport with the out-of-doors that had made Lou Henry Hoover the companion she was to her engineer-husband.

Chapter Six

FULL PARTNER

The Hoovers could not linger in Monterey to watch blueprints translated into white walls. Before Thanksgiving they were back in London, ready to plunge into new responsibilities. Hoover found that two older members of the firm had retired. Part of their interest was to be divided—twenty per cent to Hoover, ten per cent to each of two other new members, T.W. Welstead and A.S. Rowe. The latter had been chief accountant for many years.

While his wife brightened a Hyde Park Gate flat with colorful Chinese scrolls and the precious blue-and-white porcelains, Hoover studied the maps of his firm's world-wide activities.

After he had been there for about ten months, Moreing left for a tiger hunt in Manchuria, vacationing with confidence that business would proceed as usual. Rowe, middle-aged and thoroughly conversant with all phases, was in charge. The new Junior Partner had proved equal to any emergency. But the older man could not have dreamed a more difficult test than that which befell Herbert Hoover at the close of his first year in London.

He was alone in the office when he picked up a letter, marked "Private-Confidential." Startled beyond belief as he read its first words, he followed through to the end a confession from Rowe, detailing a theft of over a million dollars from the firm —$500,000 of it in forged certificates of stock. The letter ended with a threat of suicide.

There was no way to confer with the Senior Partner. Hoover called in a few trusted leaders in mining circles. When he had finished reading them the letter, each man assured him that the firm was under no legal responsibility for the defalcation. But Hoover replied without hesitation that he would make it his personal duty to pay to the last dime, "tuppence", interrupted one of the Englishmen. And pay he did, although the savings from his first five professional years were wiped out by that decision. During the next three years while he continued to pay his portion of that self-imposed obligation, Mrs. Hoover quietly saw that the wife and children of the defaulting partner did not suffer. Moreing returned and assumed seventy-five percent of the loss. Rowe fled to Canada, leaving his family destitute. Arrested and brought back to England, he served a long prison term.

Technical direction of mining and transportation operations from Australia and New Zealand to India and Russia involved personal supervision. As often as possible, Mrs. Hoover closed the London flat and accompanied her husband on his inspection trips. Whenever the stay was long, they maintained temporary homes. In them she provided an atmosphere that made friends of business associates around the world.

Even the birth of their first son, Herbert, Jr., in London, on August 4, 1903, did not detain them long in civilization. Before the baby was two months old, the Hoovers sailed for Australia. Their baggage contained ingredients for preparation of proper formula throughout the long voyage.

When their ship docked at Perth, officials said that a vessel bearing Mrs. Leland Stanford back to America had just sailed. (Months later a letter came from Lou's college friend, Evelyn Wight, who had met Mrs. Stanford when she arrived in New York. She wrote that the elderly founder of their Alma Mater knew that they were arriving and stayed on the dock until the last moment, hoping to see "my boy out in Australia."

"Just wait," she added, "until I tell you what he has accomplished. The Senator's brother in Melbourne told me that Herbert Hoover is the highest paid man of his age in the world!")

After a brief stop at Perth, the Hoovers sailed on to Melbourne. Here they were met by Waldemar Lindgren. He had come, at his former assistant's request, to aid in plans for the recovery of gold from a subterranean river under the lava beds of Victoria Province. Investors had lost several millions when the promoter of the Lodden River System had committed suicide. Hoover thought that with the advice of the distinguished geologist he could retrieve these losses. Lindgren's long study of similar buried rivers in California had taught him to cope with the unforseen geological conditions so discouraging to the earlier engineer.

The Hoovers rented a house in Melbourne. Then the two geologists traversed the hot desert. Their combined report induced mine owners to sink another two million in an attempt to reach the hidden treasure. Cornish pumps were installed to drain the subterranean river.

Spring of 1904 found the Hoovers back in London, surprised to learn that the Branners were there. They drove at once to the small hotel where Dr. Branner had settled his family. Their most important friends *must* be Hoover house guests. Over protests from both Branners, baggage was piled into the big French Panhard (the Hoovers' first automobile), and they were driven to the flat at Hyde Park Gate.

Only two years had passed since the Rowe case had been settled. Lou Hoover confided to Mrs. Branner that "all we had left in the world was what you see in this room," looking fondly at the Chinese hangings and porcelains. But she added that her husband's hard work and increasing knowledge was now putting them securely on the road to recovery.

The Branner visit was a happy interlude in a life of almost constant travel. No sooner had their guests departed than it was time to take toddler, Herbert, Jr., on another long sea voyage. This time his mother had a sturdy harness to keep him tethered to her deck chair as they sailed down the west coast of Africa. She set up housekeeping in Johannesburg. Herbert, Sr., went on an inspection tour of coal and gold mines.

He might well have been back in Tong Shan when he went

underground at The Rand. Again he heard the familiar singsong of Chinese coolies. He protested this importation of cheap labor in a speech before the Transvaal Chamber of Commerce. As always he insisted that greater productivity resulted from the employment of efficient workers, well paid and provided with decent living conditions.

Their son's first Christmas was celebrated on shipboard en route to Melbourne again, after a brief stop-over in London. This short stay in Australia was to pave the way for a project which had stimulated Hoover's imagination since his first days on those quartz-strewn deserts. Four hundred miles north of Melbourne at Broken Hill in New South Wales there were mountains of tailings in the silver-lead-zinc district. Once the silver had been extracted, miners of the past had been unable to do more with the dump.

Hoover had been giving studious attention to current research in the treatment of such residue. When he arrived at Broken Hill he found engineers trying out a new process developed by two Australians. This looked practical. He returned to London to report to Bewick-Moreing.

When he arrived in January, 1905, echoes of his China past were reverberating in the British press. Chang Yen Mao, resplendent in robes of tribute silk topped by his black mandarin skull cap with the priceless pearl given to him by the Empress, was in court pressing suit against Bewick-Moreing and the Chinese Engineering and Mining Company, Ltd. With him was Gustav Detring, the former German customs official who had acted as advisor in the negotiations leading to the formation of this foreign company after the Boxer troubles. Their purpose was to establish Chang's "rights" under the agreement which Francqui had repudiated five years ago.

Hoover, who had resigned in protest over Francqui's action, had always stood by his Chinese associates. Now both he and the Belgian diplomat de Wouters, who had negotiated the original agreement, testified as to its validity. As he looked across the court room at six-foot Chang in all his splendor, he saw in memory flickering torches lighting the mock trial of this same man on the river bank in China. He had stayed the executioner's hand that night. He knew, as few in that court room did, the amount of behind-the-scenes intrigue which had now sent the mandarin across the world. Chang was there to fight not only for the mine property, but also for his very life. The Dowager Empress, at the insistence of the new Viceroy, Yuan Shi Kai, had ordered Chang to recover the property deeded to the British firm, or to forfeit his life. Once more Hoover's straightforward words saved this man, who returned to his former position as director-general of the Chinese company.

Hoover's action was not forgotten. Twenty-three years later in the midst of the 1928 Presidential campaign in the United States, Tong Shao-yi, who had subsequently been Prime Minister of China twice, gave a *New York Times* interviewer a long refutation of slurs on Herbert Hoover which had been dug up by political opponents on the basis of this trial. In the interview, the man Hoover had rescued during the Boxer uprising testified to the complete loyalty of all Chinese who had been associated with the American engineer in those early years.

Many problems disturbed the Hoovers as they traveled from country to country. Sometimes he must have wondered if George Starr had been right in advising him to stick to the profession which kept him so constantly on the move, allowing so little time for home life. There was a brief sojourn in the United States in the summer following the conclusion of the Chinese case. Then the Hoovers sailed across the Pacific so that he could inspect the Talisman Mine in New Zealand under Bewick-Moreing management, with Hoover on the Board.

From there they proceeded to Melbourne. Reports from the Lodden River were bad. The Cornish pumps had been performing up to expectation, removing undiminishing volumes of water from the flooded mines. Yet the main lead was still elusive. The Directors concluded that there was no use sinking any more money in further effort. They entered that project on the red side of the ledger.

Prospects at Broken Hill were brighter. A new company, the Zinc Corporation, which was formed late in 1905, gave promise of fulfilling his dreams of recovering wealth hidden in those mountains of tailings. He appointed a Stanford classmate, Deane P. Mitchell, as manager.

Nearby the Sulphide Corporation had engaged the Minerals Separation Company of London, whose new "agitation-froth process" was averaging a seventy-two percent recovery of zinc at their Central Mine. Zinc Corporation engineers decided to switch to this method.

Theodore Hoover had just come to London as Consulting Engineer and General Manager for the Minerals Separation Company. Perhaps, at long last the brothers would achieve their ambition of close association in business.

Return of the Herbert Hoovers to England meant that for the first time in their adult lives the two families were together. Theodore had married his childhood sweetheart, Mildred Brooke of Baltimore. Her Quaker family had gone east from West Branch about the same time that Herbert had become a westerner. She loved to recall the days when she and Bertie's cousins, Alice and Walter, had shared their farm-cooked lunches in the Iowa schoolyard, and the chubby orphan who was now her brother-in-law had joined their circle.

But the Hoover professional tie-up was short-lived. Word came from Mitchell in New South Wales that the Minerals Separation process was unsuccessful for the Zinc Corporation. He recommended that they try a new Elmore Vacuum Process. Herbert Hoover okayed the change, despite his confidence that his brother's creative ability would ultimately succeed in adapting to their needs the apparatus used by the neighboring Sulphide Corporation.

In February, 1907, another Australian tour took the Herbert Hoovers back to Melbourne and later to Broken Hill. To their surprise they found David Starr Jordan lecturing in Melbourne. He was scheduled to give more lectures in Adelaide, capital of South Australia. Hoover was on his way to that part of the country. As the two traveled together, the young engineer discussed his future.

He told his friend that he felt he had gone as far as he

wanted to in his profession—that all there was ahead now was the accumulation of more money. He had all he needed of that. He was receiving $5,000 a year as a mining expert and $95,000 as "financial expert," managing partner in Bewick-Moreing. He planned to return to London, resign, and complete the translation of an ancient treatise on metallurgy, on which he and Mrs. Hoover were spending spare time. Then he would go back to America in search of some sort of executive work where he could be of service.

Dr. Jordan listened, but he gave no advice. He had just heard Professor Kernot of the engineering faculty at Melbourne remark: "Your friend looks too young to be an engineer."

He reminded Hoover that he was rendering service in what he was doing and changed the subject. In Sydney, Jordan had run into a member of the Stanford History Department, Payson Treat, who was purchasing books for his new course on the Far East. Hoover had personal interest in this project, for he had joined Thomas Welton Stanford and Deane Mitchell in providing funds for this, the first course of its kind in any American university.

Soon after this visit with Dr. Jordan the Hoovers returned to London. They hoped now to carry out the program outlined in the Australian conversation. The translation of "De Re Metallica," first undertaken as a pastime, was becoming an absorbing task. They discovered that their combined talents—her knowledge of Latin and his understanding of the material described in the ancient text—were making it possible to unravel the obscure passages. Scholars had been baffled since the German, George Bauer (his name Latinized to Agricola by his teachers), had published this first treatise on mineralogy, mining, and metallurgy in 1550.

The Hoovers had spent long companionable hours puzzling over the old text which he had found in a London second-hand bookshop. Whenever they could not understand the process, they tried out what they thought Agricola meant in a home laboratory set up for the purpose. This, like their other equipment, was portable. Their growing accumulation of notes and collateral reference books had become part of the essential baggage wherever they went. Now, as they were waiting in London for the birth of their second child, they worked with renewed eagerness toward the completion of the project.

Allan Hoover, born in mid-summer, was named for the uncle in West Branch who had first taken his orphaned nephew into heart and home. But the name happened to have a double significance. His mother's Stanford chum, Evelyn Wight, had been promised a namesake, should the baby be a girl. Now the widow of a New York writer, Mansfield Allan, she could divide the honor with Uncle Allan.

This baby did not have any more peaceful nursery than his older brother. In spite of what Herbert Hoover had said to Dr. Jordan about terminating his professional career, his reputation as a diagnostician of sick mines kept him in great demand. He could not retire yet. The next patient was in Upper Burma.

On September 18, when Allan was five weeks old, the family packed baby food, folding crib, Agricola notes, and the portable laboratory, and boarded ship again. They sailed southward along the coast of Africa, across the Indian Ocean and into the Bay of Bengal. From Rangoon they went by rail to Mandalay, where once more a foreign rented house became their home.

Although this was the first time his family had come here with him, Kipling-land was already familiar to Herbert Hoover. A considerable amount of his own fortune was in fact invested in the jungle mines of northern Burma.

Curiosity about them as a probable source of Ming silver had dated from his own early days in China. The Hoovers' history-gathering instinct had unearthed tales of luxury-loving rulers who had sent treasure hunters to the upper reaches of the Irrawaddy River, just across the China border in neighboring Burma. They had heard of jade, rubies and other precious stones, as well as vast quantities of silver brought from there to adorn the Celestial Court in Peking.

It had not surprised the junior partner of Bewick-Moreing

three years before when a shipboard acquaintance had sounded out his possible interest in re-developing some ancient Burmese mines. At the time Hoover was returning to Colombo after examining some tin mines in Penang. His deck companion, A. C. Martin, had described experiences in building a railroad from Mandalay to Lashio. Here, he said, he had acquired a lease on these abandoned properties and enlisted the backing of a London promotor.

When Martin mentioned the name of this promotor, Hoover had immediately recalled meeting Tilden Smith at Broken Hill. One of his first calls when he reached London was at Smith's office. He listened to a long recital of the difficulties Smith's company had encountered. All of these could be overcome with sufficient capital. To that end, he persuaded some of Bewick-Moreing's clients to join him and Smith in taking an option on a controlling interest in the enterprise.

The young engineering scout they sent had cabled encouraging estimates. There were hundreds of thousands of tons of reclaimable lead in slag heaped around the ancient workings. This sounded so preposterous that Hoover dispatched an experienced American to make an independent check. C. D. Clark's report seemed even more unbelievable. Hoover decided to see for himself and directed his advance guard to begin surveys for extension of the existing railroad to the old mines.

That first trip, made in 1905, provided Hoover with some of his best adventure stories and marked the beginning of one of the world's greatest lead-silver-zinc developments. After he and Clark had traveled about one-hundred and thirty miles up the railroad built by his earlier acquaintance, they were greeted at Hsipaw, capital of Upper Shan Province, by a native prince who spoke perfect Oxford English. The Swabwa was, however, a troubled man. His British schooling had almost lost him the respect of his subjects, who resented his preference for a foreign tongue. Furthermore, he had no white elephant, a basic necessity for royal prestige.

Before he had broached his engineering project to the Swabwa, Hoover had made it his personal responsibility to search for and find a white elephant. That gift paved the way for one of his great engineering accomplishments. For the grateful prince responded generously to the American's vision.

Assured of this cooperation, Hoover had organized an exploratory expedition. He had returned to Mandalay full of schemes that he felt would bring the mines back to profitable productivity. He would build roads, lay a roadroad across Himalaya-like mountains and construct bridges over terrifying gorges. The Swabwa ordered his tribesmen to work for the American who promised them wages beyond their fondest dreams. Twenty-thousand responded.

Now, two years later, Hoover was returning to inspect the results of their labor. The railroad was completed. A smelter in Mandalay was ready to melt the slag. The Hoovers' stay lengthened into months. 1907 ended without a glimpse of home, the first year since he had engaged in foreign work that he had not been in America for even a short period. But it was not until after he returned to London in January, 1908, that the Burma Corporation began its fabulous production of lead, production that in the decades that followed ran into millions of tons, including great quantities of silver and zinc.

CHAPTER SEVEN

ENGINEER-AT-LARGE

THAT WINTER HERBERT Hoover made a start toward carrying out the intention he had confided to Dr. Jordan on the train to Adelaide. He resigned as outside man for Bewick-Moreing, although he retained a financial share in many of the firm's projects. Then he opened his own office as a Consulting Engineer.

Rather than ending his travels, his mileage increased year after year. His interests expanded from Australia to Nicaragua and on to Nigeria. In April he was in Singapore. In August he was back in London. He reported to the shareholders of the Zinc Corporation that, even with the current low price of metals, they were making a profit of about £48,000 a year. He added that if they succeeded in contemplated technical improvements, the profits would soon be £100,000.

Everywhere he had resident engineers to whom he had become "The Chief." Mitchell remained as Australian Manager. Another Stanford classmate, Jack Means, was running the tin mines in Nigeria. Fred Nobs, a younger Stanford-trained engineer, was sent to Nicaragua.

The family accompanied him on most of his travels. Work on "De Re Metallica" progressed slowly. The summer of 1908 found the Hoovers in London with a new address: The Red House, Hornton Street, Kensington.

This rambling red brick Georgian house soon became the unofficial meeting place of Americans in London. French windows extending to the floor revealed intimate glimpses of beautiful lawns and a well-kept walled-in garden, which shut off the roar of London traffic.

They enjoyed this privacy for only a few months. An invitation then came from Dr. Branner, asking Hoover to give a series of lectures in the Geology Department at Stanford during the coming semester, an opportunity the Hoovers could not resist. He accepted with alacrity.

Once more Lou Henry Hoover packed up babies and their equipment. They sailed across the Atlantic in the midst of winter storms, journeyed by rail to California, had a brief visit with the Henrys in Monterey, and arrived at Stanford on January 13, 1909. For one night they were guests of the Branners; but this time there was another friend ready to share her home with them for the three months they expected to be at the University.

Evelyn Wight Allan, who had returned that fall to become the first Dean of Women, welcomed her friends to one of the brown-shingled double houses on Salvatierra Row in the rapidly expanding residential section of the campus. Behind its privet hedge she showed them a yard where "her baby" and his older brother could play in the California sunshine.

The *Stanford Daily* heralded the arrival of "one of our best known graduates" with an enthusiasm that sharply increased enrollment in *Geology and Mining 10-B*. The announcement promised that the closing lecture of the series would be open to the community and would cover some phase of world activity.

Faculty members and old friends flocked to see the Hoovers and to share, around intimate dinner tables, the fabulous tales the two would tell in such an environment. These people heard about the turquoise mines Hoover had uncovered near Mt. Sinai, and of his trips across the Abyssinian desert, making a survey of mineral resources for the Conquering Lion of Judah.

Those weeks on the Stanford campus were happy ones for Lou and Herbert Hoover. They took long walks in the hills. They could visit the Branners, "J.P.," and Dr. Jordan. They began to realize that here, on the campus, was where their dream house must stand someday. The one they had built for the Henrys in Monterey would do for visits, but this was the place where they really belonged.

Herbert Hoover, however, was doing more than lecture to a selected group of future mining engineers and enjoying old friends. He was making mental notes of campus needs and beginning to fulfill a vow he had made long ago in China.

Across the Pacific he had worried over threats to the very existence of the University that had given him and so many other struggling students a start. After Senator Stanford's death he had watched from afar as the widowed Jane Lathrop Stanford used all her wits and her resources to keep the doors open. When friends at home sent clippings relating the story of the law suit over the inheritance, he had resented slurs on the Senator's name. And he was filled with ire by the picture of the black-bonneted widow traveling to the Victoria Jubilee in London with her satchel full of precious gems to sell so that the "children of California" could continue to be educated. "Some day," he had promised himself, "I will go back to look after *her* interests and her money."

A student assembly was the first to hear his plans. He described the $50,000 clubhouse and trophy room he envisioned as a rallying point for the development of student spirit. This, he said, should be built and maintained by students and alumni, independent of university funds and authority. He had $10,000 of alumni money ready to start the fund, money he refused to acknowledge as his own, in spite of persistent rumors.

He was disturbed by the lack of dining facilities for Encina Hall. The room in which he had once "hashed" was now a game and lounge room. Members of the Eating Clubs used temporary shacks or walked the mile-long Palm Drive to "Larkin's-on-the-circle," or to some other Palo Alto or Mayfield restaurant. He found three of his classmates planning to build some one-story quadrangles next to Encina where the clubs could have independent dining rooms. He gave them substantial backing.

Dr. Jordan invited him to join the faculty and make Stanford his permanent home, a tempting offer to the wandering Hoovers. But there were too many other commitments. He had obligations hard to sever.

Nevertheless, he established a San Francisco office and began to renew acquaintance with western mining men. Among them was T. A. Rickard, now associated with his cousin, Edgar, in publishing the *Mining and Scientific Press.* Hoover urged the Rickards to join him in starting a similar journal in London. He supported his invitation with promise of financial backing.

They agreed to meet him in London in the coming fall. Then Hoover accepted an invitation to repeat the Stanford lectures at Columbia University and left for New York. He established a second American office at 71 Broadway and accepted membership in the National Republican Club. Thus, he registered loyalty to the political ideals of his forefathers. Then he made a quick trip to South Russia to investigate rumors of oil in the Maikop field.

His family did not accompany him on this journey. Instead, Mrs. Hoover invited Dr. Jordan's daughter, Edith, to sail with her on the S.S. *Lusitania,* so they could have the house ready for her husband's return to London in early May. Ordinarily, Mrs. Hoover preferred a less pretentious and slower mode of travel. Now time was important. Hoover had taken his lecture notes with him to prepare them for publication in book form. She wanted to be free to help in the editing.

Red House was full of activity all summer. Traveling Americans had already discovered that here, in spite of its typically British exterior, was a bit of their homeland abroad. Dinner hour was a time when the busy Hoovers laid work aside and opened their doors to friends from near and far. Edith Jordan noted in her diary one evening that she was the only guest who had not been through the siege of Tientsin. Writers and publishers, both American and British, added zest to their dinner parties. Mary Austin was in London. One evening she, too, was a guest, entertaining a small group by reading the manuscript of her latest book, "Christ in Italy."

Other nights the guest list included New Yorkers from Wall

Street, in London with large funds to invest. Hoover maintained a room adjacent to his office in the London Wall Buildings for such visitors so that they could watch the London stock market and time their investments accordingly. Of course, too, there were always mining men from the farflung scenes of his interests.

Then the Ray Lyman Wilburs arrived, with their four children, en route to Munich for a year. After these friends had gone on to Germany, Hoover received the first copies of his "Principles of Mining," just off the press of the Hill Publishing Company in New York.

Volume I of the Rickards' *London Mining Magazine* in September carried a review. This said in part ". . . while the book would have gained from closer editing and re-arrangement of involved sentences . . . it was delightful to receive a book full of first-hand information and enriched with notes taken from the personal experience of a mining engineer who ranks among the first in the profession." The reviewer reserved his highest praise for the chapters on administration: "They are written by one having authority in these difficult matters, and they are re-enforced by facts of an eloquent nature . . . the author in his concluding paragraphs dwells with enthusiasm on the part played by the engineer in the complex civilization of our day and appeals to the *esprit de corps* of the profession."

Early in the summer of 1910 the Wilburs returned to make a tour of Scotland with the Hoovers. In their Edinburgh hotel they chanced on another Stanford faculty couple, Dr. and Mrs. Henry Rushton Fairclough, Lou Henry's former professor of Latin. The tall, aesthetic Scot and his stocky wife, who was also his cousin, were going in a different direction at the time, but they accepted an invitation to dine in Kensington late in the summer.

The Faircloughs arrived in London just as Hoover returned from another trip to Russia. This time he had gone to investigate iron and copper mines in the Ural Mountains at the request of the British promotor Leslie Urquhart. Hoover entertained his visitors with stories and pictures, showing the vast estate in the Urals, "half as big as Maryland," which he said had belonged to a branch of the Romanoff family for generations. He told them that these people had lived off the riches of the great iron ore deposits. The Directors' house was "larger than Buckingham Palace." But in recent years the present Baron had called upon Urquhart for financial help in restoring the productivity of the mines. After sinking thousands of dollars of investors' money in a futile attempt, Urquhart had called in the doctor of sick mines.

The plight of the thousands of peasants dependent upon the operation of the Kyshtim properties had appealed to Hoover's heart, as the engineering challenge had to his brain. He told Dr. Fairclough that the introduction of modern mining methods and the encouragement of the people could result in increased returns to the investors, and certainly, it would give all these human beings a new incentive toward decent living. Hoover had estimated carefully what would be needed in the way of modern furnaces, transportation facilities and factories to process the iron and steel, and also to develop the latent copper and other mineral deposits. He was now directing the purchase of needed machinery and engaging engineers trained in a similar geologic environment. These he expected to find among men who had had experience in the mines of Butte, Montana.

Their Stanford visitors found more personal interest in the conversation on another night when the two couples dined alone. This time the Hoovers brought out what they had finished of the Agricola translation, the first inkling that Dr. Fairclough had of this project undertaken by his former pupil.

The professor was impressed with the practical approach to this difficult self-assignment. Their conversation revealed first-hand knowledge of Saxony where Agricola had grown up. Hoover was thoroughly familiar with the prolific mining district of Joachimsthal near Freiburg, for they had visited this little Bohemian town in which Agricola had once practiced medicine. Dr. Fairclough took the Latin text of Book I and a galley proof of the Hoover translation with him as he left for home.

Another Stanford visitor made Red House his London headquarters that summer. David Starr Jordan arrived, with Herbert Stolz, a newly appointed Rhodes Scholar as his secretary. They were enroute to Austria to attend the World Congress of Zoologists. Under the auspices of the World Peace Foundation, they would also meet the pacificists of Europe.

Hoover took time to drive his guests to many historic places in the British Isles. They stopped for picnic lunches in the forests of the Cotswolds, in the shadow of Tintern Abbey, along the silvery Trent where Izaak Walton had fished three-hundred years before. In Wales they observed the decline in the smelting industry due to reluctance to use modern methods; and they followed enticing roads through the Irish countryside.

Their conversation was naturally concerned with the growing peace movement, although Hoover remarked that he had "never before heard so much talk of peace, nor seen so many men buckling on their side arms." Dr. Jordan made much of what he called "The Unseen Empire of Finance," holding that the civilized nations of the day, except the United States, Canada, and a few of the smaller European nations, were virtually in the hands of their creditors who pyramided war debts to encourage production of arms.

Hoover did not agree. He did not think that wars could be attributed to individuals or to groups of individuals. He felt that a diagnosis of world conditions should, like that of physical illness, be based on deep study of underlying causes. As these discussions revealed the many problems involved, he determined that some day he would collect material for basic study in the realm of permanent peace.

Chapter Eight

SERVICE IN MANY FIELDS

Dr. Jordan crossed the channel to attend his meetings on the continent; the Wilburs sailed home to America; and Hoover found his multitudinous responsibilities more demanding than ever. Production from the Burma mines continued to increase. Kyshtim was beginning to be recognized as the most important metallurgical center in Russia. The Zinc Corporation was considering another change of process. Mitchell reported that Elmore could not cope with the current admixture of slimes and he recommended a return to the now more flexible Minerals Separation Process.

The *Mining and Scientific Press* for August 6, 1910, commented on this change: "the mechanical details have been worked out by Theodore J. Hoover, whose practical and theoretical skill as an engineer has been of the greatest possible value." But T.J. had resigned from the Minerals Separation Company to establish his own consulting offices on the same floor of Salisbury House as those of his brother. Several other former associates of both Hoovers had gathered in that building, where they began to be known in mining circles as The Syndicate, although their offices were actually all independent.

While the Herbert Hoovers were devoting much time to the completion of "De Re Metallica," T.J. was also at work on a book. The preface to his textbook, "Concentration of Ores by Flotation," was dated July 4, 1912.

That same month the Authors' Preface to "De Re Metallica" was signed at Red House. Before the end of the year the vellum-bound tome was issued by the *Mining Magazine.* Edgar Rickard had spared no effort toward making the work as nearly a replica of the original as possible. The dedication read:

To John Casper Branner, Ph.D.
The inspiration of whose teaching is not
less great than his contribution to science.

During this year, Hoover's professional interest had shifted partially from metals to petroleum. This brought him to California again. In the fall of 1912 the family was settled in a house on Pacific Avenue in San Francisco.

With a British associate, Chester A. Beatty, he had acquired a dominant share in the Continental Oil Company, which owned large acreage in several California fields, as well as in eastern Mexico. When that company sold out to the newly-organized General Petroleum, Hoover was elected a director of the larger company on November 29, 1912. At the same time, he loaned a considerable sum to the company on a short term note to assist in their ambitious program of building a pipe line from the San Joaquin Valley to San Pedro and a refinery at Vernon.

That month, too, marked the beginning of Herbert Hoover's service on the Board of Trustees of Stanford University. Since the resignation of Judge George Crothers, who had been a personal appointee of Mrs. Stanford, was simultaneous with Hoover's selection, he found himself the only alumnus on the Board. He took this assignment with grave recognition of all that it involved. It was as if the hands of the Founders were laid on his shoulders; and he immediately gave University interests priority in his active mind.

As he had once taken student affairs in hand, he now assumed command in financial administration. He suggested that Trustee meetings be combined with luncheons and dinners. Thus, the whole membership was drawn into discussions of business matters, hitherto confined to the Finance Committee. Soon the first full statement of resources and liabilities ever presented to the public was released. Hoover pointed out to his fellow members that an overlarge proportion of University income was being laid aside for emergency and reserve funds. He demonstrated that they could afford to devote more of the current income to yearly needs.

As soon as the holiday season was over and the boys settled in school, the Hoovers and Rickards sailed for Russia. They found the mines producing well. Many side lines were also offering employment to thousands of peasants on the great estate. American engineers had encouraged the people to distill turpentine and recover acetone from nearby forests. Local artisans were making artistic figurines and decorative objects at the iron foundry, still in operation after at least a hundred years of continuous production. Mrs. Hoover purchased many of these, and her husband promised the workers that he would find markets for whatever they could produce.

They chose a wintry day for the first visit to the foundry. The four snuggled into the droshky for a ride over the snowy steppes. Sleighbells jingled as the spirited horses pulled them forward. Hoover sat with his back to the driver, facing the others. Rickard, on the outer part of the seat, was reaching through the thick layer of coats for a cigarette when a snowball, hard as ice, snapped back from the prancing horse's hoof, hitting him full in the chest. A deep chuckle came from his host. Wisdom born of experience, rather than pure courtesy, had caused him to ride backward!

When he returned to San Francisco in late spring, Hoover found the Stanford Trustees struggling with the problem of executive personnel. The World Peace Foundation was becoming insistent in its demands for the services of Dr. Jordan. Up to the present, the university president had used his two half-year sabbaticals for world lecture tours devoted to this cause. But he had seriously considered asking for retirement for the purpose. In the month preceeding Hoover's election to the Board, he had acceded to demands of educational leaders and requested, instead, that he be allowed a leave-of-absence from the University during the first semester of 1913-1914.

Hoover had other ideas. He understood the impelling concern with world affairs that was overshadowing all else in Dr. Jordan's mind. At the same time, he wanted very much to honor Dr. Branner, who, as vice president, was carrying so much of the administrative load during increasing absences of Dr. Jordan. In the spring of 1913, he proposed to the Board that a new office, that of Chancellor, be created. This would retain Dr. Jordan's prestige at the top level of University leadership, but would leave him free in the use of his time. Next he had to persuade Dr. Branner, then preparing to spend the summer on scientific research in Brazil, to assume the presidency for two years, until his retirement at sixty-five.

The change was fraught with emotion. No other member of the Board would undertake its handling; but Hoover, with characteristic directness, carried the idea through. In a letter to Dr. Jordan on May 13th, he concluded: "I am very happy, indeed, to have effected this arrangement, which, I believe, is so much in the interest of the institution to which we are all so devoted, and of two of my most esteemed friends."

Although his family had remained in San Francisco during that school year, Hoover himself had spent only one month away from his world-wide engineering projects, and in that short time had aided the Stanford Trustees in these major decisions. Dr. Jordan wrote of Hoover's contribution in a letter to Dr. Branner, who had started for Brazil as soon as the decision was made.

"It is marvellous," he said, "how Hoover is handling our Board. Almost every reform we have dreamed of has slipped through as if oiled . . . Mr. Hopkins said that Hoover gave them in ten days more ideas than they had had before in ten years, and he seems to be arranging all sorts of things so that the incoming President, as I have long prophesied, will have a soft snap as compared with the experiences of the late incumbent."

When his last meeting with the Board was held the end of May, Jordan wrote again that every member of the group seemed to feel that each projected change and reform was his own. Apparently Mr. Hoover had devoted his whole time to persuading each individual member that it was his special duty to stand for radical improvements and to convert all conservatives. The result was that everybody was busy converting everyone else, and the forward-looking schemes all went through. Jordan was particularly gratified that $15,000 a year had been set aside to increase salaries.

As soon as the boys finished the spring school term, the Hoovers left for London. In June Dr. and Mrs. Jordan with their youngest son, Eric, came to visit. This time the Jordans stayed three weeks in Red House. Although the Hoovers could not always accompany them, they sent Dr. and Mrs. Jordan touring the countryside in one of their cars, and then re-joined them later in the summer at Stratford. For the second time the Hoovers had rented a quaint old Manor House, built in 1550, and filled it with antiques as well as choice period furniture.

During the summer of 1913, Edgar Rickard had a call from an old California friend, Senator James D. Phelan. The Senator told him that he was an official representative of the coming Panama Pacific International Exposition which San Franciscans were planning in celebration of the expected completion of the Panama Canal in 1915. Phelan was greatly discouraged over the lack of response abroad. Did Rickard know anyone in the American community in London who would have the vision and the zeal to promote this idea?

Without hesitation Rickard told his friend that the leader of their group was a mining engineer by the name of Hoover, a fellow Californian. Phelan checked with others whom he knew. Their answer was the same. Herbert Hoover was the acknowledged "Chief" of these Americans who were living in London, not as exiles, but in pursuance of the world's work. They told him that Hoover was not only interested in his profession, but that he also kept up on all world affairs with comprehensive understanding.

Phelan asked Rickard to bring Hoover to meet him for dinner. He broached the idea of appointing him as European representative for the Exposition. Hoover agreed, but said that he would need a Britisher as his coordinator, someone familiar with both countries. He suggested an acquaintance named Billy Goode (later Sir William). Through this contact they were able to reach the ear of Sir Thomas Lipton, who immediately invited the Hoovers and Rickards to a dinner party on his yacht at Southampton. Here, in the spirit of good fellowship, Hoover sold the idea of the importance of British participation in a project with valuable significance to world trade.

Sir Thomas promised to carry his enthusiasm not only to the British Board of Trade, but also to his many friends and associates on the continent. Satisfied that this project was in good hands, the Hoovers prepared to return to America.

They arrived in California in December, rented a house on the Stanford Campus, and hoped to settle down for a period of home life.

The day after Christmas his fellow Trustee, Frank Anderson, President of the Bank of California, one of the men who had added endorsement to Janin's recommendation for Hoover's Australian appointment sixteen years before, brought him a new problem. It had nothing to do with mining, but it required the same kind of financial expertise for which Bewick-Moreing had paid him the bulk of his salary.

Anderson told Hoover that the Sloss-Lilienthal family, pioneers in the business and industrial development of California, were on the verge of bankruptcy. Such a failure, he said, could involve hundreds of business associates and strike a blow at the economic structure of the State. He wondered if Hoover could spare the time to study the implications, talk with the principals, and suggest some method of salvaging the toppling estate. One member of the family, Leon Sloss, a fellow-Director of General Petroleum, was also on the Stanford Board of Trustees. The approach was easy, if Hoover could be sure that his services were welcome. Anderson had no doubt of that. He brought them together in his office. Sloss gratefully agreed to place all the facts at his colleague's disposal.

Hoover found that the families had over-extended credit in developing such enterprises as the Northern Electric Railway, and great land schemes in West Sacramento County.

This was not exactly the kind of public service Hoover had envisioned when he spoke with Dr. Jordan in Australia, but it was a job that needed to be done. He put aside all personal business and concentrated for three months on the facts as he found them. All of the family, their lawyers and their bankers cooperated. Even the matriach, Mrs. Louis Sloss, Sr., eighty-four years old, living comfortably in ignorance of the real state of affairs, had a call from Herbert Hoover. He found that her inheritance was legally untouchable, that her sons did not wish to excite her with their troubles; but he was sure that she would understand. She did. With her cooperation and Mr. Hoover's good offices, affairs were finally set in order, creditors satisfied, and the family name and fortune saved.

When all the details of this operation were completed, Sloss asked what he owed. "Nothing," replied Hoover. That was a service to his State and for his friends. Unconsciously his action portrayed the spirit of lines he had recently translated from Agricola, a quotation from the ancient Greek philosopher, Antiphanes:

"Now, by the gods, why is it necessary for a man to grow rich? Why does he possess much money unless that he may, as much as possible, help his friends, and sow the seeds of a harvest of gratitude, sweetest of the goddesses?"

Appreciation of the Hoover contribution to the mining profession began to take tangible form. On March 9, 1914, Lou Henry and Herbert Hoover were honor guests at a banquet given by the American Institute of Mining Engineers at the Biltmore in New York. The first gold medal awarded by the Institute for outstanding service was given that night to the translators of "De Re Metallica" as a reward for work of the highest scholarship, unusual in a profession which the world regarded as essentially materialistic.

Mrs. Hoover returned to Stanford to remain there with the boys until the close of the school year while her husband crossed the Atlantic again. The Board of Directors of the Exposition were anxious to complete arrangements for British and

European participation, and there were other business affairs that necessitated Hoover's presence abroad.

He visited the capitals of Europe as he had done in behalf of the bondholders of the Chinese Mining and Engineering Company a little more than twelve years before. Now he came, not as a financier, but as an envoy of goodwill from his native land. He saw and heard much that made him fear for the immediate future of Europe—although in many places he listened to discussions of the World Peace Movement.

After Hoover returned to London in May, he had a brief visit from the Jordans, who had spent that entire year abroad. In spite of all Jordan had seen, in the Balkans, Egypt, and the Near East, as well as all of Europe, the Stanford Chancellor was still optimistic. He was sure that world peace could be preserved. He was about to join Norman Angell and his group of young pacifists at a summer school of Internationalism at Old Jordan's in Buckinghamshire, once the home of William Penn.

Hoover was more practical. He told his brother that he felt the war was coming, and that if it did, it would wreck Western individualism.

"Let's go home," he said to Theodore, "get out what we have and retire on the income."

Part Two

ACTIVE SERVICE

CHAPTER NINE

HELP FOR STRANDED AMERICANS

ON THE FIRST of August the Jordans were guests at Red House, preparing to sail to America within a week. The Chancellor, taking as his secretary, Emile Holman, recently appointed as a Rhodes Scholar from California, had just completed a tour of Ireland.

They had picked up Mrs. Jordan in Wales and then had stopped in Cambridge to call on Dr. Lawrence Oppenheim, professor of International Law. Despite the gathering war clouds over Europe following the murder of Franz Ferdinand and the attack on Serbia, these students of world affairs did not feel that Great Britain would be vitally concerned. The Peace Movement was strong. Difficult situations had been patched up in 1908 and 1911. Probably things would straighten out again.

Two days later Germany declared war on France! Americans on the continent found all boundary lines closed, banks suspended, transportation canceled. As soon as frontiers were reopened to neutrals, these travelers flocked across the Channel, arriving in London panic-stricken, out of funds, but with the one idea to escape to the far-away safety of home and America.

Among them was a young student from Carmel-by-the-Sea, in California, with her mother and two sisters. Lillian Devendorf had been studying violin in Brussels, where they had expected to remain two years. They had managed to get passage on a Channel boat but had lost half the value of the money they had with them in the exchange. They were among the lucky ones who had secured passage home. That ticket had used every farthing. They had a week to spend in London before the ship sailed from Liverpool. The proprietors of the Morley Hotel were understanding.

"We know you will hear from your husband soon," they said, "in the meantime, whatever you need is yours."

Mrs. Devendorf was not in the habit of asking for help. She had her letter of credit, but no place to use it. Then she remembered something. Their home account was in the Bank of Monterey.

"Mr. Henry's son-in-law, Herbert Hoover, lives in London," she told her daughter, "perhaps he will cash our check!"

The Devendorfs found "Mr. Henry's son-in-law" at The Savoy. The iridescent prisms of its ballroom chandeliers no longer glittered above gay waltzers. Rather, its walls echoed voices of American travelers anxiously seeking help from an American Relief Committee.

Of course, Herbert Hoover, working with his Committee, would cash the check of a client of his father-in-law! He had been cashing checks for many days. Sometimes it was a friend who asked. More often it was an obscure American school teacher. Once an Indian Chief, complete with paint and feathers, from a touring Wild West Show, had come for assistance. The experienced engineer appraised them all with penetrating eyes. His faith in honest Yankees was seldom misplaced.

Hoover's presence at The Savoy was far from the intention he had confided to Theodore. Instead of "getting out and going home" with the rest of the fleeing Americans, he had found himself drawn into emergency service before the war was one day old. In the midst of that first frenzy, a call from the United States Consul had brought him hastening down the block that separated their two offices. One look at the mob of bewildered tourists storming the consulate sent Hoover to the telephone. Would his mining associates bring over immediately the few hundred pounds of British currency then in their vaults?

Quick consultation with Consul-General Skinner brought some semblance of order. Visitors were lined up. For those who had American money, British currency was exchanged at the usual rates. For those without funds, a loan of ten shillings apiece was made to provide a night's lodging.

As soon as this horde was cared for, Skinner called Ambassador Page, offering to send Hoover to his office in the West End at once. Worse confusion greeted the American engineer there. But he learned of a mass meeting called for that evening at the Waldorf by influential American bankers who had just arrived from the continent. Hoover hurried over to this meeting to offer what assistance he could.

He found Fred I. Kent of Bankers' Trust Company of New York standing on a table in the midst of frenzied Americans. The banker's tone was commanding as he outlined his relief plans. He told them that before leaving Hamburg enroute to London, he had cabled his home bank to ship $3 million in gold to London to cover anticipated demands for cash. At the same time another cable had requested Congress to appropriate $300 thousand in gold to buy passage home for Americans without sufficient credit to purchase their own tickets. Kent explained to the crowd, too, that he had been drafted by London bankers to head a special committee supervising credits by British banks to Americans. Since these duties would prevent his handling details of relief himself, he had appointed a temporary chairman, Theodore Hetzler, President of the Fifth Avenue Bank of New York.

Hoover offered to organize Americans-resident-in-London. The next morning he was at The Savoy with his loyal engineer friends. Kent, acting for the Bankers' Trust Company, had transformed the hotel ballroom into a temporary bank. Momentarily unemployed British bank clerks had been loaned by their firms, since the bank holiday had closed all banks as soon as war had been declared. Through personal acquaintances, Kent had borrowed fifteen thousand pounds in gold, silver, and pennies. Across tables arranged in a semi-circle against one wall, the clerks were doling out essential funds. Travelers checks to a maximum of $40 a day were cashed to tide Americans over until ships began sailing the Atlantic again.

It was here, some days later, that the Devendorfs found the son-in-law of their Monterey banker surrounded by patriotic volunteers who had heeded Hoover's call to enlarge the Relief Committee. They discovered, too, that this committee was responsible for the leniency of their hotel manager; that it was needling the steamship companies to fill all boats as soon as they were allowed to sail, using staterooms reserved for Americans still on the continent for others who were at hand; that it had even offered service to the harassed Ambassador, now suddenly besieged with demands for passports.

From the first, Kent had realized how fortunate it was that the leader of Americans living in London was a man with the force and efficiency of Herbert Hoover. As soon as the cruiser *U.S.S. Tennessee* arrived at Falmouth with its load of precious gold, and he had accomplished his basic banking functions, he asked Hoover to carry on the work of the London committee. The temporary American post office installed at the Savoy was instructed to re-direct to Hoover all mail addressed to Kent and the Relief Committee. The large sum left in the committee's benevolence fund was deposited in Hoover's care, and Kent prepared to follow his associates Hetzler, Oscar Straus, and other home-sailing Americans.

Thus, Herbert Hoover, who would soon become the world's most effective relief administrator, began to speak the authoritative lines of a new role. Ambassador Page was quick to comprehend what an aide he had. In a letter to Colonel House he paid personal tribute: "Hoover, himself, gave $5,000 for helping stranded Americans and he goes to the trains to meet them, while the war has stopped his big business and his big income. This is a sample of the noble American end of the story."

Mrs. Hoover was as active as her husband. Remembering Boxer days in Tientsin, she knew what war would mean to women and children. Almost as quickly as her husband had persuaded his associates to open their strong boxes, she had organized her friends to care for those in temporary distress. Emergency housing became her special concern. She also arranged educational and sight-seeing tours to fill the interim of waiting and thus keep minds active and free from hysteria.

Then the Belgians came! The American Women's Committee was meeting when they heard of the impending arrival of the first train-load of refugees.

"Let's go down and meet them" said Lou Henry Hoover, emptying the contents of her purse into a sewing basket where the others could add their contributions. "Those women and children will need everything."

Page's letter to Colonel House described the night-and-day labors of Londoners and Americans who were succoring these innocent victims of the German invasion of Belgium. Again referring to Hoover's activities, he wrote of the plight of an old woman who had been forbidden to meet the trains with bottles of milk for starving babies because she was not a member of any official relief organization. Hoover noticed her pleading with an officer, and stopped to inquire the trouble. He discovered that she was spending half of her fifteen-dollars-a week income on the milk. He escorted her to the American Relief Headquarters, saying to the workers,

"Do you see this good old lady? She puts you and me to shame!"

Among other Americans whose passage was finally arranged were Mrs. Hoover and their two boys. They sailed for home on October 3, with promises from the father that he would follow shortly. There were a few responsibilities still to be discharged; but it would not be long before they would be together on the Stanford Campus.

CHAPTER TEN

BEGINNINGS OF BELGIAN RELIEF

AS IT TURNED OUT, it was a long time before the Hoovers' reunion on the Stanford campus took place. Just before the family left, Edgar Rickard had come to Hoover's office with Millard Shaler. This American engineer had extensive interests in gold and diamonds in the Congo. Now he brought an urgent plea for the starving people of Belgium.

Hoover listened as Shaler outlined his mission. He was representing the Comité Central, composed of Belgian philanthropists and men of affairs, as well as American businessmen of Brussels. With £12,000, and permission from the Germans to import foodstuffs to provision soup kitchens for the destitute, he had first tried to purchase flour, beans, peas and rice in Holland. The Lowlanders had no food to spare; but U.S. Ambassador Van Dyke had secured government permission for free transit through their country for whatever could be procured elsewhere.

Shaler had made his purchases in England; but authorities had refused to give an export permit. There was a stiff blockade around Belgium. The British were sure that the Germans would not keep their word. They would commandeer any food. Anyway, it was the duty of invaders to feed the civilian populace.

This British opposition was not the only obstacle he had encountered. With M. Edgar Sengier of the Banque Belge pour l'Etranger, he had hoped to form a subcommittee of the *Comité Centrale* in London, which would continue to raise funds and send a steady stream of purchases to the starving Belgians. To this the Belgian Ambassador objected. Britain had been generous to refugees. A new committee would seem superfluous. Instead he would appeal to the Belgian Government-in-Exile for appropriations from the already existing Belgian Relief Fund.

The Chairman of the American Refugee Committee was thinking ahead of his visitor. He recognized a problem that would grow in intensity. Its ramifications would take it far beyond a local volunteer committee. He took Shaler to Ambassador Page. Neutral America must offer its good offices to meet this emergency.

Page, in turn, made an appointment for them with the British Foreign Minister, Sir Edward Grey. They were received with courtesy and understanding. Sir Edward was deeply sympathetic with the plight of eight million people of that little country, dependent upon the outside world for eighty percent of its food. He pointed out that England had offered hospice to more refugees than any other nation had ever done for a foreign people. They would continue to assist the Belgians in every practicable way, but it was useless to consider shipping foodstuffs. Suppose the ships would get safely through the mine-infested Channel, the Germans would be sure to commandeer the cargo for their armies. The war would be prolonged and more suffering would come to more people.

In a few days Hugh Gibson, first secretary of the American Legation in Brussels, arrived with a desperate plea that his country should use its benevolent powers to save the lives of the innocent starving victims of the German raid. He was followed by three eminent Belgians, who had been given permission by the occupying Germans under oath and bond, to take their case to the American Ambassador in London. At their head was Emil Francqui, with whom Hoover had last tangled in Tientsin! Page received the Belgians and their American friends, including Hoover, at the Embassy.

Francqui and his compatriots brought dire word of shortages that made starvation imminent unless outside help could come quickly. But who could persuade the British authorities that food purchased for relief would reach the starving people and not the German Army?

Page knew that there was only one answer. Some strong neutral government must guarantee that it would be safely distributed, and he added, "There is only one nation that can do that, The United States of America." Then Hoover broke in to say that any such guarantee involved the problems of transportation, that whatever government undertook such a venture must control shipping and railroads.

"Which means," said Page, "that there must be an experienced and forceful director." Turning to Hoover, he continued, "Hoover, you are *it!*"

At that, Francqui turned his searching eyes on the man who had stood so firmly against him in China.

"I owe you an apology," he said. "You were right. My people face death. Only a man with your convictions can save them."

Hoover made no reply. He glanced at the clock and quickly left the room. When he returned in a few minutes, he slipped quietly into his chair, participating in the current discussion; but Page interrupted with a question concerning his abrupt disappearance.

"I saw that there was an hour before the New York Commodities Exchange would close. I went to send a cable, buying a few million bushels of wheat—for the Belgians, of course."

The visitors stared at Hoover incredulously.

"But we have not money enough for such a purchase," they exclaimed.

"It will be found," answered Hoover quietly. "The important thing is to secure the wheat."

That instinctive acceptance of responsibility, coupled with his practical knowledge of world resources, made Herbert Hoover "The Chief" in a new sense. The spurs of leadership, won on the hot sands of Australia, had equipped him to direct this great humanitarian undertaking.

In the same spirit in which Huldah Hoover had laid down her needle to heed any call to a preaching mission, so now her son closed the door to his engineering office, left his brother to speak for them both on the many Directorates on which they now served, and put everything he had of time, talent and material resources into the service of a starving nation. Instructions to Theodore Hoover were that he, with the assistance of others in the Syndicate, should gradually liquidate his various mining interests. Then he called on Edgar Rickard to become his first assistant in the relief enterprise.

Together these two explored their knowledge of global conditions. They were no longer concerned with the profit possibilities of base metals. World-wide supplies of war materiels like zinc and lead could easily have been controlled by Hoover and his mining associates—to their tremendous gain. Instead, their search now was for available food, transportation, and men equipped to handle this new problem on an international scale. As a headquarters for this effort, they immediately established a small office at Number Three London Wall Buildings.

In this crowded little room, smelly and sooty from bituminous coal burning in an open grate, the two men shut out all the world except key persons in their concentrated search for help to the Belgians. Nothing could be done until they could persuade Lloyd George and Sir Edward Grey to see their point of view. Then they must obtain German guarantees of safe conduct for their men and supplies. At the same time, there were ships to find, and complicated international financial arrangements to be made that the enterprise might be self-supporting from the start.

They had not been established long when they had a caller who introduced himself as Lord Eustace Percy, secretary to Sir Edward Grey. He reported to them that he had been commissioned by the Foreign Minister to present his compliments and ask Mr. Hoover to read the draft of a speech which Sir Edward proposed to make in Parliament.

Hoover took the papers without ceremony, read the pages quickly, then slapped them on the table and reached for a pencil.

Lord Percy stared incredulously as Hoover blacked out line

after line and scribbled notes in the wide margins of the neatly typed pages.

"It is my thought," said the American engineer, as he handed back the manuscript, "that such an important speech must be factually correct in every detail. Present my compliments to His Excellency and tell him these are my suggestions."

Some days passed. Then the messenger returned. Again he presented the compliments of the Foreign Minister, who, he said, thanked Mr. Hoover for his significant ideas and requested that he read the revised pages.

Out came the pencil as the previous performance was repeated. Lord Percy shuttled back and forth several times, expressing in tone and manner his growing respect for the rugged individual from across the seas who dared to pit his knowledge and his use of language against the scholarly Foreign Minister. Finally the day came when both men were satisfied. The issue of Britain's attitude toward Belgian Relief was debated in Parliament.

"What is the policy?" asked a member. Sir Edward was on his feet with the Hoover-corrected speech. He explained plans for saving the Belgian people as worked out by the young American engineer, who could be found by reporters at Red House on Hornton Street.

This was step number one of the Hoover agenda for winning British cooperation in the task of feeding the Belgians. As the result of Sir Edward's speech, Parliament gave them a provisional go-ahead to follow the Hoover blueprint.

It was natural that Hoover would look to his mining associates for cooperation in this new venture. With the exception of Hugh Gibson, representing the State Department, the men he called to the initial meeting of the American Committee for the Relief of Belgium on October 22, 1914, were all fellow engineers—men who had worked with him on the American Relief Committee.

Hoover outlined to his associates a three-fold task. They must find and purchase enough food for a nation. They must guarantee safe transportation on land and sea, which meant control of trains, ships, and barges. They must enlist financial support on a far larger scale than any privately endowed philanthropic project had ever attempted.

Before any work was undertaken, however, he had called upon an international firm of accountants, not only to audit, but to *keep* the books from the first day of their existence. This, said the chairman, was more than a move toward efficiency. He had made these arrangements in order that the honor of the Commission and of the country represented in this trusteeship should never be challenged.

In accepting the chairmanship, Hoover made it clear at once that all administrative positions were without salary. Following his example, shipping firms, accountants, insurance agencies, purchasing organizations, as well as his principal staff officers, gave freely of their time, compensated only for actual out-of-pocket expense.

Headquarters was, of course, London. Here the Chief remained, except to cross the Channel or make perilous journeys into enemy territory to confer with authorities at top level. Two other offices were opened immediately, one in New York, for propaganda and purchasing purposes, with Lindon Bates in charge; and the other in Rotterdam. Here Captain Lucey would transship food stuffs made available to the C.R.B. Agents of the Commission were soon operating from Bergen to Kalgoorlie, from Karachi to Rio.

Within ten days after the Commission was set up, the American S.S. *Coblentz*, loaded with 2,300 tons of flour, rice and beans purchased in England, steamed into Rotterdam. Its cargo was assigned to the American Minister in Brussels, Brand Whitlock. From the beginning he, with the Spanish and Dutch Ministers, the Marqués de Villalobar and Mynheer von Vollenhoven, had been the patrons of the Relief Committees. In mid-Atlantic, another ship laden with wheat consigned to Liverpool received radio orders from its American owners: "Proceed to Rotterdam."

The press of the world was soon headlining the story. Shaler had first enlisted Philip Patchin of the *New York Tribune*. His dispatches of October 11 and 14 had prepared the American public for the flood of stories that followed the organization of the C.R.B. Then Hoover's friend, Melville Stone, General Manager of the Associated Press, in London at the time, alerted his correspondents in Berlin and in Brussels.

Will Irwin, a Stanford friend, was a guest at Red House. As a War Correspondent, he represented various U.S. dailies and the *Saturday Evening Post*. He had met Shaler, Gibson, and Francqui. His vivid pen helped arouse the sympathies of the neutral nations of a world shocked almost beyond belief by atrocity stories of the German march through Belgium. He pictured the Meuse running red with the blood of innocent defenders of peasant homes. Flames seemed to sear the words that described the burning of the ancient university city of Louvain with its irreplaceable library. He personalized long lines of gaunt women and hungry children waiting before charity-supported soup kitchens in Antwerp.

Money, clothing, food gifts began to pour into the hands of the Commission. But Hoover knew that volunteer private funds would not be enough. Within a few days of the organization of the Commission, the British Government allotted $5,000,000 of its own previously-initiated fund for relief of Belgian refugees. By October 25 the word "American" was removed from the name, which was soon known the world over simply as "C.R.B." (Commission for Relief in Belgium). *The Comité Centrale* of Brussels was reorganized as the *Comité Nationale de Secours et d'Alimentation* to take over the task of distribution under the supervision of American, Dutch, and Spanish neutrals.

It was necessary to find energetic and trustworthy young men to serve as the American contingent in carrying out this dangerous mission. What about Rhodes Scholars like the young secretaries Dr. Jordan had brought with him? As Hoover considered this, a Yale graduate, Perrin Galpin, then a student at Oxford, came in to volunteer his services. Hoover's invitation relayed by Galpin brought fifteen others eager to join the organization. Among them was Emile Holman, whom he had last seen with Dr. Jordan in August. There were also men from Nevada and Kentucky, Williams College, and the Universities of Indiana and North Dakota, a cross-section of specially selected young Americans ready and willing to take orders from a leader they trusted. With the idealism and exuberance of their youth, they entered into the task that Herbert Hoover outlined to them at their one meeting with him in London.

"Now men," he said, as he handed each his specific commission, "this is yours to accomplish. If you meet any difficulties or have questions, I'll be right here." They started across the Channel full of confidence because they knew they were trusted.

That was in December. By the last of January, Hoover was summoned to a meeting with Lloyd George. Chancellor of the Exchequer Lord Emmott represented the Committee on Trading with the Enemy. Lord Eustace Percy came for the Foreign Office. Attorney-General Sir John Simon completed the roster. Hoover sensed what this meant. He knew that the agreements under which the Commission had been operating for the past two and a half months were provisional. The British Government still felt that the relief work was a military disadvantage for the Allies because it spared the Germans the necessity of feeding the subjugated Belgians. Hoover was also cognizant of the pressure which had been brought to bear on the heads of the government by the military to curtail, or even to terminate the work of the C.R.B. He was thoroughly prepared to answer every argument of the shaggy-haired Welshman.

While the meeting had been called ostensibly to discuss financial arrangements, the talk was soon diverted to the question of the advisability of continuing the Commission. Hoover listened quietly as Lloyd George stated his reasons for objecting to the relief work. They covered all of the points about which rumors had been reaching Hoover.

The Prime Minister maintained that without the help of the

C.R.B. the Germans in the long run would be compelled to feed the people. C.R.B. help was like providing for the population of a besieged city, thus prolonging the resistance.

Hoover was ready with documented answers. He had proof that the Germans were abiding by their promise not to requisition any more food; that none of what had been sent thus far had reached Germans; that no new money was being introduced into Belgium. Because the Commission was making it possible for Belgians with funds to purchase food, he pointed out that they were keeping what money there was in circulation. There was no danger of the Germans taking any of the funds collected for foodstuffs because whatever the C.R.B. had were in the custody of the American Minister.

He quoted the German statement that there was no clause in the Hague Convention obligating them to feed the civilians, but that rather the civilians should support the military. As Hoover elaborated on the German attitude of blaming Belgian resistance and hostility for existing conditions, Lloyd George finally broke in to denounce this as a monstrous attitude. Then Hoover played his trump. He replied that the English people had gone into this war to protect the existence of small nations. It would be an empty victory, indeed, if one of the most democratic of the world's peoples should be extinguished in a battle of democracy versus autocracy.

Lloyd George turned abruptly to his colleagues: "I am convinced," he said. "You have my permission. I would be obliged if you gentlemen would settle the details of the machinery necessary to carry it out."

Then he apologized to Hoover for running away to other more pressing duties, but predicted that the world would yet be indebted to the American people for the "most magnanimous action which neutrality had yet given rise to."

That victory for the C.R.B. eventually resulted in grants of $5,000,000 monthly from the British and a like sum from the French Governments for the continuation of the work. But the path was never free of obstructions. Germans like Reventlow cried: "Abolish Belgian Relief and kick the Americans out."

Such relief, they contended, permitted the continuance of the Allied Blockade and thus inflicted great hardship on the German people.

Finally Hoover made a trip to the German Great Headquarters. The Commanding General was infuriated beyond control by foreign newspaper accounts of outrages being committed by Germans in Belgium. He told Hoover that the C.R.B. was "nothing but a set of Entente spies." He would see that they were kicked out of the country.

Once more Hoover explained the details of the methods used by this neutral committee. Then he said bluntly:

"You have the deciding vote. Would you go down in history as the butcher of a whole people?"

The blustering German gradually grew calmer as the quiet voice of Hoover penetrated his rage.

"Come back to see me tomorrow morning," he answered.

The work went on, but Hoover was even more explicit in his admonitions to his workers. No matter what their personal feelings might be his fundamental instructions called for maintenance of strict neutrality. "There is only one way in which you can do your duty," he would say to each one. "That is by ignoring the war. You are only stewards of grain, of bacon, of dried peas. It is your business to see that they arrive safely, to count and weigh them accurately, and to make sure that they reach the mouths for which they are intended."

Despite meticulous adherence to their "strict neutrality" rule, the C.R.B. was operating under all the hazards of war. One night the Zeppelins dropped bombs around the London Wall Buildings. When Hoover arrived at his office next morning, he found that one of them had ripped through the roof grazing his desk enroute to the basement where it had exploded. Another time a bomb blew the railing off a ship on which he was crossing the Channel. When a submarine torpedoed one of the Commission ships and a week later a hydroplane tried to bomb another, Hoover hastened to Berlin. The High Command assured him such a mistake would not occur again.

"Your Excellency," said the Director of the C.R.B., "have you ever heard the story of the man who was nipped by his neighbor's dog? He reported to the owner and asked him to muzzle the dog.

" 'But that dog would never really bite you,' the man replied.

" 'You know he won't bite me, and I may know that, too, but the question is—does the dog know?'

"Herr Hoover, will you excuse me a moment?' asked Bethman-Hollweg. 'I am going to let the dog know.' "

Chapter Eleven

BUILDING A LOYAL STAFF

As the months of war lengthened into years, the international standing of the organization directed by Herbert Hoover brought unprecedented power. The C.R.B. flag flew from masts of more than two thousand vessels. Their representatives traveled on passports issued from their own headquarters. They operated mills and factories. They could even requisition local crops, and ration the product to Belgian and French people. It was, in fact, as one Allied diplomat phrased it, a piratical State, organized for benevolence.

It became a mark of distinction to be identified with this group. Young men came from all over America to offer their services. Hoover insisted that their credentials be screened with eagle eyes. Then, once accepted, each was received as a member of his personal family group. The guest rooms at Red House were continually occupied by those in transit, sometimes old friends; more often, new ones.

When it became apparent that the C.R.B. must have an Ambassador to the German Great Headquarters at Charleville, Hoover sent for a Stanford Professor, Vernon Kellogg. He was sure that Kellogg's reputation as a scientist and his knowledge of the Germans and their language would give standing to that post. The professor arrived in June, 1915, and was dispatched at once to his lonely assignment in the captured French village —a small gray town on the Meuse, where the river flows out of its canyon course through the deep green forest of Ardennes. Attended night and day by a watchful German officer assigned as "protector," Hoover's emissary lived among the men of the High Command. He was conscious that every word he spoke, every waking act, could affect the millions who were dependent upon this organization for their very lives. His quiet dignity, his sense of right and wrong balanced with fairness and tolerance, made Kellogg equal to every tense situation. Hoover was fully justified in his trust that the innate tact and whimsical humor that illumined this unusually intelligent mind would deal effectively with the ponderous Prussians.

Before he left for the front Kellogg had told Hoover of eager young men in California who had besieged him for appointments to the staff of the C.R.B. Two of them, John L. Simpson and Clare M. Torrey, had even accosted him in the dentist's chair as he was preparing to depart. These two enthusiastic graduates of the State University seemed full of drive; but he had not encouraged them because they did not speak French.

The ambitious would-be helpers had another spokesman. Hugh Gibson knew them. He advised Hoover to investigate these applicants further. At the same time, Gibson spoke of two others, Newton Drury, also from Berkeley, and Prentiss Gray, a young shipping man from Oakland. He thought the experience of the latter might be useful. By fall Hoover had found places for all four and cabled for them to come. Torrey, by then, had just been appointed secretary to the University President, Benjamin Ide Wheeler. Drury was also on the administrative staff. When the president said that he could release only one, Drury offered to take on Torrey's work at the university, and the latter left immediately with a year's leave of absence.

Hoover was at Red House when the Californian arrived in December. "I checked up on you," said the Chief, "and decided that we could use you without the language."

Early in January Hoover's thoughts were diverted from European cares to an event in California. Mrs. Hoover represented him at the inauguration of Ray Lyman Wilbur as the third President of Stanford University. At a student assembly held in connection with the ceremonies, her vibrant voice stirred her audience with stories of young Americans like themselves ministering to stricken Belgium.

Echoes of this talk spread far. A Denver father, trying to dissuade his son, Maurice Pate, from volunteering for the Canadian Army showed the young Princeton graduate a *Saturday Evening Post* article on Belgian Relief. That spring of 1916, the C.R.B. Headquarters of the Commission in New York was besieged with applicants. In spite of a letter of reference from President Hibben of Princeton, Maurice Pate was almost rejected by the C.R.B., a cause that molded all his later years of constructive devotion to Hoover's humanitarian service. Pate was twenty-two, but looked seventeen. His French was halting. But he had determination. After a month's study, he passed an interview with the Belgian Consul-General and was sent to Rotterdam, where supplies were transshipped. That office had all the help they neeed. Pate was re-assigned to Brussels just in time to replace a field representative in the Tournai District, who had met with an accident.

A few months later he was in a group called to a conference with The Chief at Brussels. Prentiss Gray was there, having arrived in February. Vernon Kellogg had relinquished the Charleville post to Tracy Kittredge, one of the first volunteers among the Oxford group of 1914, and was in command of all relief in Belgium and Northern France. In a meeting of such experienced workers it took courage for one of the newest recruits to present a problem to Hoover, but Pate was deeply concerned over German tactics of sending able-bodied men, including employees of the C.R.B., as slave labor to unknown places. He asserted that the whole Tournai operation was threatened. A note from Hoover was on his desk next morning: "My dear Pate," it said. "I envy your opportunity to work so closely with the people in the field. I know you are doing a wonderful job. Remember that whatever you do, I am 100 per cent behind you. H.H."

When he returned to Tournai and took his Hoover-backed complaint to the German Commanding General, Pate learned the depth of the enemy's respect for the Quaker Chief of the C.R.B. The next day orders came to exempt from German requisition of manpower all C.R.B. men in the region.

Hoover returned to London burdened with the thought that his own country was assuming too much credit for the accomplishments of the small staff of overseers, while the world knew little of the gruelling work of the 55,000 Belgians and French who were succoring their fellows. He asked Kellogg if he thought that his wife, Charlotte, could arrange to leave their baby in California.

The cable which reached Mrs. Kellogg on a camping trip in the California High Sierra merely said, "Come. Hoover."

Months had passed without letters from her husband during his long assignment at Charleville, but she had received word that he was in Brussels. With longing in her heart she journeyed out of the California mountains to make quick arrangements for her child and home. Before she left America she knew that she was to be the first and only woman on the official roll of the C.R.B.

Lou Henry Hoover met her in London with a strange request. Would she take a little dog with her to Ambassador Whitlock in Brussels? She was horrified. Take an animal to consume even a scrap of the food so precious to those starving babies! No, of course, she would not. She was amazed that the wife of the Chief would make such a suggestion. Nothing more was said, but on the way to the boat train Mrs. Hoover told the driver to stop their car in front of a shop on Bond Street. There she picked up a Pekingese snuggled in a carrying basket equipped with all its needs. Charlotte Kellogg turned on her heel and rushed out, slamming the door so violently that the sound echoed down the staid street. In the end, however, she had to give in to the wise and firm older woman. She arrived in Flushing, Holland, with the small dog draped over her arm, knowing that Vernon Kellogg waiting on the dock, must be watching her with unbelieving eyes.

When they finally reached Brussels, however, and delivered the dog to the grateful American Minister and his lonely wife,

Mrs. Kellogg regretted her reluctance to bring this one mite of comfort to the childless couple who had endured so much in the name of the people they represented. She learned that another dog, which had been a companion to the ailing author-diplomat, had died, and Brand Whitlock had asked for this new one to cheer his many wakeful anxious nights. She marvelled at the insight of people like the Hoovers who in the midst of overwhelming responsibilities had thought for the minor details that made life bearable for others.

Charlotte Kellogg, herself, was thrust into heartbreaking tasks as she went daily among the unbowed women of Belgium. Her notebooks filled with memos of scenes that would become immortal symbols of courage and high spirit. She was given a car and a Belgian driver. (He confessed later that it made his hair rise to comply with the orders of this intrepid Western woman who went wherever duty called her day or night, regardless of shell holes and darkened streets.) But she experienced the soul-searching trials of the valiant people who had staked their all against the arrogant invaders.

Hoover's strict neutrality rule was almost more than she could take. She often rode alone with her chauffeur on some errand of mercy as near the Etappe (forbidden fighting territory) as she, the only woman allowed a car in that area, could go. The C.R.B. flag flying bravely from the little Renault seemed to invite the outstretched hand of an old peasant woman, or a mother trudging along the muddy roads dragging weary children by their arms. She longed to give them a lift. But she knew that help to one of these might endanger the whole relief program for millions of people. She shut her eyes and drove on. Orders were that no one else should share that car.

During the six months that she lived with the other C.R.B. staff at 42 Rue de Commerce, she was constantly disciplined in the difficult school of neutral diplomacy. It was necessary many times to entertain high-ranking Germans when their only other guests could be the three neutral Ministers. One afternoon just before she returned to America in December, she came in from a gathering at which the Belgian women had presented her with a beautiful lace medallion. Before she had removed her hat or coat, a German officer appeared with a bouquet as his farewell token. He caught sight of the medallion.

"I see the Belgians have been saying good-bye," he remarked. "May I, too, ask a favor of you? Will you tell your people the truth about what we are trying to do in Belgium; and not the lies the Entente press spreads abroad?"

"I know all that," answered Charlotte Kellogg. "You ask me to explain this or that, but you cannot expect me to make American women understand why you cannot send just an open postcard to these anxious mothers and wives, saying simply, 'your son, your husband, your brother, is dead'—or 'he is alive and a prisoner of war.' "

"These Belgians!" The officer spoke in a tone that unconsciously revealed his sense of German defeat. "They are all like ostriches. In spite of all we do, they refuse to take their heads out of the sand."

And so, Charlotte Kellogg sailed for America—not to arouse passions through repeating atrocity tales; but to hold before the world the picture of a nation whose soul had survived unthinkable torture. She could tell of starving shop keepers who would decorate their windows with cabbages that the green color of hope might symbolize their undimmed belief in the future. She could recall women who would lift their lace work to reveal the secret pattern of the Belgian lion or the roses of the Queen. She could remember a day shortly after her arrival, the eighty-sixth anniversary of the Independence of the country. Cardinal Mercier rose in the St. Gudule to predict that fourteen years hence, on the hundredth anniversary of this event then being celebrated under guard of a Conqueror, their victorious King would lead his people in a Te Deum. She would describe the riot on the Cathedral steps when the crowd threw caution to the wind and shouted, "Vive le Roi—Vive Monseigneur!"

She had not needed to smuggle out the copy of the forbidden underground *La Libre Belgique* which the maid had found in the metal mail box at 42 Rue de Commerce the morning she left. Its poignant appeal from Belgian workers, protesting their deportation to Germany as slave labor, was etched in her mind. Her eyes had raced down the pages in the brief moment while the white-faced girl had gone for matches to burn the paper in the fireplace.

While she was filling the pages of American magazines with such stories, Hoover was arranging that other qualified wives could join their husbands, although no one except Charlotte Kellogg was ever on the official staff.

Mrs. Prentiss Gray came to keep open house for her husband's young assistants in Brussels. Almost a "diplomat without portfolio", she helped maintain dignified social relations with Belgians and Germans alike. Long-standing acquaintance with the Spanish Minister, the Marqués de Villalobar, dated from his days at the Embassy in Washington. The Marqués was the prototype of an Old World aristocrat, strange contrast to the blunt American Quaker, in whose efforts he was collaborating so wholeheartedly. As these two met in the congenial atmosphere of their mutual friends' home, their conversation revealed equally benevolent impulses. The one operated with the suave polish of a born diplomat; the other, with the stern and stubborn conviction of a man subservient only to a Higher Law.

Hoover was constantly bolstering the men who worked with him. One of them, homesick and longing for the girl he expected to marry, told the Chief that he must resign. Without a word to his young friend, the Director of the C.R.B. quietly investigated the girl's background and then asked Mrs. Prentiss Gray if she would chaperone the prospective bride across the Atlantic after a trip home, if the girl was willing to come.

One night the young man was interrupted by a servant as he was dressing for dinner at the Brussels staff house.

"*Un messieur en bas*", the man announced.

At the foot of the long stairway stood Herbert Hoover. "Son, that girl does not want to marry you", he blurted without a word of greeting.

"How do you know?" queried the young assistant.

"She cabled me, and I caught the boat right over here to tell you personally. Will you return to London with me and we will talk it over."

As the two discussed the situation far into the night on the boat train, Hoover spoke as an understanding father. "I know something of the difficulties of persuading a girl to marry and go a long way from her family," he said with an understanding smile, "and if you want to go home and try to get her to change her mind, it is all right with me. However, in this case, I think I would stay here."

By the time they reached London the question was settled. The assistant had decided to take the cabled "No" as final and turned his whole energy into new tasks assigned by The Chief.

There was little time, however, for Hoover to spend in such fatherly excursions. Before the end of that summer of 1916, the Germans were threatening to requisition the crops of Northern France. Firmin von Bree, one of the original members of the Comité Centrale now represented the CN in this area. Unable to make headway with the commanding officers, he sent for the Chairman of the C.R.B. He knew from experience that when there was trouble, Hoover would find a way out. Many a time the Chief had sent word when ships had been sunk: "You'll have to cut rations temporarily, but we'll soon have more." Never had more than two weeks passed without a fulfilled promise.

This time, however, Major von Kessler at Charleville could do nothing. Orders from Berlin were adamant.

"Very well," said Hoover, "I'll go to Berlin and take you and Kellogg as interpreter."

Their mission was two-fold. Not only were they insistent that French farmers should be allowed to consume a portion of their own crops, they wanted permission to import dairy products and a limited amount of meat from Holland through Belgium to make up deficiencies in the diet of children and old people in this part of France.

En route, they were invited to view through field glasses the terrific battle then raging on the Somme. Hoover arrived in Berlin sickened by the sight of wasted manpower hurled en masse against each other in the smoke and dust, of the wounded staggering back through the unending cavalcade of ambulances. He was in no mood to temporize with the instigators of this horror.

In Berlin the Americans were not invited to sit in on official discussion of their case as they had been by Lloyd George. Major von Kessler came back from his first interview with the Ministers of State disheartened and frustrated. They would make no compromise. Worse than that, they threatened to abolish the Commission. General von Sauberzweig, who came with the Major, was in an especially sullen mood, not in the least relaxed by the continuous whiskies he was served. von Kessler apologized. The General's son had just been blinded in a gas attack on the Western Front. Savage in his grief and desperate with whiskey, von Sauberzweig launched a verbal barrage on meddling civilians, finally relating his "necessary" order for the shooting of "that defiant spy, Edith Cavell." For that deed, "vital to the protection of the Germany Army" he had been, he said, unjustly reviled as an "infamous murderer."

Hoover was quick to sense an Achilles heel. He would appeal to the wounded pride of the Prussian. The usually mild-spoken Quaker was righteously indignant. He spoke emphatically. He pounded on the table. If he could not get agreement on his request for aid to Northern France, he would order all revictualment stopped, blaming it on von Sauberzweig. If the General added the demise of the C.R.B. to his other cruel deeds, he would become an even more horrifying monster in the eyes of the neutral world.

Sensitive Vernon Kellogg winced at this vehemence.

"I cannot translate these remarks," he stated. "They are too strongly worded."

"But I will," spoke up von Kessler. In crisp staccato he gave an unexpurgated version, burning the acid of Hoover's indignation into the quivering mind of his superior officer. The General glowered in gloomy silence. Then he gave his command, von Kessler would inform Minister Lewald that negotiations would go on.

Some weeks later an agreement was signed, doubling the proportion of French crops given to the hungry people. And later still a few proteins were made available to those people whose vitality was ebbing.

More often Hoover won his point without oratory. M. Labbé, Secretary-General of the Comite de Ravitaillement for Northern France, wrote to ask for increased food allotments for the people of Lille. The letter went by necessity through the German Headquarters. When Hoover and his assistants arrived to investigate the need they were accompanied by German officers.

In M. Labbé's office, Hoover asked his representative to outline the details of the citizen's needs. In poignant phrases, the Frenchman described the poverty of his people.

"You exaggerate," interrupted the German officer. "We have just come through the city. The people are gay, well dressed. They do not seem to suffer."

"Do not trust appearances," answered Labbé. "The people make the best of things, but there is no more. Our stores are closed."

"*Pardon, monsieur,*" the officer replied in polite French, "we have seen them open."

Hoover had said nothing; but now he interrupted the German who was insisting that food was for sale in all the stores.

"Show me," he demanded.

The markets were indeed empty, deserted; but the officers were unconvinced.

"They are open in the mornings."

The Chief ran his finger over the marble counter as they talked, tracing a pattern in the dust.

"We must get on to Brussels," he remarked without other comment. M. Labbé's request was granted within a few days, unrestricted by the German Headquarters.

During these months of constant strain Hoover looked forward to his stops in Rotterdam. Here he could find respite in the home of Walter Lyman Brown, a California engineer whom he had known in South Africa. When an earlier assistant had moved on to another C.R.B. assignment, Hoover had approached Brown. Would he take charge of the Rotterdam office for three months? Brown had protested that he knew nothing about shipping; but that was unimportant to The Chief.

"All right, what are my orders?"

"Just keep the food moving." That was the only instruction Hoover had given for what proved to be three years of strenuous service in that one key port.

Brown's family had come with him to Holland. An opportunity to relax and play with the two little girls became as important to Hoover as the efficiently run office. Betty, the older one, had been born in Africa, in the days when the two families had been briefly together there. Herbert Hoover always had an instinctive understanding of small children. His happy relationship with these two lasted through the years. No matter how busy he was there were always Christmas dolls for them, often accompanied by personally-written letters.

Housekeeping in wartime Rotterdam was fraught with difficulties. Mrs. Brown's homesickness was not unnoticed by Hoover. As he said good-bye after one of these visits, there was a pleading tone in his parting words: "Oh, do try to stick it out a little longer!"

This concern to keep his staff satisfied in uncomfortable surroundings was part of the secret of the success of this great humanitarian undertaking. But Red House in London was often a lonely place these days. Mrs. Hoover tried to divide her time between the school boys in California and her husband, and he did make an occasional trip home. They never traveled together. They had an adamant rule not to be on the same ship, with the ever-present danger of submarines. Their boys would not be orphans if they could avoid it!

On one of Hoover's trips he was invited to be the banquet speaker for the Rocky Mountain Club in New York, of which his friend, John Hays Hammond, was the organizer and president. Hoover's appeal was so persuasive that the group voted at once to contribute the sum they had been collecting for ten years for the purpose of erecting a clubhouse. And they all left the meeting so embued with the enthusiasm of their guest that within two months two million dollars were added to the American contributions.

Chapter Twelve

"FRIEND OF THE BELGIAN PEOPLE"

Hoover's foresight in the administration of the C.R.B. made it unique in the history of philanthropy. His own dedication and that of the volunteers who worked with him evoked trust that resulted in the large allocations from Allied governments, as well as in major giving such as that of the Rocky Mountain Club. The fact that no administrative salaries were paid at top level, reduced overhead cost to less than one-half of one percent. His business experience and acumen made savings possible in every phase of operation. In Rotterdam, for instance, Hoover had seen to it that a "dispatch charge" was included in contracts with shipowners. This meant that the C.R.B. was paid a bonus by the shipowners because their cargo handlers were so imbued with the spirit of the organization that they speeded unloading, rather than incurring demurrage charges paid by owners whose ships waited in dock beyond a certain time. Even the sale of bread to those Belgians who could afford to pay included a small profit to add to the general fund, although prices were lower than in any Allied country.

With all of this, however, overwhelming needs continued to exceed contributions from all sources. The Director was heartened by a surprise gift from admirers in The American Institute of Mining Engineers. They wrote that study of a recent report of the Commission had shocked them by the small per capita contributions from the United States in comparison with other countries. Thus, they had incorporated Belgian Kiddies, Ltd., with offices at 120 Broadway, New York. Shares were sold at

$12 each—enough to feed one child for a year!—resulting in a contribution of nearly $120,000.

Hoover and Francqui recognized the magnitude of the financial resources accumulating in their care. During one of their meetings in the summer of 1916, they faced the problem that would surely be theirs sometime in the future. What should be done with moneys left in the treasury if and when the war should cease? Remote as that time looked then, the two men knew they should have a plan for disbursement at the liquidation of this emergency organization. In the midst of war—and not knowing from what sources their urgent daily needs would then be met—they decided that whatever might be left in the unforeseen future should be devoted to educational purposes. Francqui was self-made, without a college education. Hoover had labored hard for his. The contribution of Rhodes Scholars to the C.R.B. was proving vital. By providing for future scholars, the result of their common effort could become permanent.

Francqui took the proposal to the Government-in-exile in le Havre. At first they demurred. Then Hoover addressed a letter to M. Van de Vyvere, Minister of Finance, on July 18, 1916. In it he reminded the government that if the administrative staffs of the C.N. and the C.R.B. had been paid, there would never be a balance. The Commission had earned the right to dispose of the money as they wished. "We have fed the bodies of these people," he argued. "Let us, in the years to come, provide for their mental growth."

In this communication, which was to be kept confidential until the appropriate time to implement it, Hoover outlined plans for an educational foundation. Details of its function would, he suggested, need to be worked out by a committee representing the various universities in Belgium.

After the Government's tentative acceptance of this plan, Hoover returned to his London headquarters. Financial worries continued to plague him. France was behind in her payments. The British Foreign Office was gravely concerned with its large contribution. Complicated correspondence between that office and Francqui dealt with the question of authority. The C.N.

represented work of influential Belgian leaders. Was it to dictate to C.R.B. staffs? Or did the pledge of the C.R.B. to see that all foodstuffs were imported and distributed under the direction and control of neutrals give it final responsibility? Hoover insisted that Americans cared only that Belgians be fed, and not an iota about individual position.

By December 30 an agreement satisfactory to all was reached. The Chief was now free to sail to America. For two years he had realized that if the Commission was to be released from hand-to-mouth existence, it must have permanent financial stability.

After crossing the submarine-infested Atlantic in the first week of January, he hastened to Wall Street. There he subjected New York bankers to the same sort of roughshod insistence that had won Hoover his way with everyone, from Lloyd George to the German High Command. He succeeded in assuring these men that a loan sufficient to cover the Commission's expenditures for a year would be covered by the pledges of the governments of Britain, France, and Belgium.

American neutrality was being replaced rapidly by crusading desire to help the Allies win the war for democracy. When Berlin continued to ignore President Wilson's notes of protest over German submarine attacks on neutral shipping, diplomatic relations were broken.

Hoover was in Washington on a February evening soon after this breach occurred. This night he dined at the home of a fellow Californian, Franklin K. Lane, then Secretary of the Interior. His heart was heavy as he foresaw the end of American participation in the relief work which claimed his whole attention. He could not shift his thoughts to the level of his table companions; but one, Adolph Miller of the Federal Reserve Board, seemed to share his concern for the Belgian people. Hoover immediately singled out this former University of California professor. As soon as the four men present retired to the Library after dinner, Hoover took Miller by the arm and led him into an adjoining parlor, saying with evident relief,

"There seems to be no one in here. We can have a little

quiet. You are the only person here who seems to sense the vital importance of this relief work. When can we have a good long talk together?"

It was Saturday night.

"Would you like to come to my house tomorrow?" asked Miller. "Suppose you come for lunch, or about eleven o'clock."

"That is not early enough", replied Hoover. "I want *plenty* of time."

"Fine," said Miller. "Come to breakfast."

Hoover was at the Miller home on "S" Street promptly on Sunday morning. He stayed on through lunch and most of the day, talking with intense concentration about the tremendous task he was directing. The two men parted at the end of that day firmly started on a friendship that would prove increasingly valuable as future years would bring them together in attempts to solve even greater problems.

It was March before Hoover sailed for Europe again. This time he had a perilous and uncomfortable voyage on a Spanish freighter. He knew by now that sooner or later Americans would have to withdraw from active participation in Belgian Relief. Germans had been demanding that from the moment that diplomatic relations had been broken. Belgians, backed by Villalobar and the British Foreign Office, had been equally insistent that the work should go on as agreed in December.

The stop in Madrid offered opportunity to discuss just how the transfer of authority should be made in case it became necessary to leave the C.R.B. in the care of neutral Spain and Holland. Then he journeyed on to Paris and Brussels.

Everywhere he found his C.R.B. staff diminishing daily. He knew that their "neutrality" had been maintained in contradiction to hidden emotions for two long years after the sinking of the *Lusitania*. That vessel had carried with it two of their number, C.T. Broderick and Lindon W. Bates, Jr., son of one of Hoover's London mining associates. Even before he had left for America, one of the young assistants, Hallam Tuck, had come into his Brussels office infuriated over mass deportation of forced labor.

"Tell my people at Mons," Tuck had said, "that I will be back with the British Army."

By the time Hoover reached Brussels this time, many more of his aides had followed Tuck into British or French forces.

Then, on April 6, 1917, all "neutrality" ceased abruptly. The United States had at last thrown her strength into the war on the side of the Allies. Only Prentiss Gray of the C.R.B. remained in Belgium, with special permission from German military authorities, to carry on until local supervision could be transferred smoothly to two highly competent and trusted Belgians, Fernand Baetens and Walter Blaess. Well laid plans prepared during Hoover's Madrid stop enabled Spanish and Dutch to carry on. The Marqués de Villalobar became guiding patron.

Hoover agreed to maintain offices in New York, London, and Rotterdam in order that financing, purchasing, transportation, and record keeping should go on without interruption. Edgar Rickard became New York Director, W. B. Poland remained in London, and Walter Brown in Rotterdam. *The Comité Nationale* under Francqui operated as usual, distributing supplies inside Belgium.

But before all this was arranged, Hoover himself had had a new call. On the very day that war was declared, Hugh Gibson had come to him in London, bringing a message via Colonel House to say that President Wilson needed him to organize the food resources of the United States.

The nebulous ambition confided to Dr. Jordan in Australia some ten years before suddenly had dramatic fulfillment! His "some sort of executive work where I can be of service" would now have significance beyond any demand either of them could have imagined in those days of a seemingly peaceful future. There was no hesitation about assuming the great responsibility; but Hoover stipulated two conditions. He would serve as an unpaid volunteer, and he must retain his leadership of the Belgian Relief Commission outside of Belgium.

Without realizing that he was preparing for responsibilities of this importance, he had already begun to lay a foundation. One night in the early fall a young C.R.B. assistant, George I.

Gay, had brought a friend to Red House—a man whose store of knowledge regarding world food conditions would prove invaluable in the task now at hand. At the time Alonzo Taylor had been making a survey of prison camps in England and Scotland, but they had not conversed long before Hoover sensed that he was talking with a nutrition expert of wide experience. He had asked Taylor to remain after other guests left. In that late night conversation, he made a friend, whose association would continue in many mutual efforts then unguessed.

The immediate result of their talk was to commission Clare Torrey to make a survey of British Food Regulations before Torrey departed on his intended enlistment in the French Army. Now Hoover knew how much he would use the report which Torrey was about to bring him.

Before Hoover left London, Baron Edmond Carton de Wiart, acting as emissary from King Albert, came to offer a royal decoration. With Quaker reticence, Hoover replied that as a citizen of a democracy he could not accept foreign honors. All that he wanted was to be considered a friend of the Belgian people. The Baron, who had been a delegate from the C.N. to the C.R.B., understood. He had grown accustomed to Hoover ways. Something about this simple direct American had won his growing admiration—after he had overcome his first shock at Hoover's brusque ignoring of Old World customs.

When they had first met, the Baron, who had spent his youth as secretary to Albert's father, King Leopold II, had raised his hat, bowed and inquired politely about the health of the American. He had soon learned that this busy Relief Director had neither time nor concern for such amenities. In all their subsequent dealings, he had proceeded to the business in hand with no preliminaries. He had watched the progress of the C.R.B. with growing regard for the man who could command so much respect from younger members of the Commission and get so much done in a short time. He realized that Hoover was right in avoiding unnecessary ceremony. Now, as the two men parted, the Baron was already formulating in his mind the alternative suggestion he would make to the King.

C.R.B. staff members, then in London, accompanied Hoover to the boat train as he started across the Channel for three days in France before sailing from Le Havre. Clare Torrey was among them with his recently completed survey. As he stood with the others waving farewell to The Chief, who had lived and worked so intimately with them all, he turned to his companion.

"He'll never come back to this way of life!" he sighed. He was proud of the honor that had come to their leader. He rejoiced for his country that such a man had been chosen for a vital task. But he feared that henceforth The Chief would be too pre-occupied with affairs of state to allow younger colleagues the free access members of the C.R.B. staff had enjoyed in the three years just passed.

At Senlis, Hoover joined a group of French volunteers who had worked under him, but whom he had never seen. One of them, Madame Saint-René-Tallandier, recognized at once that the terribly grave young man could only be Hoover, the Quaker from America. His thin-lipped obstinate mouth spoke without words of the ancestry that had prepared him for this service. His taciturnity silenced the thanks that sprang involuntarily to her own lips.

When the party came to Noyon, they saw this self-control subjected to severe test. A group of old villagers, mayors of ninety liberated towns, who had traveled miles, some on foot, others in carts, over nearly impassable roads, waited in a large room to voice their gratitude. The Major of the Prefecture whispered in Hoover's ear that he must meet them. The Chief stopped short, removed his hat and stood motionless a moment as if trying to master emotions his strong will would not disclose. Then he listened with tears in his eyes as the leader spoke, the sinews of the old man's leathery neck pulsing with agititation as he recalled longs days of trial. The speaker took a morsel of bread in reverent fingers.

"This is the bread of France," he said, "and thanks to you Americans, our sweat has never moistened the bread of slavery;

we and our wives and our children have eaten the bread of France."

Hoover was able to respond briefly. As he looked into the faces of those men who had suffered so keenly, he said, "We have left invaded France because we are coming to fight for the France that is free."

Then they went on through the ghost-villages. The brave spring flowers were shedding fragrance over ruins. The hopes of surviving people were rising out of torn hearts in the sun of promised American aid.

Before he sailed, Hoover kept the promise made to Baron Carton de Wiart that he would pay a farewell visit to the exiled King in the seacoast town near Le Havre. Albert had crystallized the idea presented by his emissary. He told his guests that he had decided to create a new decoration. Herbert Hoover would henceforth be known as "A Friend of the Belgian People and an Honorary Citizen of Belgium."

Chapter Thirteen

UNITED STATES FOOD ADMINISTRATOR

Welcome to official circles in Washington was not as full of appreciation as the leave-taking from France and Belgium. Too many people had listened to echoes of German accusation pointed at the business dealings of the C.R.B. Many more were resentful that the President had summoned a man who had spent most of his adult life on foreign soil.

Hoover was too engrossed with the urgency of the task President Wilson was ready to lay on his shoulders to heed public opinion. Before he presented himself at the White House, he had mapped his course. He was certain that his countrymen, once convinced of the basic importance of food in winning a war, would cooperate in a voluntary program. Of one thing he was sure, whoever headed that program must be an Administrator, not a Food Director. He would present the facts, confident that self-discipline would evoke necessary sacrifice.

President Wilson, also an idealist, concurred; his satisfaction with the outlined program led to a press announcement in early May. Herbert Hoover was appointed Food Administrator, subject to Senate ratification.

A flood of congratulatory telegrams seemed to justify the choice. Governor Arthur Capper voiced the universal endorsement of agricultural states in a wire that said in part, "you can count on heartiest support and cooperation." A special committee of the Grain Exchanges wrote that "private rights and private interests should sacrifice themselves at this time." They suggested, too, that Julius Barnes, who later became one of Hoover's chief lieutenants, should represent them on his committee. Millers, restaurant owners, the Housewives League, the A.F. of L. and Motion Picture Councils were among those who sent assurances. Ohio farmers were emphatic in saying that "real farmers everywhere are patriotic to the core and will welcome food control . . . the legislators opposing this do not represent producers."

Opposition on Capitol Hill, which had spurred Ohioans to send this message, was a new experience for Hoover. He had been away from the political scene too long to remember how cumbersome democratic red tape could be.

As an engineer and as a relief administrator, he had been accustomed to marshalling facts, presenting them to authorities with power to act, and getting down to the business at hand with a minimum of delay. He rebelled at the long debates over ratification of his appointment, and over granting such authority as the President asked of Congress to implement that appointment. He started the work of building up the machinery of office when his only authorization was the President's letter.

Alonzo Taylor was now Assistant to the Secretary of Agriculture. Hoover wrote to him for cooperation and advice. His reply summarized world food conditions, with the conclusion that "we have enough, if pooled with the wheat and cereals of the Allies, to feed us and them, providing distribution is under control, demand expresses need and is not influenced by manipulation and extortion, and hoarding is prevented."

With the details of Taylor's description of what reasonable control should accomplish in mind, Hoover began to draw together a reliable staff. Vernon Kellogg came home to join him. On May 23, Hoover wrote Secretary Lansing, requesting Hugh Gibson's assignment as a liaison between the State Department and Food Administration. "I could make use of Mr. Gibson practically at once," he wrote, "in formulating plans of organization as to relations between our various commodity executives and those of the Allies for the approval of your Department."

While Hoover was going forward with his plans, the Democratic Senator from California, James D. Phelan, was pleading eloquently for his ratification. Senator Reed of Missouri shouted "Un-American." Phelan argued back that Hoover was a better American for his travels. Garnered experience was an asset placed at the disposal of his country in time of need. The Senator related his first personal contact in 1913 when Hoover, the acknowledged leader of Americans in London, had so willingly put aside personal business to carry on in Phelan's stead in promoting the Panama-Pacific Exposition.

"When a man has traveled," asserted Phelan, "he has learned better to understand his fellowmen. Herbert Hoover is a pioneer American in realms of usefulness, both in world development of resources and in practical expression of humane sentiments."

Eventually, such arguments were convincing. In August the United States Food Administration was officially organized under the man President Wilson had chosen. All of America became a civilian army under Hoover's generalship, competing to produce and to utilize every possible food resource.

Under the Lever Act for the purchase and sale of food, two legal bodies were established—the Grain Corporation, with a capital of $150,000,000; and the Sugar Equalization Board with $5,000,000—both underwritten by the United States Treasury.

Ben Allen, a Stanford alumnus associated with the C.R.B. from its beginning, established an educational division in Washington that reached every town and hamlet in the United States with the slogan, "Food Will Win the War." Housewives and school children took up the cry. Wheatless bread and sugarless cake recipes brought honor to competing homemakers. Reversible "Hoover aprons," useable on both sides became symbols of efficiency. Children were taught to eat their plates clean. "Hooverizing" developed into a national synonym for waste prevention. Mimeographed news releases were re-written with local color by thousands of volunteer publicity chairmen contributing to their home newspapers.

Young men, deferred from front line service by physical disability, flocked to enlist under the Food Administration banner. William C. Mullendore, who eventually became its official historian, was such a recruit. His "disability" was temporary, convalescence from an operation; but his appeal to Senator Curtis of Kansas brought him an introduction to Hoover's attorney. Judge Curtis Lindley welcomed the young law student as an assistant in preparing the draft of the Food Control Act. The judge immediately recognized Mullendore's potential and passed that word on to The Chief, who kept in touch after the young man left to serve with the Air Corps. Once the war was over, Mullendore was at Hoover's right hand, recording in detail the magnificent service of the eight thousand full-time volunteers and the 750,000 part-time patriots who had supplemented the three thousand salaried personnel needed to maintain this nation-wide effort.

When the final accounting was made after the Armistice, the Food Administration was able to hand back to the U. S. Treasury the entire capital of $155,000,000 plus profits from the two corporations of $60,000,000. Increased production had been achieved; there had been a marked reduction in consumption and waste. Profiteering had been controlled, with minimum prosecution of even flagrant cases. The only legal action possible under the Enabling Act passed by Congress was cancellation of the purveyer's license for the duration. Hoover was reluctant to apply such drastic treatment lest it interfere with the offender's means of livelihood. Thus, in consultation with his lawyers a plan was evolved under which an offender could retain his license by making a voluntary contribution to the Red Cross or by agreeing to sell food to other government agencies for a nominal consideration.

Nearly ninety-eight percent of the 400,000 firms dealt with during the Administration won the rating of "complete honesty." Of the 8,800 cases of reported violation only about 100 received the drastic penalty. The balance made contributions to the Red Cross aggregating some $500,000, or sold food to other government departments at a nominal consideration having a value in excess of $1,000,000. Furthermore, at the end of hostilities flour millers turned back to the Grain Corporation profits exceeding the original agreed amount by more than $6,000,000.

This accomplishment required unceasing attention to innumerable details, even with the experienced and loyal staff that Hoover gathered around him. He spent long hours in the plain little office which was staffed around the clock. Sometimes his family became impatient for at least a little of their father's time. Herbert Jr. and Allan were waiting in the outer office one dark evening, playing with Alpheus Walter, night page boy. With nothing better to do, they thought of experimenting with gem clips stuck into the light circuit. Allen held on too long. His scream, "Dad," brought the Food Administrator hurrying from his desk. Both sons were turned over their father's knee, and Alpheus had his ears boxed. What hurt worse was the sound of Hoover's voice calling Mr. Walter on the telephone.

"I've just spanked your son," he said. The boy trembled for his job!

The Hoover family, gratefully re-united after the long period of separation by danger-filled miles between London and Stanford, lived at 1701 Massachusetts Avenue. Here, again, Lou Henry Hoover maintained an atmosphere of normal living, despite the strain of world tension that occupied nearly every waking hour of her husband's time. The moments were rare when he could relax in the pleasant rooms and gardens; but when he did, he entered into his sons' pursuits as naturally as any less harassed father. In August, 1918, he described his household in a handwritten letter to Betty Brown, aged seven, in Rotterdam.

"My dear Betty," he wrote, "I was glad to get your nice letter of August 3rd. I was in London then and it did not catch up with me until I got to Washington.

"I am much astonished at Dickey fighting; its not proper for small dogs; I however think he may recover; they do that generally.

"I was sorry not to be able to come over to see you when I was in England. I was very much worked so I apologize. We have in our family

2 small Boys
1 dog
11 goldfish
1 canary
3 frogs
14 chickens
2 Turtles
1 Rabbit

and every morning 2 mice. They don't get through the day usually as Allan needs the traps to catch more and thinks they should be drowned.

"We also have 12,000,000 misquitoes (sic). I am expecting the war to finish in just 12 months and then I will come over to see you.

"Love to your Mother and Daddy,
H. Hoover."

In the neighborhood, at 2131 "R" Street, lived another family with a few more small boys and one sister. Their father, too, was concerned with bringing an end to the war. He was the Third Assistant Secretary of the Navy Franklin Delano Roosevelt!

CHAPTER FOURTEEN

SUCCORING STARVING EUROPEANS

WHEN THE ARMISTICE came suddenly on November 11, 1918, Hoover found himself with huge surplusses of food in storage for the coming winter. But he had to leave the question of its disposal for his staff. On November 18th he was bound for France, starting for Versailles with presidential approval of a broad plan for relief in Europe. Before he sailed he had arranged with the War Department to ship 140,000 tons of food to Gibraltar. The Grain Corporation was also sending another 120,000 tons to Falmouth for emergency use in northern Europe.

The new assignment had far-reaching implications. In October, Hoover had discussed the menacing threat of Bolshevism in post-war Europe with Secretary Lansing. It was apparent that starving people must be fed as rapidly as possible after the close of hostilities. Otherwise, inevitable unrest would turn sufferers into ready tools of the Bolsheviks.

Now he was on shipboard, steaming across the Atlantic with authority to institute a program that he hoped would bring succor to starving people and forestall any Bolshevik invasion. He had capable aides with him—Vernon Kellogg, Robert Taft, Lewis Strauss. As the ship ploughed through great waves they talked and planned; but there was little they could do until they were on the scene. He had leisure and he made good use of it. Stretched in a deck chair, he read "The Memoirs of Andrew D. White," who was the president of Cornell for twenty years.

Suddenly his mind was alerted to another need—something far in the future, but it seemed to him then, a burden he might shoulder. White's plaint that documentation of the French Revolution had been lost in the turmoil of a broken Europe stirred his imagination. He would not let this happen to records in this era. The only hope for an eventually peaceful world lay in understanding and correcting the mistakes of the past.

The idea was not really new to him. He had already made a small beginning. Two years before a letter from the head of Stanford's History Department, Dr. E. D. Adams, had started him thinking. Dr. Adams had suggested that "at least the private and confidential letters in regard to the work of the C.R.B. might well be sealed up and kept at Stanford." All of these, with promise of more to come, were now in Adams' care.

Almost as soon as he arrived in Paris, and before he became involved in the intricacies of his new task, he cabled Dr. Wilbur at Stanford. There was a sum available for an historical collection of records of the World War, if the University would send a suitable committee to Europe. Wilbur's immediate response started Dr. Adams and a group of young scholars on the task of assembling what later became the nucleus of the world-famous Hoover Institution on War, Revolution and Peace.

The new assignment, which now commanded his full attention, loomed large. His first task was to enlarge his staff. He sent for some of his most effective State Food Administrators. Howard Heinz from Pennsylvania, Eric Swenson of Wisconsin, and E. A. Peden from Texas arrived early in January on the ship that brought Bernard Baruch, Vance McCormick, and other advisors to the American Peace Delegation.

As fast as he could, Hoover gathered the former members of the C.R.B. to work alongside the men from the Food Administration. Service men like Clare Torrey, then a Captain in the Field Artillery, received orders from General Pershing to report to Hoover at the Crillon in Paris. There he found Bill Poland, Walter Brown, and many other old associates.

Whenever he saw a likely recruit Hoover was quick to invite him to join his force. He was deep in conversation in the lobby of the Crillon when he spied Captain T.T.C. Gregory, a San Franciscan and member of the Stanford Board of Trustees. Extending his hand to Gregory, Hoover motioned him to wait. The result of that conversation was that his friend did not proceed home on leave. Instead, at Hoover's request, he was detached from military service and ordered to Berne to join Dr. Alonzo Taylor as a member of the Allied Mission investigating the food problem in Vienna.

Taylor's earlier survey of conditions in Austria-Hungary and the Balkans had disclosed distressing conditions. He had found that food was practically non-existent everywhere. Hoover men were now sent in many directions to make similar surveys. Heinz went to the Golden Crescent to investigate the plight of Armenians in Turkey. Swenson investigated the situation in Scandinavia. These missions were instructed to study needs and available supplies, with the promise that there would be resident directors of relief in each country as soon as necessary arrangements could be made.

In Paris, Hoover and his staff were settling in at 19 Rue Lubeck, where the former steward of the Menlo Country Club in California was looking after their comfort. Private Kosta Boris, who had been "striker" for Captain Gregory, had requested permission to be assigned to Hoover in Paris. As soon as this request had been granted, the tall efficient Boris arrived to look after The Chief with a devotion that was to last over thirty years. In this establishment Clare Torrey found that the fears he had expressed at Le Havre two years before were unfounded. Herbert Hoover was one of the intimate circle again, like a real father of the family, paying bills and sharing the camaraderie that his staff had feared would be lost in the greater demands. Before many months, he was assisting with a wedding in the new establishment when one of their number married a Red Cross worker. Herbert Hoover presided at the Bachelor Dinner, joining spontaneously in the speech making. The next day he assumed the role of "Father of the Bride," giving her away at a happy ceremony.

Most of his days, however, were filled with burdens. His

advice was constantly sought. General Tasker H. Bliss, Head of the American Peace Delegation, recognized that this experienced fellow-citizen carried significant knowledge of the world's needs in his mind. The General called for Hoover after he received a memo from Major Lawrence Martin suggesting that in view of the stringent fuel shortage in France and other parts of Europe a conference be called while Herbert Hoover was still in Paris to consider the possible exchange of Allied food for German coal. The memo continued. "As Mr. Hoover was a Geologist and Mining Engineer before the War he doubtless knows who could tell us best of the situation of the Belgian coal fields since the Germans left."

The resultant conference with the Chief Geologist from General Headquarters eventually led to an arrangement with the "Big Four" that Hoover would receive a "mandate" to control the distribution of all Central European coal. After he had set up a Coal Section in his Administration, Hoover asked General Pershing to assign "the best coal man in the Army" to this post. Colonel Anson C. Goodyear, who received this assignment, proved so efficient and tactful that soon coal was moving all over Europe.

Other important requests continued to cross Hoover's desk, diverting attention only until he could find the right assistant to carry out the details involved. His own paramount concern was that of food, as a "bumper" against Bolshevik control of middle Europe. In all his communications to General Bliss, he insisted upon adherence to the principle outlined in his pre-Armistice cable to Joseph Cotton, London representative of the Food Administration. In this he had said that relief should be administered mainly by Americans, not on an Inter-Allied basis.

Hoover was also convinced that urgent food problems and other passion-fraught details should be assigned to Commissions and not be part of the discussions at the Peace Table. In this he concurred with Presidential Advisor House, as he did in objections to Wilson's personal participation. Secretary Lansing and Bernard Baruch also agreed that if an ocean could be kept between the American President and the emotional sessions at Versailles, Wilson could practically dictate the terms of peace.

But the Crusader for the League of Nations paid no heed. Wilson arrived in Paris on December 15. Very soon after that, he sent for Hoover. He wished to discuss the immediate necessities of food and relief; but he also wanted to gain from Hoover's long experience with foreign affairs some perspective on the situation in Paris. Hoover's summary was brutally frank, sparing the idealist none of the harsh facts he knew to be so starkly true. The impatient President clung to his bright stars of hope, indignant that anyone should suggest possibilities of tarnishing.

Nevertheless, he, as well as General Bliss, leaned on Hoover for constructive ideas as the peace negotiations progressed. Hoover had already won the respect of Lloyd George, who, since his conversion to the support of Belgian Relief, had continued to back this American engineer. The fact that Hoover had taken measure of the nimble-witted Welshman, and at the same time admired his moral courage and administrative ability, gave force to his analysis of the British point of view as he presented it to his American colleagues.

Just as Hoover understood Lloyd George in his reliance on expediency, so he grasped at once the blunt realism of Clemenceau, a man relentlessly bitter over the suffering of the French people. Hoover, the humanitarian, and Clemenceau, the avenger, were equally rugged. The great difference was that Hoover insisted upon right based on justice; Clemenceau, on might. With Orlando and his insistence upon territorial concessions based on secret promises, Hoover had less basis for understanding. Yet, he was always able to get direct audience with any of these leaders because his mission was completely detached from political objectives. His comprehension of basic intentions, gained from all these contacts, made his counsel invaluable to the American leaders.

Hoover was insistent on several points. He did not hesitate to say so in blunt communications to General Bliss and, if necessary, to the President. Primarily, he hammered home the vital importance of lifting the blockade, encouraging German trade with neutral nations, the re-establishment of production, and the stabilization of currency. He sensed that the President was not receiving sufficient advice on economic matters. Early in January he suggested the formation of the Supreme Economic Council.

When the detailed memo came back marked, "Approved, W.W.," Hoover was named to serve as its general executive, as well as a rotating chairman, along with Lord Robert Cecil, Clementel of France, and Italy's Crespi. Also on the American delegation were Bernard Baruch and Vance McCormick, with whom he had served on the War Council in Washington. Norman Davis and Henry M. Robinson represented the interests of the United States Treasury, a liaison suggested in Hoover's original memo. Because the group included General Bliss in most of their discussions, they were able to influence the thinking of the American Peace Delegation on economic problems.

While Hoover still retained his title of United States Food Administrator, he was given the added one of Director of Relief and Rehabilitation. During this period all overhead and traveling expenses of his staff were met from the Food Administration budget, although Hoover, himself, stuck to his traditional routine of drawing no salary and paying his own expenses. Eventually, Congress made an emergency appropriation of $100 million to aid liberated countries, and Hoover became the Director of the American Relief Administration, a technical organization set up to account for the expenditure of these funds.

In February, he wrote General Bliss that he was exhausting every resource and only meeting about sixty percent of a minimum program to keep people alive, and this after the United States Treasury had added advances to the governments of Belgium, Rumania, Czecho-Slovakia, and Serbia.

Hoover urged that the Peace Commission should make it clear that the United States would withdraw from all Inter-Allied food organizations unless they could be assured that the other victors would share in the relief. To this, he added the practical suggestion that the United States should be allowed to sell some of its surplus food in storage at Rotterdam to Germany, if the money was forthcoming. As a possible alternative, he suggested that food be bartered with Germany in exchange for use of her ships to transport American soldiers home.

The offices of the American Relief Administration at 51 Avenue Montaigne were rapidly becoming a reference library for those who wanted real facts about the peoples of the world. Its representatives were working in twenty-five nations, not only distributing food to the hungry, but also acting as economic advisors to governments struggling to rise out of chaos. The charts and maps that covered the walls of this fifty-room establishment reflected humanitarian effort at its zenith. Little blue flags dotted the ocean spaces on the maps to indicate shiploads of supplies sailing in safety over the seven seas.

By the middle of March, Hoover had the railways of the old Austrian Empire under his command. Shipments of food from Trieste rose from eight hundred to twenty-five hundred tons per day in the space of three weeks.

In that same month, Hoover won his battle for lifting the blockade of Germany by a straightforward presentation of facts to Lloyd George. As in the case of Belgian Relief the British Prime Minister was convinced by Hoover's indictment of a nation that would assume a philanthropic attitude and at the same time deny sustenance to innocent women and children. Lloyd George rose in the War Council to sweep even the uncompromising French into willingness to accept Hoover's dictum that "we must write into history such acts as will stand credibly in the minds of our grandchildren."

"You may start your shipments now," said one of the French delegates to Hoover with a wry smile.

"They have been on the way for weeks," replied the Food Administrator. He had believed so firmly in the final triumph of right thinking that he had not waited for authority.

Nevertheless, Hoover continued to find many obstacles that warranted the dark picture he had painted for President Wilson in their first interview in Paris. When the Chief Executive returned to France after a trip home in mid-March to try to sell the preliminary draft of the League of Nations to the American people (a draft which, incidentally, had elicited severe but constructive criticism from Hoover) he found that the peacemaking had become mired. The very intolerance, insincerity, and greedy nationalism of which the Relief Administrator had warned had muddied all the issues. Wilson acknowledged that Hoover's wider world experience had given him a clearer insight. He now agreed with the position he had repudiated so impatiently a few months earlier.

In April, the President's illness left the American Peace Delegation rudderless. By the time he took the helm again the going was very rough. He even sent for the S.S. *George Washington* to take him home; but he gave in to advisors who persuaded him to stay because of the adverse effect his retreat would have on the American public. Stay he did to fight a losing battle for his ideals.

Hoover wrote to the President on April 11, pleading that the United States should withdraw from Europe, "lock, stock, and barrel if the Allies cannot be brought to adopt peace on the basis of the Fourteen Points. . . .

"It grows upon me daily," he wrote, "that the United States is the one great moral reserve in the world today and that we cannot maintain the independence of action through which this reserve is to be maintained if we allow ourselves to be dragged into detailed European entanglements over a period of years."

The President replied that he was in whole-hearted agreement, except that the United States was committed to membership on the Financial Commission on Reparation, "because that commission will undoubtedly need an umpire, and I am afraid we must take the necessary risks in that matter."

CHAPTER FIFTEEN

"THE LASTING GRATITUDE OF EUROPE"

HOOVER'S EARLY MORNING sleep was rudely interrupted at four o'clock on May 7. His servant explained that a messenger in the hall below refused to leave without delivering his document in person. He was wakened into full command of his mental forces when he found that he was reading the first printed draft of the Peace Treaty. His worst fears were confirmed. Throughout its lengthy pages ran an undercurrent of hatred and revenge. Conditions were imposed that would make permanent peace impossible!

He pulled on his clothes quickly and walked into the deserted streets. As he passed rows of houses he knew that their occupants were still dreaming of the hard-won peace this vicious document would deny them. Suddenly another figure emerged out of the gray mist. Hoover recognized the tall military bearing of General Jan Smuts. Soon the two were walking together, each pointing out how he detected the evil threads in the pattern, Smuts in the political field, Hoover in the economic. Before they reached the Etoile, they agreed to make their representatives aware of the poison in the draft treaty.

Hoover called the top staff of A.R.A. for breakfast. These men knew the heart of Europe; they were objective, free from any desire except to clean up the alley ways of the Old World. They pondered over the problem, trying to formulate a practical way to temper the vindictive peace-makers. They charitably assumed that many of the provisions resulted from an ineptness and ignorance of the probable outcome.

As he left the conference Hoover met one of the brilliant young economists of the British delegation, John Maynard Keynes. They agreed in their estimate of the probable economic consequences of such a peace. Together they called on General Smuts, with the result that some members of the British Cabinet came to Paris to urge Lloyd George to work for revisions.

In the meantime the Supreme Economic Council tackled the problem of post-war international finance. Hoover's long experience in re-vitalizing sick mines and industries had prepared him to undertake the rehabilitation of European business. He outlined a plan in a memo to General Bliss, pencilling in the margin: "This is probably not the first one you have seen."

The General replied that Hoover's sound ideas on re-establishing the banking structure interested him particularly, although as he was not a financial expert he was not qualified to evaluate the details. He was, however, anxious to have Hoover come before the Council to discuss lifting the blockade of Hungary.

Bliss wrote: "As about the only thing to fight in Hungary is Bolshevism and as that can be fought as well as any other way (as far as I know) by food and raw material for work, I see no reason why the blockade should not be lifted."

Hoover agreed emphatically. He had consistently maintained that the food blockade was a crime against civilization. Shortly the blockade was lifted, not only from Hungary, but also from Bulgaria and Turkey.

That achievement was one step in his drive against Bolshevism. But like a true physician he sought to combat pestilence at its source. He had lived in Russia. He knew the feelings of the peasants who had risen in revolt against those who had kept them in age-long servitude. He had urged the Allies to give food and other supplies to the struggling democracy led by Kerensky. Now Lenin had swept a new regime into power with police tyranny and controlled propaganda. Hoover's sympathies were with the suffering common people. In a long letter to President Wilson he explained that his desire to help these people was not new. He called attention to the real grievances behind the Revolution and made an eloquent plea for the appointment of a commission headed by a prominent neutral to administer relief in Russia along the lines of the C.R.B. He suggested that perhaps the Polar explorer Nansen could assume this task.

This idea was acceptable. Nansen outlined a plan in letters to Wilson, Lloyd George, Clemenceau, and Orlando. Although France was reluctant and contemptuous, the four gave the explorer permission to propose the idea to Moscow. By the middle of May, 1919, Nansen's cable to the Peace Commission gave the substance of the Russian reply with the added note: "Please tell Hoover that I intend to meet Lenin's delegate, perhaps at Stockholm, but shall be glad to have Hoover's opinion as soon as possible."

Neither Hoover's opinion nor Nansen's diplomatic efforts succeeded. French obstruction finally thwarted negotiations. The matter was dropped.

While it had been impossible to bring relief to Russia at this time, Hoover was now able to accomplish another long-cherished mission. In the early days of the C.R.B. he had been besieged by Polish-Americans to organize a similar plan to help their countrymen. The man who had sought him out was an acquaintance of his undergraduate days at Stanford, Ignace Paderewski!

The pianist, who had generously waived his claim for a minimum guarantee at the campus concert series a quarter century earlier, had been so eloquent that Hoover had even spared Vernon Kellogg from arduous duties in Belgium to survey the needs of the suffering peasants of Poland. Those people whose fatherland had been divided between Germany, Austria, and Russia for over a century were then being forced to fight unwillingly in the ranks of opposing armies. In spite of the dark picture painted by Kellogg and the obvious necessity for neutral aid, no amount of logic could gain consent of the Allies and

Germany at that time to let Hoover's planned organization function.

Shortly after America entered the war Paderewski came to Washington representing the "Kosciuszko Squadron," named for the volunteer General who had served under Washington in the Revolutionary War. The squadron was composed of Polish immigrants who had not yet obtained American citizenship, but who were so eager to fight alongside the Allies for the freedom of Poland that they had formed a special unit then training at Niagara-on-the Lake, Canada.

While in Washington Paderewski had been a frequent guest at the Hoovers' Massachusetts Avenue dinner table. He longed for his own invalid son left with friends in Switzerland. Thus he took pleasure in visiting with the young Hoovers, especially ten-year-old Allan.

It had been natural that after the war when Paderewski came to Paris in December, 1918, en route home to serve his newly-liberated country, he would find the Director-General of European Relief prepared to send substantial help to Poland. Within a few days of their meeting Hoover had a new Mission to Poland ready to follow Paderewski to Warsaw.

Vernon Kellogg with Colonel W. R. Grove and Vance McCormick arrived in that stricken city January 4, 1919. Chaos was worse than anything they had feared. Typhus was raging among the starving people. Internecine wars between Bolshevist elements threatened to add this new republic to the Russian debacle. Poles were denied the opportunity to hold public office or attain military rank of consequence for over a century. Now they were floundering in their attempt to establish an independent government. Kellogg, a man of tact and wisdom, was able to persuade the military government under Pilsudski that Paderewski was the one man who should be Premier, that he alone could establish the Allies' confidence in Poland.

Thus, the country was able to present a united front at the Peace Conference, with Paderewski at the head of her delegation. During the next vital months the Premier commuted between Paris and Warsaw.

This time, in contrast to the frustration of 1915, the A.R.A. Food Mission could bring prompt and effective help. Kellogg wired urgently that starving babies must have sustenance at once. Several carloads of condensed and malted milk were shipped from Switzerland. The first three vessels carrying wheat flour trans-shipped from Rotterdam reached Danzig on February 17. Again, Hoover had not waited for red tape to unwind!

At the head of an efficient organization for feeding Polish children was Maurice Pate, who was as decisive as The Chief when action was needed. His task was to provide one warm meal a day for 1,300,000 Polish children. Once he had to ride the locomotive of a freight train loaded with rice, tinned meats, sugar and cocoa to get to the Mayor of Katowice, a town in Upper Silesia where Poles, Germans and Czechs were disputing borders, to get food stuffs moving. Before the day was over the Mayor had a committee of Poles, Germans, Czechs—Protestants, Catholics and Jews—ready to assume responsibility for impartial distribution of foodstuffs from America.

The Polish situation had been ticklish. As he had done in Belgium, Hoover issued instructions to all Americans overseeing food distribution in Poland to keep out of politics. "There are political missions assigned to that work," he wrote. "We should forward to them any matters of interest . . . yours is entirely that of relief.

"Remember that you are representing the American nation in a great enterprise and the task is one requiring day and night work when necessary. You are now playing personally a large part in the broad reconstruction work of the Peace Conference, and the Allies look to you to do your part to give Poland the start she so well deserves."

During those months, President Wilson, ill and disillusioned, was increasingly difficult to approach. Even after Lloyd George had agreed to press for revisions in the proposed Treaty, Wilson vacillated about calling the leading Americans in Paris for consultation. When he finally did this on June 3, they got no further than to point out some of the major weaknesses in the document.

Consequently, Hoover wrote to the President on the following day, detailing the needed modifications. This was followed with a letter to the President's Economic Committee in which he indicated that he saw in the British change of heart a tendency to recognize the President's original intentions. He urged that Wilson now *insist* on the changes.

A few days later in a personal plea, Hoover drew on himself the implacable wrath of the President when he insisted that the treaty as it stood would make for destruction and not reconstruction; for instability, not peace. He was never again invited to his private councils.

On the 28th of June, Hoover stood with the other observers in the Hall of Mirrors in Versailles Palace when official signatures were placed on the Peace Treaty; but his mind was far away, seeing with prophetic clarity the stultifying effect on the millions of "just hopeful" people whose lives he and his associates were laboring to save. Depressed, he walked out of the room and into the great courtyard of the Palace where mobs had once called down vengeance on their luxury-loving rulers.

But there was no time on his agenda for regret. The signing he had just witnessed only added to his burdens of Relief. He saw now that the Allied purpose of devitalizing Germany would start forces that could bring economic degeneration to the world; but all he could do for the moment was to try to sustain life in those people who would have to bear these crushing levies.

Sympathy for the German people was exceedingly unpopular, yet Hoover sensed that these reparations and controls would stifle German recovery; that her ultimate collapse could drag the whole world with her into an abyss. The plight of German babies had touched him as deeply as had that of the little Belgians and French for whom he had worked so long. But the grants of aid from the American Government had specified that none of that money should be spent in former enemy territory. Hoover had other sources of help. Since the Armistice his fellow-Quakers in The American Friends' Service had done yeoman work in this field. They would continue.

Further appropriations for the A.R.A. ceased with the signing of the Peace Treaty. But the millions of children all over Europe, whose only future lay in continued help from America, were not to be let down. With the approval of the President the A.R.A. was transformed from a public into a private organization. The main office moved from Avenue Montaigne in Paris to 42 Broadway in New York. Walter Lyman Brown was left in charge of European activities operating out of London.

Hoover associates from New York to San Francisco and from Maine to New Mexico went immediately to work raising funds to carry on. All profits that had accrued to the Food Administration during the Armistice, some $40 million, went into the coffers of the new Childrens' Relief Fund. American Relief warehouses sold the surplus that had been piling up in preparation for another year of war, turning the profits to the enlarging program for the children of Europe.

Sure now that the work would be carried on, the Chairman of the A.R.A. made a quick personal survey of the needs of the liberated countries before returning permanently to America. Wherever he went he suggested that the various governments invite American technical advisors to assist in economic and food problems. Paderewski in Poland was one of the first to act. In fact, Hoover's welcome to Warsaw was poignantly personal. Thousands of barefoot children in tattered clothes marched across the pavements to Mokolowski Park. Each carried a paper American flag to express appreciation to the people of that land represented by the quiet man with bowed head sitting between Pilsudski and Paderewski. Then the Mayor offered a traditional Polish welcome, bread and salt on an especially carved wooden tray.

During the ceremony Hoover's eyes wandered to a little child who had broken ranks to chase a white rabbit. The lad suddenly laid his furry tribute at the feet of the man who had made life possible for him and all these others.

"It is only an hour until dark," Hoover whispered to Hugh

Gibson, America's first Minister to the new Republic. "How far do these children have to go to reach home?"

"Some came from as far away as twenty miles," answered Gibson.

Hoover quietly left the official party and hurried down the line of eager children and Polish dignitaries, shaking hands as he went. He was unceremoniously hastening the procedure so that the youngsters could start their homeward trek before the twilight passed.

At the tomb of Kosciuszkio in Cracow, Paderewski again seized an opportunity to put his gratitude into words. The Premier's translation of Hoover's terse ten-minute speech lengthened into three-quarters of an hour, as he added his personal account of the sequence of events that had linked the two since their first meeting on the Stanford Campus.

"For twenty-five years this man has thought that he owed me a debt," said Paderewski, "but he has repaid it a thousandfold in what he has done for you, my people, in making life possible for the children of Poland."

Hoover did not look at it that way. Before he left the country, he paid his debt to Paderewski personally with a gift to the Premier of a shiny black Cadillac, the first of its kind to be seen of the streets of a Polish city.

There were a few more stops before Herbert Hoover boarded the S.S. *Aquitania* at Liverpool, bound for home at last. In Brussels he sat once more in his accustomed seat among his old associates of the C.N. and C.R.B., around the long dining table of Francqui's palatial home on Avenue Louise on August 28. The time had come to try to crystallize the plans he and Francqui had formulated in 1916. There was money enough in the unexpended funds in their coffers to enlarge the endowments of the four great Universities of Belgium, Liége, Ghent, Brussels, and Louvain, as well as the Institute of Tropical Medicine in Antwerp. There was also enough to erect in the heart of the Belgian capital a permanent educational center, the Fondation Universitaire.

Hoover explained to his colleagues what such an institution

could do to promote better understanding between the intellectual leaders of the country. Hitherto religious and political differences had separated members of the faculties of the various universities; but Hoover's vision laid the foundation for cooperative action that would extend far into the future.

From Brussels he went to Paris for a farewell call on Premier Clemenceau. With the Old Tiger's gloomy prediction of another world war that would demand his return to humanitarian service again in Europe indelibly imprinted on his mind, Hoover returned to London.

Here, he was honored at a dinner given by Cecil Harmsworth, M.P., Under-Secretary of State for Foreign Affairs. A message from Lloyd George brought warm thanks from the British Government for the ability and energy expended by the Director of Relief in Europe. Hoover sailed for home with the Welshman's assurance that he had "earned the lasting gratitude of the people of Europe."

Chapter Sixteen

BACK TO THE HOME FRONT

THIS TIME HE WAS welcomed with acclaim. Three days after he landed in New York, on September 16, the ballroom of the Waldorf was crowded with thirteen hundred fellow-engineers. This was the third largest dinner ever held in that city, the two previous ones having been for Theodore Roosevelt and General Pershing.

Toastmaster W. L. Saunders introduced the honored guest as "a man of rugged personality; strong of conviction, modest; thinking never of self; practical, far-seeing, wise, human, brave; with a mind clear in action; a conscience that always functions; one who saved lives while all others were engaged in destroying them; a rare combination of physical, mental, and moral courage; a real American . . . the example of an engineer who typifies the modern definition of engineering which is thus written in large letters on the wall of the Engineers' Library in New York: 'Engineering, the Art of Organizing and Directing Men, and Controlling Forces and Materials of Nature for the Benefit of the Human Race.' "

Pages at each table were filled with signatures and bound in a book later presented to Hoover. On the first page these professional associates of the American Institute of Mining Engineers had expressed their appreciation in four short paragraphs, ending with the thought that since no gift of gold or precious stones could convey their deep feelings, they simply subscribed their names as fellow engineers, co-workers, and admiring friends.

A few weeks later these men voiced their confidence in the more tangible form by electing Herbert Hoover president of the Institute for 1920, succeeding the eminent Horace Winchell, who had created the profession of consulting geologist. There was a brief prospect that as soon as the affairs of the relief organizations could be wound up Hoover would withdraw from public life into the professional circle for which his training and personality were suited.

He traveled on to California to establish legal residence on the Stanford Campus and to relax for at least a month before these new duties would demand his major time on the East Coast. He yielded, however, to student clamor to speak at the University assembly, explaining the plans and purposes of the League of Nations; and to the Engineering Societies of San Francisco to be honor guest at a dinner presided over by T. A. Rickard.

A command request from the White House asked him to act as host for the visiting King and Queen of the Belgians. Due to President Wilson's serious illness, it was impossible to entertain the royal visitors as had been planned in Washington. A California tour seemed the most appropriate substitute. Because the Hoovers' temporary campus home had only one spare bedroom, he arranged through mutual friends an invitation for the visiting monarchs to use the Robert Bliss estate in Montecito in the outskirts of Santa Barbara. Here King Albert's party were entertained in a mansion hidden among woods that could carry the monarch's thoughts back to Château d'Ardennes, his grandfather's hunting lodge in the October-tinted Belgian forest.

The Hoovers rode down San Francisco's Market Street in a brilliant parade with King Albert and his Queen. Later the Director of the C.R.B. saved the Mayor's political face when he suggested that James Rolph accept the proferred Order of the Crown in the name of the city, not for himself.

During this month in the West, Hoover also gave much time to the Stanford Board of Trustees. Due to his presence at the October meeting, he was able to persuade the others that the time had come to charge tuition at the University. For the past six years he had tried unsuccessfully to bring Dr. Wilbur to this point of view. Now he met a storm of protest from alumni and students as this vote changed the institution from its original status. Hoover took time to explain his reasons in the student *Daily,* quoting Mrs. Stanford's opinion that great gifts without some obligation to make return, either directly, or by furnishing equal opportunities for others, lower moral responsibility. He added that a fund had been made available to provide for those who could not afford the $40 a quarter to be charged for tuition. This loan could be repaid over a long period after graduation without interest.

At the same time, he was laying the foundation for another venture which would bring more world interest to his Alma Mater. Shortly after returning from Europe he had discussed the world food situation with the president of the Carnegie Corporation, Dr. James Angell. Hoover felt that some institution should assemble all significant data and provide for continued research in the field of food production, distribution, and consumption.

With Dr. Angell's concurrence, he had asked Alonzo Taylor to report on the possibility of setting up such an institution. Hoover took advantage of this time on the campus to present the idea to Dr. Wilbur, who agreed that Stanford offered ideal opportunity for this undertaking. Scholars would be attracted by easy access to the growing accumulation of war documents now being filed in the University Library. Stanford was willing to provide quarters, facilities, and faculty position for the personnel of the projected Carnegie Food Research Institute for a ten-year period. This gave weight to Hoover's request to the Carnegie Corporation to underwrite the project. It was brought to fruition a year later with a gift of $704,000.

Even before the funds were assured, Hoover had helped with the selection of three eminent men to act as Directors, Alonzo Taylor, Dr. Carl Alsberg, representative of the American Chemical Society on the National Research Council, and Dr.

Joseph Davis, a member of the Social Science Research Council and Contributing Editor of the Harvard Economic Service.

While Hoover was thus concerned with the business of the University, the Stanford family had been eager to plan an official welcome. This had been postponed until his return from New York in late December. Then they finally gathered for a gala dinner at the Commercial Club in San Francisco. Hoover's classmate, Charlie Field, presided.

"Bert, here are your friends of Stanford," he said in introducing the illustrious Son of the Stanford Red. "Fellow Alumni, here he is, Hoover '95!"

Dr. Branner's was the most personal of all the speeches, recalling student days when his young assistant would take off his coat, fix attention on the task assigned, and see it through whether he liked it or not. Although he said that after graduation Herbert Hoover had started at the bottom of the ladder, he had never cultivated "the bottom of the ladder habit, but did his work promptly and just as promptly went forward and upward. And from the very outset he always enjoyed the process of getting things done, and of making a success of whatever he put his hand to. Indeed, I never knew him to fail to do anything he ever undertook, if it were humanly and physically possible to do it."

Lou Henry Hoover was not forgotten in this tribute, as she listened to Dr. Banner's description of her as a well qualified, thoroughly competent and loyal partner. Her serious blue eyes involuntarily turned toward the dignified man who had first brought them together, then dropped modestly as he concluded, "Not a small part of Mr. Hoover's success in life has been due to her able and cheerful cooperation. Our country has no honors too high for such a man and such a woman."

Their Stanford friends were not the only Americans to feel that gratitude. In the leading article of the New Year issue of the *Saturday Evening Post* "Consider Mr. Hoover" Samuel Blythe discussed the possibility of a business man as the next candidate for the Presidency. Blythe seemed to feel that because Hoover's political affiliations were as yet undeclared, he could be commandeered by the expressed wish of the people, regardless of politicians.

Other magazines and newspapers throughout the country began to write in the same vein. The *New York World* of January 21, 1920, in an editorial announced that they would be glad to support Hoover as the Democratic candidate on a platform that represented the historic principles of that party; or as an independent on a platform of progressive liberalism. Also, they would not hesitate to support him as the Republician candidate on a platform presenting the kind of government Mr. Hoover had exemplified in his public career.

Partisan objections were regarded as arguments in his favor by this avowedly Democratic paper, which maintained that Americans were tired of professional politicians; that Hoover alone measured up to the Presidency. The editorial recounted that he had worked with his hands, and had been a director of labor, knowing from wide personal experience the responsibilities of employers. As a further argument, they said that Hoover knew the economic condition of the world perhaps better than any other American; that he was thoroughly familiar with the diplomacy and politics of Europe in a way that few of his countrymen had ever experienced; and that those who wanted a business man for President would find here a man who had managed brilliantly one of the most successful business undertakings in history.

While his proponents were writing in superlatives, Hoover was shouldering new cares. The American Friends' Service had persuaded him that the starving children of Germany must have more help than their organization could provide. He realized that the European Children's Fund must be enlarged to save not only the children of the liberated countries, but these little Germans as well. He wanted, too, to achieve this through a business-like program that would not make beggars of the recipients nor self-righteous patrons of the donors.

German-Americans were ready to aid overseas relatives. Hoover sought the cooperation of bankers on both sides of the ocean. Then he sent for Bill Mullendore, who had just completed his "History of the Food Administration." This young man, in later years the president and chairman of the Southern California Edison Company, went first to London and then to Berlin to become Hoover's liaison in handling the food drafts. These drafts, a precedent for CARE after the second World War, made it possible to accomplish this purpose.

Quantities of cocoa, flour, and rice were purchased in bulk in the United States, shipped to Hamburg, and packaged to be sent to distribution stations throughout Germany and Poland. Relatives in America bought food drafts at their local banks and sent them to the intended recipients in Europe. The drafts were presented at the A.R.A. stations in exchange for the food parcels. A slight charge for this service covered all overhead expenses.

Others beside Mullendore were called back to Hoover service as he sought to enlarge the scope of the European Children's Fund. Among them was Mrs. Hoover's former Latin Professor, Dr. Fairclough, who had been serving the Red Cross in the Balkans. Hoover persuaded him to stay in Europe to carry on the child feeding program in Montenegro. The W. P. Fullers, Stanford friends from San Francisco, went to Poland. Lincoln Hutchinson, University of California Professor, became his aide in Czechoslovakia. Christian Herter, one of the secretaries who had been with him at Versailles, and who years later would become Governor of Massachusetts and after that, Secretary of State of the U.S.A., was appointed Executive Secretary of the whole organization.

During this period, the C.R.B. was winding up its service. The $33 million residue in its treasury had already been committed to educational purposes by the agreements made with Francqui in 1916 and 1919 and implemented in the Brussels Conference the preceding year. Edgar Rickard and Bill Poland, as joint liquidators, made a cash advance of $18 million to Belgian universities and technical schools. The remaining funds were then divided, nearly seven million dollars to the Foundation and another eight million to the C.R.B. Educational

Foundation set up in New York. The income from these two closely cooperating foundations, one in America and the other in Belgium, would make it possible (1) for young Belgians to obtain university training; (2) to advance scientific research in Belgium; and (3) through exchange of scholars to help knit closer ties between the two peoples. Perrin Galpin, who had been a Hoover aide continually since the beginning of C.R.B., became the executive director.

In his inaugural speech at the annual meeting of the American Institute of Mining Engineers, Hoover paid high tribute to fellow engineers who formed and supported free advisory boards in Washington to discuss national problems. His words were self-revealing. He said that these men wanted nothing for themselves; they merely sought efficiency in government. And he outlined how he thought this objective could be reached, picturing an ideal society in which every man could find a place consistent with his ability.

"Its inspiration is individual initiative; its stimulus is competition. Its safeguard is education. Its greatest mentor is free speech and organization for public good."

Braced with such hope for the future, these engineers went from that meeting to add their voices to the clamor that this man should apply his business acumen and wide experience to the problems of his own country. In addition to these engineers, people from all over the nation were insistent. Housewives who had enlisted in the Food Administration, volunteers who had raised Belgian Relief and A.R.A. funds, loyal Stanford alumni everywhere, all wanted their Chief to become the nation's Chief. But Hoover had no yen nor taste for politics. He announced that he was not a candidate. He assured his associates in the offices of the Engineering Societies that he was preparing to return to his profession.

Dr. Wilbur became his spokesman in answering urgent letters from alumni who wanted to organize Hoover Clubs. He told them that he felt that his friend's strong sense of duty might ultimately impel him to respond to a call if the public was insistent enough. On the other hand, respect for Hoover's wishes seemed to make organized effort to secure delegates' votes undesirable. He was sure, however, that the country needed to know more about their great alumnus; he advised "plenty of conversation, but no organization."

In Washington, Carter Glass called on Adolph Miller. Could this old friend persuade Hoover to become the Democratic candidate?

"I should think that he is a Democrat," said Glass, "since he supported Wilson in the Congressional election of 1918, trying to help elect a Congress that would back the Presidential program."

Miller agreed to sound Hoover out. He dropped in one evening after dinner as was his habit when the two had serious problems to ponder. Before he could finish relaying the Senator's suggestion, Hoover got up quickly from the sofa. He walked across the room to the mantel and turned to face his friend, his back braced against the marble. Then he said, slowly,

"I can never forget the enthusiasm with which I supported Theodore Roosevelt. As you know, I was one of his great backers."

"So was I," said Miller, "but that did not prevent my support of Woodrow Wilson, whom I consider one of the greatest men of our generation. I am really what you would call an Independent Democrat."

Hoover interrupted, vehemently. "No! You are a Republican."

Nevertheless, the idea of selecting Hoover for the Democratic ticket did not die readily. Another neighbor, Franklin Roosevelt, came to Miller to discuss the prospect, saying that he had heard of the proposal made by Glass.

"I feel," said this mutual friend of Franklin Lane, "that Hoover should be a Democrat. The men he has associated with most in Washington are younger Democrats. You might press home to him that he is closer in his thinking to them than to the Republicans."

Hoover, however, remained loyal to his traditional political affiliations. Across the continent his close California associates ignored the candidacy of their senior Senator and former Governor, Hiram Johnson, to work openly for Hoover's nomination at the approaching Republican Convention.

June came, and Hoover finally wired Warren Gregory, one of his faithful C.R.B. staff, that he would accept the nomination on a platform conforming to his ideas on public questions.

As soon as Hoover's decision was announced, Judge Curtis Lindley registered as a Republican and wired his client that he had joined a "Hoover-for-President Club." His wire said that he had been reluctant to see the humanitarian enter the precarious field of politics, but his message expressed full knowledge of the strength of the Johnson machine and his realization that every ounce of effort must go toward its defeat.

Hoover replied that although reluctant he had made his decision only because he felt it an absolute duty. Forces beyond his control were sweeping him away from the seclusion of his desk to the rostrum on which he would be at the mercy of a public who would demand oratory as the price of votes.

He would have no truck with political machines. If the people wanted him, he was ready; if they did not, he had other things to do. He could not and would not speak for himself; but if Governor Nathan Miller of New York wanted to ask the Republicans to nominate him in Chicago he would not refuse to do his duty.

June 22 found perspiring crowds tense with excitement in the Chicago Convention Hall. There were banners for General Leonard Wood, Governor Lowden of Illinois, Calvin Coolidge, Nicholas Murray Butler, vociferous calls for Hiram Johnson. Up in the gallery a determined minority had gathered to challenge the Republican machine. Blasco Ibañez, reporting for the *Kansas City Star,* looked up at this group electioneering for Hoover and jotted the observation that they were all women, "some very pretty and chic."

"Why do women prefer a candidate so enigmatic and undemonstrative?" he asked, "Hoover holds the world's record for silence. No man can boast of hearing him speak a dozen words consecutively. . . . This must be the law of contrasts."

When the time came for Judge Miller to speak, Senator

Smoot of Utah was temporarily in the chair in place of the elected chairman, Henry Cabot Lodge. The galleries cheered and cheered, completely oblivious to the pounding gavel after Miller's speech. Finally, he told Hugh Brown of Nevada, another Stanford alumnus, to go ahead with his seconding speech. Continuing din from the galleries was so great that Brown's enthusiastic speech went unheard.

Arthur Brisbane in the *Chicago Herald and Examiner* reflected that "someone has been working intelligently for Hoover and he has friends and plenty, but in spite of Judge Miller, Brown, and the other second, Mary Miller Morrison who was like a beautiful character from 'Little Women,' not one delegate is for him. Goodbye, Hoover boom for Chicago. Try San Francisco!"

In the smoke-filled committee room, too, Hoover was unnoticed. The weary Convention finally cast its vote for the straight-line politician Warren Gamaliel Harding, whom these men had produced to whip the non-conformists into line.

Now at last world-embracing responsibilities could be shed. The Hoovers could return to the home overlooking the Stanford campus, and the man who believed in the recuperative value of fishing could take his sons up to the Klamath River whenever school vacation allowed.

Hoover was thinking in terms of Stanford again, too. Dr. Wilbur announced at a June student assembly that an anonymous donor in the East had given $100,000 for an eating commons to be built connecting the Stanford Union and the Women's Clubhouse, with the proviso that the Trustees advance another $150,000 to be repaid out of earnings. It did not take much thinking to penetrate that "secret." Any Stanford alumnus who kept in touch knew that there was only one member of their family with such money and loyalty.

At home or abroad, the Hoovers could not escape recognition. Requests for speeches on many subjects came from all sections.

October was a full month. On the eleventh he was in St. Louis, promising the American Hygiene Association that if the nation would grapple with the whole child situation for one generation, its public health, economic efficiency, moral character, sanity, and stability would advance three generations in one. He journeyed along the farm lands bordering the Missouri, speaking for the Farmers' Cooperative in Topeka, urging that they apply their cooperative methods to remedy the marketing system. Next he was in Cleveland helping to inaugurate a Community Chest. Here he seized the opportunity to look beyond the needs at home. He explained in detail the suffering of the children of Europe and enlisted that philanthropically-minded city in his program for the European Children's Fund.

Four days later, the Federated Engineering Societies in Washington heard Hoover urge them to apply their trained minds to a solution of economic strife and differences between capital and labor.

It was not strange, then, that Warren Harding, grappling with the selection of acceptable men for his Cabinet, turned a deaf ear to politicians who had procured his nomination and election to the Presidency, and listened to wiser ones among his advisors, like Will Hays, who told him that if he honestly wanted a business-like administration, he must have Hoover in his Cabinet.

Over the vigorous protests of Senators Reed and Penrose, Hiram Johnson, and even a personal plea from Alice Roosevelt Longworth, the President-elect followed the mandate of the people and invited Herbert Hoover to become Business Manager of the Nation—the Secretary of Commerce.

Chapter Seventeen

BUSINESS MANAGER OF THE NATION

While American senators were still wrangling over Hoover's appointment to the Harding Cabinet, the *New York Times* carried an item under a Vienna dateline, saying that a message from Herbert Hoover translated and placarded on the city wall, had been the only ray of hope on a gloomy New Year's Day. His words had assured that, due to the magnanimity of the American people, he was in a position to continue feeding the children of Austria. At the same time, the administrative offices of the A.R.A. European Children's Fund in London received a testimonial from Cracow, signed by fifty thousand children of Western Galicia, who had come with hands carefully washed with A.R.A. soap to sign the precious document of thanks.

Senator Hitchcock of Nebraska rose indignantly in the Senate to answer Senator Reed's questioning of Hoover's use of the $100 million appropriated for European relief. "Never in the history of the world has there been a more careful organization," asserted Hitchcock, "and never a more prompt report. We should give the Director credit as Europe has done."

The great heart of America said "Yes" to this in tangible form. Before the end of January, Hoover announced that he had an offer of fifteen million bushels of corn from farmers in the Mid-West, to be used by the European Relief Council.

"I am confident, too," he said, "that money for the transportation of this grain will be volunteered, for the money in our treasury cannot be diverted from the Children's Fund."

He estimated that it would cost fifty cents a bushel to move the corn from an Iowa farm to Europe, so they needed $7,500,000.

"Let us make the slogan of our farms this year: 'Market surplus in relief and take our pay in good will,' " he said.

When the Senate finally agreed with Harding that the nation should commandeer the services of a man who had done so much for the world, the Hoovers again gave up their dream of living permanently in sunny California. That newly-completed house on San Juan Hill above the Stanford campus had finally, but briefly, sheltered a re-united Hoover family. The great lift vans, tightly packed with possessions stored in London since they had closed Red House, had crossed oceans and arrived at what their owners hoped would be a final destination. For just a few weeks, Herbert Hoover had begun to enjoy the unsurpassed view of the Santa Clara Valley through the plate glass windows of his study. That room was Lou Henry Hoover's concession to her husband's wish to have his outlook unobstructed. Otherwise, she had insisted upon leaded glass in all the windows, in keeping with her dream of preserving some of the atmosphere of Old England in the interior of this house with its Algerian exterior.

Now they had to repack personal possessions and cross the continent again to go house-hunting in Washington.

By March, they had purchased and settled in a gracious Colonial-type house at 2300 "S" Street. Hoover was ready to undertake the next task. Since that day on the train between Melbourne and Adelaide when he had confided to Dr. Jordan his ambition to return to America and find some work where he could be of service he had looked forward to a peacetime place in the normal life of the United States.

As with the C.R.B., he had again taken on responsibility at the cost of personal fortune. During the period when he was considering Harding's offer, Daniel Guggenheim invited him into full partnership in theirs, the greatest mining and metallurgical company in the world. They told him that the minimum guaranteed salary would be five hundred thousand dollars a year!

It had taken no time for him to decide. If the nation needed his services, he was home for good. He settled into his Washington office with idealistic dreams of bettering the economic life of his own country.

In the April issue of *Industrial Management,* as the Secretary of Commerce Hoover outlined his conception of "What America Faces." Editorial comment pointed to his achievements at the age of forty-seven as an inspiration to other executives to apply accumulated knowledge to the needs of their country.

Although most of his own life he had followed the nomad existence of a mining engineer, Hoover felt that the family unit, dwelling in comfortable and clean surroundings, was the cornerstone of the commonwealth.

He told the American Institute of Architects that national banks should be given greater freedom to apply savings accounts to mortgage purpose, and promised to devote the facilities of his Department to a program of better homes. Because of his recent experience in building, he started a survey leading to standardization of such items as pipes, bricks, plumbing fixtures, building hardware.

He established a National Committee on Wood Utilization, which was to encourage the fuller use of cheaper and more plentiful varieties of lumber, of short lengths and imperfect stock. Advisory committees on all phases of home building were formed to furnish facts to the public through the Department. His own small book, "How To Own Your Own Home," became a best seller.

The inevitable aftermath of war with its growing unemployment and the industrial confusion inherent in adaptation to a peace economy raised many problems. Hoover leaned on Adolph Miller for advice. An interruption in one of these conferences in the office of the Secretary illustrates Hoover's spontaneous response to need. A long-distance call for Miller was relayed from his home. It came from the Mayo Clinic in Rochester, Minnesota, telling him that his closest friend, Franklin K. Lane, had died. Hoover walked to the door with his caller, deep sorrow reflected in every line of his quiet face.

"Do you know how he leaves his widow?" he asked, as he pressed Miller's hand.

The older man replied that he did not have exact knowledge, but that he presumed that a man who had given so much of his life to public service had not been able to lay aside much.

"We must do something about this," pursued Hoover. "It's up to you to find out for me what is necessary."

A few days later several men joined Miller as they walked out of the Washington memorial service for Lane.

"Let's go on up to your home," they said.

About thirty men, including Herbert Hoover, gathered at Miller's home. Out of their informal discussion, the Franklin K. Lane Memorial Fund was established and a committee appointed to receive, not to solicit, gifts. The income would go to Mrs. Lane while she lived. Later, the capital should be devoted to some philanthropic purpose determined by the three guardians, Herbert Hoover, Adolph Miller, and Franklin Delano Roosevelt!

In the summer of 1920 Hoover's sympathies were diverted to a new humanitarian call. Walter Lyman Brown, still in charge of the European office of the A.R.A., relayed to him a telegram from the Russian novelist, Maxim Gorky, an urgent plea for help as famine was claiming millions of lives.

Another telegram, 1,400 words, came about the same time from Maurice Pate, adding pressure for immediate action in this crisis. Pate and a companion had managed to get to Moscow to negotiate for the safety of Hoover Commission personnel in Poland, then at war with Russia. Officials had been so impressed with these direct-speaking young men that they were invited to remain three weeks to make a study of Russian food-distribution problems. Their report of appalling famine conditions stirred The Chief to action.

Hoover replied to Gorky that if Russia would send a responsible representative, he would instruct Brown to meet such a person in Riga. Maxim Litvinoff came to the Latvian capital. Despite the "lack of confidence on one side and suspicion on the other," as Walter Duranty reported their conversations, they reached an agreement. This included a promise that all Americans still detained in Russia should be released.

But Brown reported to his Chairman that it was not easy to obtain the concessions granted so readily in the liberated countries. Russians were sensitive to the American fight against Communism. "Food is a veapon!" reiterated Litvinoff, whenever Brown asked for immunity for his American aides and for other special considerations.

Nevertheless, when Litvinoff assured Brown that every American he knew about was free to leave the country, the A.R.A. began preparations to extend relief beyond the Polish and Roumanian boundaries.

Final arrangements were complete on August 20. One month later hungry little Russians were eating their first American meal. Funds came from several sources. Hoover still had $7 million in the coffers of the A.R.A.; the Grain Corporation had a balance of $20 million. He convinced Congress that world security demanded that these moneys should be used in an effort to save the victims of the terrible winter of 1921 which, combined with the ruthless economic practices of the Soviet rulers, had brought disaster to these far-away people.

Colonel William N. Haskell, veteran European Relief worker, and a corps of experienced Hoover aides arrived to supervise the task. At first, it covered only child feeding and food drafts. Eventually, after one of the aides, Sam Keeney, pointed out the urgent need to save students and scholars, as well as children, millions of adults were also rescued from imminent starvation. Typhus and other famine diseases were brought under control; and later, seeds, bought with Russian money, were planted to prevent future famine.

Although hard times were beginning to grip the American people, there was generous response to Hoover's appeal. Soon, with the addition of $25 million from Russian gold reserves, total relief funds amounted to $78 million. As the work progressed, Lincoln Hutchinson moved from Czechoslovakia to Moscow to join Dr. Frank Golder, a Stanford faculty member who had been on Dr. Adams' staff collecting tons of valuable documents for the growing Hoover Collection on War, Revolution, and Peace. As these two fought the ravages of famine they often traded food for such books.

In this same summer of 1921 the President asked his Secretary of Commerce to attempt to find a solution for the growing problem of unemployment in the U.S.A. At the first meeting of a Commission gathered from industry and labor, Hoover outlined his philosophy, emphasizing his belief that it is not consonant with the spirit of America to make demands on the public treasury for the solution of every difficulty.

Until now the Department of Commerce had been inconspicuous. Now the new Secretary was developing it into a potent factor in many phases of American life. Almost coincident with his appointment, he was faced with the regulation of radio, a new invention that would eventually affect every home. Until now, radio had been used mainly for ship-to-shore communication. Within a few months after Hoover became Secretary growing personal radio use began to clog the ether.

On February 27, 1922, Hoover called a conference of radio experts and broadcasters. There was no precedent on which to base control; but the Secretary had some definite opinions. He believed that the air channels were public property. Broadcasters, as tenants, were thus subject to regulation. He recognized that inventors had a right to earn a profit; yet no one should monopolize public communication. Fortunately, it was possible to assign certain wave lengths to each station in a given geographic area. He designated WBZ as the first licensed radio broadcasting station setting the pattern to simplify all future use of the air waves. But because he had a sympathetic understanding of the expectations of the American boy, he specified that a band of wave lengths must always be kept open and unrestricted for the use of amateurs.

It did not take President Harding long to realize that the serious man whose mind ranged the whole gamut of governmental tasks was not one to invite to White House poker games; but he called Hoover into consultation on every type of problem. Before long Washington wits referred to the Californian as "Secretary of Commerce and Assistant Secretary of everything else." Harding asked him to head the Red Cross. He appointed him High Commissioner on Inter-American Affairs. He was named advisor to the Washington Arms Conference.

Hoover asked that the Bureau of Mines be transferred to his Department. Under his direction, the activities of the Bureaus resulted in the discovery of new mineral resources and the conservation of others, notably, petroleum. Clearing long-standing congestion in the Patent Office, he encouraged inventors to apply their talents to the greater production that he envisioned as the way to American prosperity.

The Bureau of Fisheries offered an intriguing opportunity. From the day he had first learned to fish with a bent pin on the end of the string, this had been his one form of recreation. Now he applied all his personal knowledge toward the preservation of the sport as a national therapy.

"The spiritual uplift of the goodwill, cheerfulness and optimism that accompanies every fishing expedition is the peculiar spirit that our people need in these troublous times of suspicions and doubt," he told the Convention of the U.S. Fisheries Association at Atlantic City. "They ought to be sent fishing periodically, and if they are to be sent fishing, we must build up the opportunities for them to fish. Life is not comprised entirely of making a living, or of arguing about the future or defaming the past."

He also devoted endless time and thought to the commercial aspect of what he termed the "most precious of our primary food supplies." As President of the Izaak Walton League, as well as in his government capacity, Hoover helped to put through Congress much legislation that led to conservation and development of all kinds of fisheries, deep sea, littoral, and inland.

Companions on fishing trips best knew the *real* Herbert Hoover. He and a group of his intimate friends owned a camp in the wild Klamath River Canyon at the far northern boundary of California. Whenever he could take a few days away from the pressure of business he would join these men, Fred Smith, owner of the Palo Alto Sport Shop, Ray Lyman Wilbur, Pearce Mitchell (University Registrar), Dr. Alonzo Taylor, and Dr. Tom Williams (football star of Stanford pioneer days). In the glow of the campfire, he relaxed and shared the human side of his world experience.

But those who accepted the hospitality of the house on "S" Street met a different man. Old friends, invited to spend a weekend, reported that their host did not seem to know that they were in the same room as he sat at the head of his table, looking out through the great window, absorbed in the tangled affairs of a nation bewildered by its new position in an unfamiliar world.

He had no patience with the flippancy of this era in which he was tackling vital economic problems. Every waking hour, and there were often sixteen to eighteen of them per day, was devoted to finding ways and means of providing the best for every American, good education, the physical necessities for comfortable living, and independence in spiritual matters. But all around him he heard jazz bands. America was off on a post-war bender. His heart was heavy as he watched the growing orgy of stock speculation and an unnatural business boom.

Early in 1922 the Secretary warned a Los Angeles audience that until Russia could be restored to her functions of providing food and buying the manufactured products of Europe, the commerce of the world would be deranged.

The commodity crisis of 1921 and the current coal strike led him to propose that America must reorganize her economic system and utilize her great resources to maximum advantage. As one such opportunity he cited the possible development of the Colorado River with its nascent millions of horse power, making the desert bloom through irrigation.

Facts and figures about the Colorado River Project were fresh in Hoover's mind. He was in the West, attending a series of meetings with members of a recently-appointed commission, of which he was chairman by request of the Governors of the seven states involved. Hoover had long been interested in the proposal to control the great river—a subject that had been discussed before the war. On one of his earlier California visits, he had studied the project as a means of protecting the Imperial Valley from floods, and as a potential source of water for the rapidly increasing population of Southern California. Thus, he had been a natural choice of the Governors when they had met in a preliminary session late in 1921.

At the same time Hoover was proposing that the United States negotiate with Canada over the feasibility of providing the grain growers of the mid-continent with a water outlet to world markets. Experience in many places had taught him that a good canal system could keep transportation costs low. His idea, the seed of the St. Lawrence Waterways Project, was that by constructing a canal from Lake Ontario to Montreal the river could be open to permit passage for ocean-going vessels to and from the Great Lakes Region. He also foresaw vast power development.

Leaving this suggestion in the hands of a joint Engineering Commission, the Secretary turned to more immediate problems. California rice growers were bankrupt. Their crop, four million bags of paddy rice, had no market at home or abroad. Appeal for current reports on world markets reached the newly-formed division of foodstuffs in Hoover's Department, with a branch devoted to foreign markets.

Here was a typical need, such as Hoover had suggested in persuading the Carnegie Corporation to underwrite the Food Research Institute. Within a month from the time the request came across his desk, his assistants had located a market for the California rice in Japan.

One-hundred-forty-eight million pounds were shipped through the Port of San Francisco during 1922, a greater amount than had been shipped through New York or New Orleans, where rice had been one of the principal exports for more than seventy-five years.

Raisin growers, tobacco farmers, and many other producers

of specialized items found similar assistance in his Department's commodity division. Thus, the "Assistant Secretary of Everything Else" was taking on duties that normally would have been assigned to Agriculture!

In June, delegates to the National Conference of Social Work heard the Secretary of Commerce discuss human waste in industry. Child Labor, the twelve-hour day, and seasonal employment were cited as primary evils in the American system. Hoover's hope was that each state would solve the problems through individual legislation. He warned that if this were not accomplished, he would be forced to support a National Child Labor Act.

The Secretary's personal work hours were traditionally long. Nevertheless, he believed it impossible to develop proper citizenship or proper family life when men were required to work twelve hours each day. He, therefore, urged the public to stand behind the President in his recent appeal to leaders of the steel industry to abolish the long work day.

In the meantime the Department of Commerce was cooperating with a committee of economists and business leaders in an attempt to minimize intermittency of employment. The Secretary was convinced that if such funds could be accumulated for certain types of construction, such as public works and large-scale utilities, these funds could be used in times of depression. Labor could then be shifted from producing consumable goods to plant and permanent equipment. This, he said, would "clip the top from booms and the depression from slumps."

The man whose planning had saved a whole generation of Belgian, Polish, and other European children now turned his attention to child needs at home. He became President of the American Child Hygiene Association, recently consolidated with the Child Health Organization of America. His ideas were blue-printed for the delegates who heard his opening address at the Washington meeting in October. Thinking Americans should strive, he said, for a nation in which every child should be born under proper conditions, live in hygienic surroundings, have sufficient nourishment, prompt and efficient medical attention and inspection, and be given primary instructions in hygiene and health habits. "It is our purpose to supplant ten policemen with a single community nurse," he concluded.

While the settlement of European War Debts was clearly outside the province of the Secretary of Commerce, President Harding turned to the one member of his Cabinet who really knew the world. Hoover's Versailles experience made him invaluable to the commission appointed to deal with debtor nations. In a Toledo speech, Hoover explained the significance of these debts to every American taxpayer, assuring his audience that given time they would be repaid in goods or gold. A large international debt was not a new phenomenon. As proof, he cited the thirty billions owed by the rest of the world to Europe before the war, a burden which was carried without disrupting the world's commerce.

In November, Hoover left for Santa Fe, New Mexico, with two of his assistants, Christian Herter and W. C. Mullendore. They met representatives of the seven basin states to hammer out an agreement leading to the Colorado River Compact. These men had grown up with the conviction that individual and State water rights were inalienable. For three arduous weeks they met in constant tense session.

Hoover used procedures developed during the Food Administration. But the unanimity of purpose among State Food Administrators under stress of war was not so easy to attain in this vital question of peacetime progress. Hoover's patience seemed unlimited as he presided with calm and unwearied attention to compose heated arguments. Finally, through his own example of constant work and consequent long overtime sessions, he brought representatives to agreement almost in self-defense.

When the Compact was signed, subject to ratification by State Legislatures, it was regarded as a triumph of intranational diplomacy. Never since the nation had begun had so many states been able to settle a question of interstate rights by a treaty. Hoover was not satisfied to leave the final solution to his associates. He visited every state concerned and worked incessantly through press and speakers' platforms to be quite sure of its final adoption.

During the summer President Harding decided to make a personal inspection of Alaska. He invited Mr. and Mrs. Hoover to join his party in Tacoma in July. From Vancouver they sailed on the *U.S.S. Henderson* for Seward and thence by rail to Fairbanks. In the party, Hoover found Secretary of Agriculture, Henry C. Wallace, Hubert Work of the Department of the Interior, and Admiral Rodman. All were wearied by the continuous games of bridge commanded by the inwardly disturbed President.

Hoover escaped for a while with his assistant, young Mullendore, for a brief fishing trip while they were anchored at Seward. Well informed on the West and all aspects of fisheries, he was soon on friendly terms with the accompanying press. One of these men, Charles Michelson, boasted often of his cordial relations with the studious Secretary.

As in Washington, the President reserved his important questions for the ear of his Secretary of Commerce. So it was that on a day when Harding seemed most depressed, Hoover was requested to come to the Presidential cabin. He was startled with the President's question. Would he think it wise to expose a known scandal in the administration? Hoover answered bluntly in the affirmative. Then the President related with obvious concern some stories of irregularity in a governmental department. These, he told the Secretary, had preceded the suicide of one of his intimate friends, Jesse Smith, shortly before they had left Washington. When he left the cabin Hoover was burdened by the mental anguish of the President.

A few days later the party landed at Seattle with the President seriously ill. Because the doctors disagreed as to the exact nature of the ailment, Hoover wired Dr. Ray Lyman Wilbur to meet the party in San Francisco.

By the time they reached the Palace Hotel in that city, the terminal nature of his illness was indisputable. However, the President was still conscious and he recognized the voice of the brother of Judge Curtis Wilbur, his Secretary of the Navy. Dr. Wilbur brought two highly respected physicians with him as consultants. While these trained men were devoting all their skill to making the dying President's last hours as bearable as possible, Hoover did what he could for Mrs. Harding. In his quiet way Herbert Hoover made the necessary arrangements, including those for the funeral train that took the saddened party back across a shocked continent.

Chapter Eighteen

THE COOLIDGE ERA

As government routine was resumed in Washington, Hoover found himself the chosen evening companion of the new President, who outwardly surpassed him in taciturnity. Occasionally, however, in their hours together, Hoover heard the kind of homey Yankee stories and observations that he most enjoyed.

In official affairs Coolidge was not as responsive to Hoover's forward-looking ideas as his less opinionated predecessor had been. Hoover's reform plans irritated the man who preferred to let time heal all things. He remembered his Vermont childhood with its chores and hard work. To him that was the inevitable and salutary lot of youth. He opposed the Child Labor Amendment. Hoover had worked hard to control loans to foreign countries, stipulating that they should be made only for productive purposes. Coolidge repudiated this. When the Secretary predicted a dire end to the false prosperity in which Coolidge gloried, the President turned a deaf ear.

Nevertheless, Hoover's special abilities were still in demand. Coolidge appointed him Chairman of the American St. Lawrence Commission to review the Inland Waterways project in new discussions with Canada and to find a common basis for engineering and public action. Hoover uncovered plenty of objections. Lake cities were divided as to the proper route. Power companies were fearful of competition. Seaboard cities were concerned because traffic might be diverted from their ports. He worked patiently to conciliate the various elements.

Herbert Hoover's parents Huldah Minthorn Hoover and Jesse Clark Hoover.

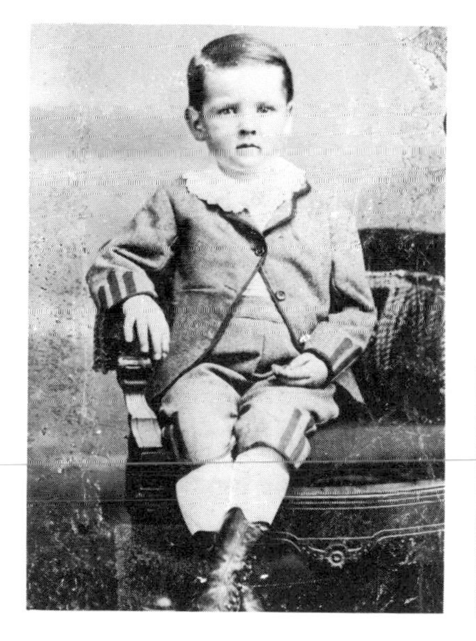

Herbert Hoover about four years old.

As a young man (1899).

Dr. Branner's geology class. Hoover is standing second from left.

Hoover leads camel train, Coolgardie, Australia, April 11, 1897.

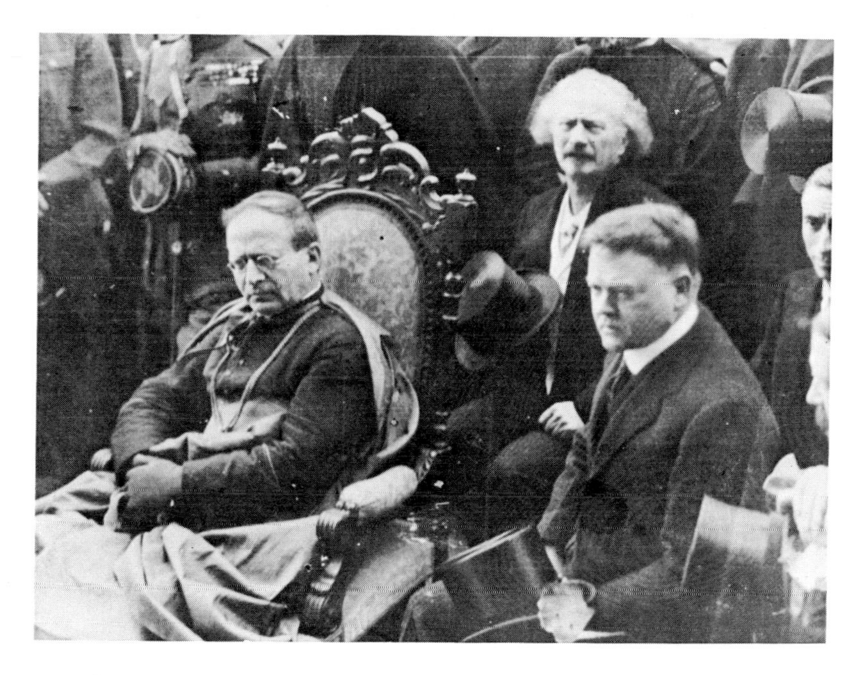

In Poland (1919) with the future Pope Pius XI and Ignace Paderewski, famed pianist and Premier of Poland.

Crowd greets President-elect and family before his Stanford home, (1928).

Flanked by Col. and Mrs. Charles A. Lindbergh at a White House ceremony August 15, 1930. Mrs. Hoover is at the far left.

President and Mrs. Hoover arrive for services at the new Friends Meeting House in Washington, D.C., April 5, 1931.

The President and his First Lady pose before the White House front portico, December 26, 1931.

Photograph sent to Gerrit J. Diekema at his request, to hang in his office at the Hague when he was Hoover's minister to The Netherlands.

Christmas card (1939) showing Hoover family at Christmas dinner the year before.

Before Hoover Institution on War, Revolution and Peace, Stanford University.

From left: Harold H. Fisher, Dr. Ray Lyman Wilbur and Edgar Rickard with Hoover in the lobby of the Hoover Institution on his 74th birthday, August 10, 1948.

Herbert Hoover at ribbon-cutting ceremony of The Boys' Club of Hunters' Point, San Francisco, July 20, 1960, with (from left) William J. Zellerbach, President of Boys' Clubs of San Francisco; E. L. McKenzie, Regional Director of Boys' Clubs of America, and Mayor George C. Christopher.

At the dedication ceremony for the Herbert Hoover Building, National Headquarters of the Boys' Clubs of America at the United Nations Plaza, N.Y., October 18, 1960.

Commercial aviation became the next object of Hoover's consideration. Early in his term the Secretary had called a conference of representatives of all interests involved in this new mode of transportation to tackle the problem of air safety methodically. In 1925 he finally persuaded President Coolidge to appoint a regulatory commission with Dwight W. Morrow as chairman. The Air Commerce Act of 1926 was based on Hoover recommendations.

Under Harding, Hoover had been appointed chairman of a Commission to investigate the status of the Merchant Marine because immediately after the war Congress had authorized continued government ownership, which had been enacted as an emergency war measure. This was contrary to all that Hoover believed. In speeches as a private citizen in 1920 and year after year as Secretary of Commerce he had reiterated his opposition. Finally, in 1925 he was ready to report his plan for the reorganization of the United States shipping to a House Committee. His solution was that "the whole fleet and other property should be transferred to an Emergency Fleet Corporation, and the president thereof should be appointed by the President of the United States." Under this plan he insisted that the Government should retire from the shipping business as soon as private firms could be assured of future policies that would enable them to operate ships with profit.

Hoover's opposition to government ownership was evidenced in all his public speeches. His arguments reflected knowledge of such experiments in many countries. American institutions, he said, were designed more for liberty and less for business. Government operations would fare far worse than in foreign lands.

Despite preoccupation with the burdens heaped on his Washington desk, Hoover found time to share his ideals with younger men. One evening, during a short respite from a speaking tour of the West, the Hoovers were taking an after-dinner walk around the crest of the Stanford hill topped by their campus home. Lights shone from the wide windows of the Payson Treat home. They rang the doorbell.

"You sound as if you were having a good time," said Hoover when the professor came to the door. "May we join you?"

The room was full of students, a gathering of graduate history majors. Treat introduced his distinguished neighbors and said, "Perhaps you might have a word for these men, Mr. Secretary?"

"Just let them ask questions," replied the unexpected guest.

In that intimate group Herbert Hoover was just another alumnus, injecting into this surprised gathering enthusiasm for the job at hand in the way that had made him The Chief at Broken Hill, at Namur, or in Warsaw. The hour was late, but the young men listened on as he answered their many questions on national and world conditions.

Such contacts deepened another plan for Stanford which had been crystallizing during these Washington days. In his dealings with American business through Commerce, he had realized more than ever that if this country were to assume leadership in the years ahead, there must be better trained men to carry responsibility. Business should be regarded as a profession, just as engineering had advanced from the pick and shovel era to a recognized order "pledged to control the forces and materials of nature for the good of the human race." He had watched the growing influence of the Harvard Graduate School of Business in the East. He knew that men so educated were achieving a broader concept of their roles in the counting room and at the order desk.

He began to discuss with men of large affairs the possibility of establishing a similar school on the Pacific Coast. Dr. Wilbur grasped the significance at once. Convinced that the important business firms of the Pacific Coast would underwrite such a project, the Board of Trustees listened to Hoover's facts and figures and voted to establish this new school.

In the spring of 1925, Hoover had a visitor from Evanston, Illinois in his Washington office. Willard E. Hotchkiss had been asked by Dr. Wilbur to become the first Dean of the Stanford Graduate School of Business. Before Hotchkiss would give his answer, he asked permission to discuss the proposal with the man at whose elbow he had sat during President Wilson's Second Industrial Conference in 1920. Hoover, as vice chairman of that Conference, had presided over many of the sessions while Hotchkiss had acted as executive secretary. Mrs. Hotchkiss, too, had been part of the Food Administration Staff. Thus, both were quite familiar with the Hoover approach to large undertakings.

As the prospective Dean discussed aims and procedure with the Secretary of Commerce, they found themselves in complete agreement and Hotchkiss accepted the position. During the following summer they met again, this time on the campus, where Hotchkiss was a guest at the president's reception for the summer faculty. Conversing with Mrs. Hoover, he found that the Secretary of Commerce was at home briefly before departing for Washington the following day. She managed to crowd in an appointment for him at nine o'clock that evening. It was midnight before the two men parted. The projected program for the school, which was to open in the autumn, had received undivided attention for three fruitful hours.

Wherever the Secretary went his eyes were alert for vital needs and his mind focused on meeting them. After a trip to Stanford to attend Herbert, Jr.'s graduation in June of 1925, Hoover spoke in Sacramento of a project close to his thoughts.

"If we were to scan the whole nation for the greatest opportunity for national development we would find that it lies right here in the central valleys of California," he told his audience.

He proposed that the State Engineer be made chairman of a committee to draw up plans for such a project, with representatives from the Railroad Commission, the Division of Water Rights, engineers from the various irrigation districts and local employees of such Federal Departments as War and Interior, and the Federal Power Commission. But his proposal fell on deaf ears.

"I am never particular," he said, "about names or details. What we want is an organism that will function."

Hoover returned to Washington, seriously concerned with

the mad race for quick money that he and his neighbor, Adolph Miller, felt was overwhelming the good sense of the American public.

Late one October afternoon Hoover charged into Miller's study.

"I have come to talk about the trends in speculation," he said. "I have a serious apprehension about what this is leading to. Some brake should be put on this orgy. As a member of the Federal Reserve Board you are in a position to do something about it."

Both men recognized that the Board itself had been contributing to spreading inflation through credit expansion and lowered discount rates.

Hoover tried to warn the President. But Coolidge stuck to a "hands off" policy. Next the Secretary appealed to the Senate Banking and Currency Committee. One member, Senator Irvine Lenroot, grasped the significance of his contentions. Ironically, Hoover's original memorandum to the Senator foretold the very calamity that was later to absorb most of his energy as President of the United States. By a strange twist of fortune, Hoover would be blamed by vast numbers of uninformed people for the results of the speculation and inflation he sought to check in its beginnings!

Senator Lenroot's hints of exposure of the effect of Federal Reserve advances to stock brokers (over a billion dollars in months when common stocks had risen forty percent), and the combined opposition of Miller and Hoover, succeeded in applying a temporary check on the inflation of credit. Two years later, however, European bankers again won over the majority of the Federal Reserve Board. The disastrous program was resumed in spite of Adolph Miller's determined opposition.

In the interim, satisfied that for the present the abnormal speculation had been checked, the Secretary of Commerce concerned himself with other phases of his official duties. He had long been challenged by a desire for better understanding between the Americas. While Latin America was one part of the world to which his personal business had not yet taken him, the strategic importance of those countries to world peace was clear in his thinking. An invitation to speak at a dinner gathering of the Motion Picture Producers and Distributors of America, in honor of the diplomatic representatives of these southern neighbors, offered him an opportunity to express some of these thoughts.

He reminded his audience that they had mutually undertaken a complex task in trying to perfect in the New World a form of government based on a unique conception of human rights.

"All men may be created free and equal," he said, "but they are not created with that sense of moral discipline and that sense of compromise between individual advantage and public right which is the basis of ordered liberty."

Turning to his hosts, Hoover characterized the industry they represented as a "skilled and potent purveyor of intellectual ideas and national ideals . . . but it can also transfer the worst within us as well as the best . . . herein lies a heavy obligation."

The relationship between nations, especially those separated by language, was likened to a situation when a strange family moves next door. Disturbing noises are often heard, over loud laughter, cries of children when disciplined. Dog fights are seen, or the painting of the fence. But the outsider does not glimpse the intimacy of family life, nor does he know the affections, the self denials, the joy and the sorrows. He does not see the family album. "So," said Hoover, "it is between nations. There is little opportunity to become acquainted with the ideals and accomplishments of each other."

Officially, he was High Commissioner for Inter-American Affairs. He was immersed in plans for the Third Pan American Commercial Conference, scheduled for Washington in late April, 1927, when he was called suddenly from his desk to the bursting levees along the lower Mississippi. Here the Red Cross was administering aid in the worst flood disaster in American history.

Will Irwin was with Hoover reporting the story to the anxious public, who now watched the famed Relief Administrator applying his vast experience to the succor of fellow Americans. Irwin wrote of the life boats and crews of ships speeding from the Atlantic Coast, of airplanes winging from Army and Navy posts, Coast Guard vessels racing up the flooded river, carpenters in a hundred construction yards throwing together emergency boats, and Red Cross units setting up sanitized camps all directed by "the magic hand of Hoover."

As soon as he began his work, he had a special telephone circuit rigged to function from his private railroad car, whether in a central depot or at a remote country siding, to every important point in the whole flood area. Hoover could reach his key men instantly with as much ease as on any inter-office communicating system.

Irwin, who had followed his friend across the face of Europe, described The Chief standing calmly on the levee above the raging flood, issuing directions to a corps of assistants he had gathered about him. He knew that they would restore order out of chaos while he journeyed back to Washington to address the delegates to the Pan American Union on May 2. That speech was a serious one dealing with international trade, tariffs, and the complicated subject of international debt. The marble halls echoed applause as Hoover urged that nations should discourage citizens from borrowing or lending money unless it was intended for productive enterprises, that would of themselves provide means of repayment. If that principle could be adopted among all nations, none should depend upon others for balancing budgets, purchasing military equipment or paying for other war purposes.

Then he returned to continue the fight against the raging Mississippi and to commence a preventive program for flood control. He took with him a gift of nearly two thousand dollars sent by school children from Poland to help their age-group who had been made homeless by the flood!

Scarcely was that task completed when a flash flood in September sent the Secretary of Commerce hurrying to Vermont. His personal secretary, Reuben Sleight, had been killed instantly as his plane landed on a water-logged airstrip while he was en route for a preliminary survey. When Hoover arrived, he learned that among other tragic results of the storm, railroad workers had been killed when lightning struck their bunks and that the Lieutenant Governor had lost his life when his automobile had been swallowed in a cave-in of the flood-soaked street in front of his own house.

Hoover found the Red Cross well organized. Each county was ready with a report of damage and relief plans. It was necessary to spend only a few days with officials in Montpelier. Then, with two secretaries, George Akerson and Bradley Nash, he started for Concord, New Hampshire, by car. Enroute, farmers talked with him, not complaining but with eyes to the future, asking advice about re-stocking with better breeds of cows and chickens, and what materials would be most durable in rebuilding bridges. These Yankees were of the stuff Herbert Hoover approved!

The railroad trip from Concord to Boston would just give time to dictate notes preparatory to further conferences there. But the Concord station was swarming with weekend excursionists. Seemingly, there would be no space where the three could even sit together. With youthful enthusiasm Nash persuaded the station master to add another coach as a traveling office for the Secretary of Commerce. Thereafter, Hoover was likely to refer to railroad coaches as "Nash Pullmans."

During that busy summer, President Coolidge stated enigmatically: "I do not choose to run." Hoover, who sensed the hidden meaning of that New England phrase as "coax me" called on the President to assure him that, public rumors to the contrary, he would prefer to remain a Cabinet member and issued a press statement calling for Coolidge's re-nomination.

The quiet Vermonter, however, had been hurt to the quick by public acceptance of the face value of his pronouncement. All he would say when the party leaders met in December was, "My statement stands."

CHAPTER NINETEEN

THE PEOPLE'S CHOICE

MEANWHILE HOOVER WENT about his daily tasks. He was not unmindful of the growing demand that he should be the next President; but he would leave the decision to the people who wanted him. He had cautiously assigned a competent Hearst newsgatherer, Henry Sell, to sample the validity of public demand. Then, on the day dedicated to his national hero, Herbert Hoover filed as a Republican candidate for the Presidency in the Ohio Primary on Lincoln's birthday, February 12, 1928.

Opposition from old-line party leaders, whose advice had gone unheeded when Harding appointed Hoover to the Cabinet in 1920, rose in a storm. These men dug up all the old canards. Hoover had urged election of a Democratic Congress to support Wilson in 1918. He had advocated the League of Nations. He had hesitated about announcing his political affiliations when Democrats like Colonel House were spreading rumors of the possible choice of Hoover for their party. They even accused him of being a British subject.

Senator William Calder of New York produced evidence of Hoover's membership in the Republican Club since 1909. Former colleagues like Harry New and Hubert Work spoke out in his favor. Senators from Wisconsin and Kentucky, and former Congressmen of New York and North Carolina added their endorsement. Among the people, the old vigor of the "Hoover-for-President" Clubs of 1920 was magnified into sufficient strength by May to promise over four hundred delegates pledged to vote for the man who had been so untiring in his devotion to the rights of the individual.

Andrew Mellon broke the silence he had maintained all summer and telephoned Hoover from Kansas City that he intended to recommend to his fellow Pennsylvanians that they vote for Hoover on the first ballot. Whatever ideas may have been in preparation for a "Draft Coolidge–Stop Hoover" movement were nipped in the bud by Mellon's call. Eight hundred and thirty-seven of the 1,084 delegates followed the lead of Pennsylvania, once John L. McNab, silver-tongued orator from California, had presented Hoover's name to the Convention. McNab's characterization of Hoover as "America's greatest administrator in human welfare, engineer, practical scientist, minister of mercy to the hungry, administrator, executive, statesman, beneficient American" promised the Republicans a leader they could support unreservedly. Hoover was nominated on the first ballot.

The *New York World* of June 21 exultantly revived the editorial published eight years before, adding just one more line: "We endorse everything we said then, in 1928."

As Hoover came through Chicago on the way home to California, William Allen White, classmate of Vernon Kellogg, reported in the *Chicago Herald-American* that nominee Hoover was pleased by the warmth of his reception, showing his response "in broad smiles and blushes." White admitted that Hoover was a man of few words, but prophesied that his election would be a "triumph of mind over mouthiness." In support, he quoted Henry Ford as saying that Hoover would make the kind of inventive and original executive who would devise new ways of building up the nation and of replacing poverty and unemployment by prosperity and industry.

Mayor Thompson disagreed. He appealed for the protection of Chicago from an invasion of King George, as Senator Reed sounded the old fake clarion call of Hoover's mythical "British citizenship."

The Hoover party reached the Stanford campus on July 20, saddened by the death of Mrs. Hoover's father, Charles D. Henry. Outwardly, they put aside their grief in the face of national demands. The planned home-coming party was canceled, however, and Hoover took advantage of the comparative quiet to concentrate on the acceptance speech to be delivered on August 11, by his own choice, in the Stanford football stadium.

The university campus was suddenly roused from the usual summertime siesta. The rambling Phi Kappa Psi house on the hill below the Hoover home was transformed into a press headquarters for the large staff of correspondents who had traveled west with the nominee's party. Both national telegraph companies established branch offices there with elaborate equipment for handling the mass of words that streamed out of this normally quiet community. True to character, Hoover himself gave little news, maintaining strict silence on political questions until his speech would be delivered; but he met with them informally at frequent intervals.

Sometimes he would hit on a favorite subject, such as the newly-completed university library building which housed the Hoover collection. Then his reserve would be lost in an enthusiastic account of the future possibilities for research; of stories told him by the scholars gathering data around the world, documents that he hoped would be studied toward the ultimate goal of establishing peace and world order.

A few days after the Hoovers came home, summer session students marched up the hill in the glow of red fire to stage an impromptu rally, welcoming the candidate with yells and college songs. At the front door, Hoover responded by saying that he would rather have a greeting from Stanford men and women than from any other group.

A week later, San Francisco citizens gave him official recognition at the City Hall, where he was cheered by a large contingent of classmates, shouting the '95 yell. Mayor Rolph reminded the crowd that Hoover's world-wide service had begun when he had been in London as the representative of their city in preparation for the Panama-Pacific Exposition.

By now his acceptance speech was finished. His close friend and advisor, Colonel William ("Wild Bill") Donovan, rumored then as the possible choice for Attorney General should Hoover win, listened with approval.

He was fifty-four on August 10. That evening, the Eastern correspondents gave him a party. Earlier in the day a giant birthday card in the form of an official ballot had arrived, bearing the signatures of President and Mrs. Coolidge, as well as many leaders of the Republican Party. Decorated with the California State poppy, the card included a few lines of verse:

> "For you who cheered vast multitudes,
> Where war's grim shadows led,
> Whose many wise and kindly deeds
> A lasting radiance spread;
> We hope this day may be enriched
> By birthday joy and cheer.
> And your election in the fall
> Will crown your fine career."

August 11, 1928 was a memorable day on the Stanford campus. Alumni journeyed far to swell the throng that listened to Hoover's first presentation of his program for America. His voice was carried by nation-wide hookup over air channels once assigned by him as Secretary of Commerce.

As he designated problems of the future as "problems of construction" he outlined his conception of the way to use "the new tools which Science has given us" in preserving "those principles upon which it has grown to greatness." Among other promises, he vowed to use the privileges of office, should voters give him the opportunity, to make life easier for families such as our forebears working on the land in what he considered the nation's basic industry, farming.

Ten days later he was adding potent arguments to his theme as he stood among his childhood neighbors in West Branch, Iowa. Just as the boyish Stanford graduate had stopped there to receive the blessings of his Quaker relatives when he started on his first world journey in 1897, so now he paused among these people who understood him best before trying to explain to the rest of America what he had in his heart to do.

In the audience that greeted the Republican candidate, he caught sight of the elementary teacher who had first guided him to a comprehension of the meaning of America. Now he acknowledged publicly his personal debt to Mollie Brown, now Mrs. Carran, describing her as the embodiment of the spirit of the vast body of women who not only teach and inspire the children of the land, but who also watch over their wider destinies.

Throughout the summer the nation listened to Hoover's impassive voice, contrasted strangely with the rousing speeches of idealists to whom he was *the* man of destiny. When he returned to his campus home to vote in November, ten thousand people met the train in Palo Alto. The Stanford band followed his car up Palm Drive to the University, playing the favorite football rally song, "Come, Join The Band." Normand Goddard, stunt aviator of the day, circled above the crowd, dropping bombs that released parachutes flying flags of all nations.

Neighbors and friends who gathered around the stone fireplace in the Hoover home listened with the family to election returns on the night of November 6. As the greatest popular vote yet cast rolled up a five million majority, with forty states casting their ballots for Hoover, students marched up San Juan Hill to salute their fellow Stanfordite. Sousa's band was there, leading exultant college songs. Hoover stepped out on one of the flat roofs of his hilltop home. Lou Henry Hoover stood at his side, her steady eyes glistening in the glare of lights focused on them and their tall sons.

Hoover spoke from a full heart that night, when he said simply, "I thank you!"

The next day his secretary, George Akerson, handed out an amplified statement of appreciation to the first official press-conference of the President-elect. This read: "I can make no adequate expression of gratitude for the overwhelming confidence of our people, who, without regard to section or interest, have selected me for President of the whole United States."

But his morning started before he stood in the grey-stucco-finished room that had served his sons for their adolescent games and now was converted into a workroom for the top correspondents of the nation's press. Long before breakfast, two quiet people had slipped away from their big house and its sleeping inmates to tramp side by side over the hills back of the campus, where they had first opened their minds and hearts to each other.

When they returned the house was surrounded by secret service men. The privacy of the hearthstone that Lou Henry Hoover had guarded so zealously, wherever duty had called them, was already invaded. She relinquished that guardianship to those who were trained, but her touch on the arm of her life-companion tightened. She, who knew him best, realized that now he would need the protection no one but she could give. Would his sensitive inner being endure the X-rays of prying public opinion? She had traveled over deserts and oceans with him; she had dared the bullets of the Boxers and the submarines of the Germans; but she trembled before the heedless intrusion of the expectant American public. In her heart she must have prayed that these people would be capable of responding to the quiet strength and trained leadership of this man she trusted. She knew that now he was entering an arena where the crowd could be so easily stampeded by demagogic oratory, so different from the cold logic that made her husband impatient with careless thinking.

These months between the election and the fourth of March offered a respite and an opportunity to do the kind of prior planning that any engineer needs before undertaking a major contract.

Hoover had sensed in his Pan American Conferences that it was necessary to make a real effort to become friends with these neighbors from the southern half of the Western Hemisphere. Accordingly, he offered to take an official party to call on the members of the Pan American Union, many of whom he knew personally from his position as High Commissioner of Inter-American Affairs.

He would pay out-of-pocket costs for his immediate party. Such members of the press as wished to go at their own or their papers' expense, would be welcome. Since the fleet was always under steam, it would mean no extra expense for the government to allow them the use of a warship. The *U.S.S. Maryland* and the *U.S.S. Utah* were placed at his disposal. The *Maryland* of the Pacific Fleet would take the party down the West Coast to Chile, and the other would meet them at Buenos Aires for the Atlantic journey up the East Coast to New York.

The first stop was in Honduras. Here he described the purpose of the neighborly call, solicitude for mutual welfare, desire to create understanding between countries of the Western Hemisphere. He told them that he planned to withdraw the troops from Nicaragua. He also investigated the dispute between Guatemala and Honduras over boundaries. Then he went on, stopping at Salvador, Nicaragua, and Costa Rica. Fishing helped to pass the time as they steamed through tropical waters. The President-elect had some proud moments when he landed several large fish.

The days on shipboard were friendly. After they commenced the longer ocean voyage, the Hoovers had time to become better acquainted with officers and men. Hoover was in a jovial mood when a huge wave shipped so much water that he was sloshing about in water inches deep in his cabin.

"Well," he said, "I've seen bigger floods."

Mrs. Hoover visited the galley. She made friends among the crew. Hoover enjoyed going with the ship engineers to the plotting room where he could study the intricate fire-control mechanism. On many a pleasant evening officers of the ship were invited to dine with the Hoovers.

Among the press representatives that Hoover had known long and well were Edward Price Bell, William Philip Sims, Mark Sullivan, and Will Irwin, who had been especially invited by The Chief. Lawrence Sullivan, of International News Service, who had been covering all major party conventions since 1920, was now assigned to the State Department, studying the current Latin-American situation. Rex Collier of the *Washington Evening Star* had covered the Hoover relief project during the Mississippi flood, along with Will Irwin.

When they reached Guayaquil in Ecuador, Hoover explained to his first listeners in South America that his idea of true democracy was that it is not and cannot be imperialistic, since the principle of brotherhood implicit in democracy is a guarantee of good will. He told them also that it was his hope that what had been called American dollar diplomacy would be abandoned. He was against government protection of private North American concessions. He pledged that his administration would never collect any debts by military force.

The party was cordially welcomed to Lima where a national holiday was declared as it had been done in Ecuador. Here, Hoover took advantage of an opportunity to study the current Tacna-Arica dispute, likening it, in many ways, to the European Alsace-Lorraine problem. He promised that this whole subject would be thoroughly considered in the coming months.

At Antofagasta the ship anchored at sea off the Chilean coast while the Bolivian delegation came by boat to pay respects, since time forbade a train trip up to La Paz, their capital-in-the sky. Among the visiting officials was a Stanford alumna, Frances Willis, U.S. Vice Consul. As she sat among the cigar smokers, she heard serious discussion of the boundary dispute between Bolivia and Paraguay over the Chaco, claimed by both countries. Hoover needed the facts, because these questions of territorial rights were basic if he were to succeed in promoting the unity he dreamed of among Western Hemisphere neighbors.

Since word of his conversations in Lima had preceded him, he made a special effort to allay the suspicions of the Chileans whose reception to Valparaiso seemed somewhat cool.

The party left the *Maryland* at this port, and crossed the Andes by train. A pilot train waited at the summit because the police had been warned of a plot to wreck the visitors' train. Across the many miles of open pampas they were thus escorted in safety. At the first Argentinian station, Hoover smiled at the crowd and praised their land as "the world's bread basket." In Buenos Aires welcoming crowds jammed the railroad station. The recently-elected Argentine President made their greetings official.

Hoover expressed public disavowal of the "Big Brother" attitude of North America. "I see in each nation of the Continent a friendly nation and each about the same age," he told business leaders. "We have no policy of intervention."

When the party reached Rio, Brazilian papers were praising the significance of this visit. Hoover was the first elected ruler of a world power to travel in South America. He spoke freely with Brazilian leaders about the future in commercial and cultural relations between the countries.

From here they sailed for home, satisfied that the weeks had been spent profitably gaining perspective on some phases of the undertaking immediately ahead.

The *Utah* arrived in the United States on the sixth of January. The Hoovers paid a brief visit to Washington to make preliminary plans for the move to the White House. The President-elect called first on President Coolidge and assured him that during the days he was in Washington, Hoover would not embarrass the outgoing administration by interfering in his legislative program. At the same time, the two leaders exchanged opinions on a few current problems, especially Reparations, which would concern them both before March fourth.

Recognizing that their California home would be too far from Washington during the following weeks when they would need detachment and as much rest as possible, they gratefully accepted the invitation of two friends to use their adjoining Florida estates.

One of them, J. C. Penney, had come into his life during Commerce days when Under-Secretary William Jardine had introduced the chain store executive as the president of the Fruit Growers Association of Florida, a cooperative marketing organization that adhered to the best Hoover pattern. Penney asked them to use his home on Belle Isle, across the beautiful Venetian causeway from Miami. There was a guest house that would be available for secretaries and assistants; while the press would be welcome in the guest quarters of his neighbor, Joseph Adams, who was one of Hoover's engineering associates. Adams, inventor of a cracking process used in oil refining, owned a comfortable houseboat, the *Amitie,* (meaning friendship in any language). This he placed at Hoover's disposal, along with its smart little fishing smack, the *Patsy,* hoping that there would be some days when the President-elect would go on expeditions off the Florida Keys, really remote from press and politicians.

As soon as the public realized that the Hoovers were interested in going to Florida, there were many other invitations to use even more palatial homes and yachts; but the Quakers were content with their choice of the white stucco house on Biscayne Bay. Surrounding gardens of oleanders, poinsettias, and bougainvillea reminded them of their home state. Here, in an environment intended for leisure, Hoover concentrated on the selection of future cabinet members from the two hundred or more names that had been submitted to him.

The *New York Evening World* said that having been chosen for the cabinet eight years before with no solicitation on his part, Hoover was at a loss to understand the psychology of men who would urge themselves for such an appointment. The evidence which he now had before him of the extremes to which men would go to win such places was a shock to his ideal of top-level American leadership. This revelation of self-seeking among men who reached for preferment in high places disgusted and disheartened one who regarded government office as an opportunity to serve, not as a reward for past deeds.

The President-elect turned from the two hundred names on the suggested list to men he *knew*. No matter who else he had in his Cabinet, he was determined that Ray Lyman Wilbur should be at his side. When Hoover's wire reached the university president at Stanford, Dr. Wilbur turned to Comptroller Almon Roth, who happened to be in his office. "I guess Hoover feels that he must have one man in his Cabinet who will not 'yes' him."

For Secretary of War, Hoover chose his Western campaign manager, James W. Good. His first assistant in the Department of Commerce, Robert W. Lamont, became his successor in that department. He kept two of the Harding Cabinet, James J. Davis, Labor; and—after much consideration—Andrew Mellon, Secretary of the Treasury. (Rumors that Hoover wanted to invite Henry M. Robinson to this or some other post were silenced by this friend's modest insistence that he preferred to remain behind the scenes, ready to become available as needed in specific advisory capacity.)

Hoover delayed his decision in choosing his Secretary of State until he could discuss it with his Washington neighbor, William R. Castle, then Chief of the Division of Western European Affairs in the State Department. He hesitated to accept Castle's suggestion that Henry L. Stimson, Governor General of the Philippines, was the best prepared and most acceptable candidate, because he felt that he did not know him well enough. But he recalled Stimson's energetic activity when Wilson had appointed him on a commission overseeing American participation in Belgian Relief. Hoover called Stimson home to assume the high office, naming Joseph Cotton, former Food Administration representative in London, as Under Secretary.

With his roster complete, Hoover prepared his inaugural address. With the calm of an engineer rolling up well-detailed blueprints, he waited for the ground breaking of his own four-year building program which was to be girded with high hopes and cemented with an understanding of the world he had served so widely.

Chapter Twenty

PRESIDENT OF THE UNITED STATES

On March 4, 1929, Herbert Hoover raised his right hand over the Book from which his mother had preached so often, repeating the oath that made him the thirty-first President of the United States. Few other Chief Executives had assumed that position as a first elective office. But Hoover brought to it a world experience more extensive than any predecessor had ever known. And he could boast an American lineage almost as long as that of any President. Tracing his ancestry through his maternal great-grandmother, Lucindy Sherwood Minthorn, he was a direct descendant of two Colonial Governors of Massachusetts, Thomas Dudley and his son-in-law Simon Bradstreet.

His inaugural address reflected allegiance to the principles for which his forefathers had struggled. It rang with belief in the destiny of the nation that had chosen him its leader. He appealed to all his constituents for *voluntary* cooperation in a common effort to attain social betterment for all citizens. All that he had achieved thus far in the realms of engineering, relief, and government service had resulted from faith in the integrity of fellow workers. He pointed out this need for mutual effort to leaders of industry, finance, agriculture, and communications. In addition to his domestic agenda, he presented a program for international cooperation aimed to insure American leadership in the cause of world peace.

"Surely civilization is old enough," he said to the expectant throng, "surely mankind is mature enough so that we ought, in our own lifetime, to find a way to permanent peace."

But Herbert Hoover's faith in the maturity of mankind was destined to brutal disillusionment. His ideals for America had never swerved from the fundamental precepts of his Iowa school teacher, who sat proudly among the intimate guests gathered for luncheon that day in the White House. Hoover had no room in his mind for men of low aim and selfish thinking.

He had come to Washington, ready to dedicate all that he had of personal courage, world-wide experience, and trust in God to the service of the land he loved. That four years hence he would leave the Capitol, weighted with blame for all the ills he had labored to avoid, could not have clouded the vision of that solemn day in 1929.

The center piece of the Inaugural Luncheon table was symbolic. Ten ears of Iowa's finest red, yellow, and white corn decorated their first meal as White House hosts. Lou Henry Hoover had expressed her wish for it to an old neighbor when her husband had delivered his first campaign speech in West Branch the previous August. Humble acknowledgment of a debt to the steadfast men and women of that hard-working farm community, as well as his firm reliance on his Quaker associates, were deeply ingrained in the being of the new Chief Executive. The Hoovers were at heart pioneer Americans whose branches had spread world-wide, but whose roots went deep into familiar soil.

They clung to old friends with tenacity. New ones were admitted only on the basis of genuine respect. Yet, in following this regime, they semed to shut themselves away from the clamoring public. People who had expected an extension of personal interest from the grass roots President were almost immediately rebuffed. Thousands who had voted hopefully for this silent man of deeds thronged the national doorstep, hands outstretched in trustful greeting, as soon as he was settled in office.

His long working hours were spent in the Lincoln Study. One of the first changes he had insisted upon in the White House was the reconversion of this room from its then current use as a bed room, so that he might work in an atmosphere charged with the spirit of one who embodied his highest ideals of patriotism. Above the white marble mantel he had hung a steel engraving of Lincoln and his Cabinet, a treasured possession that had always traveled with the Hoovers to their farflung temporary homes. An inscription below the picture designated this as the room in which the Emancipation Proclamation had been signed.

As the Hoover Cabinet pondered the problems threatening the post-war world, they sat on the very chairs that had once supported those other serious men fighting for the life of the nation. Guidance from the revered yet humble statesman seemed still to emanate from those compassionate eyes above the mantel.

In this study, too, the President unrolled his blueprints for a better America. He needed practical support, not from the past, but from present day leaders of the country he now was serving. Thus, he continued the program that had proved successful in Commerce days. Men and women familiar with all phases of American life were invited to presidential conferences in Washington. They came from industry and from labor. There were bankers and railroad executives, social workers, housing experts, community planners. From all he sought facts and cooperation.

He appointed his administrative assistant, French Strother, executive of a Commission to correlate these facts and to pursue further studies of *Social Trends in America.*

His eight years in top level Washington had convinced him that government could not function efficiently with the unwieldly mass of bureaus and agencies that had grown Topsy-like through the years. Thus, he assigned a prophetic task to one of his secretaries, Walter H. Newton. This young man was told to assemble all available data, preparatory to a practical reorganization of the ten major departments of government. Little did either of them suspect that nearly a quarter of a century later Herbert Hoover would struggle again to bring order out of that chaos!

While the President's working hours were spent in constant

conferences with these many people, then strangers to him, Mrs. Hoover bent every effort toward making the routine of this new home familiar and as informal as she could within the limits of protocol.

She soon dispensed with the services of Mrs. Coolidge's former social secretary and built her staff from old acquaintances and younger Stanford women. The White House menage became Quaker-like in simplicity, yet Californian in hospitality.

Just as in Red House in London, she prepared guest rooms for innumerable visitors from far places. The President followed his life-long custom of reaching important decisions around breakfast, luncheon, or dinner tables, over which she presided with easy informality. Yet back of this home-like atmosphere was Mrs. Hoover's quiet determination to keep their home free from unnecessary intrusion. And this very effort toward privacy contributed to misunderstanding between the President and the people.

There was loss both ways from the Hoovers' over-emphasis on seclusion. Had their social base been broader, they might have detected shifting opinion long before it became politically fatal. Had more people sensed the simple humanity of their President, he might have had greater cooperation in his far-reaching plans for the common good.

A California guest arriving with an invitation to Mrs. Hoover to become an honorary member of one of the State's oldest clubs understood this intuitively. They were already seated at the luncheon table when the President came in, worry and dejection in every line of his troubled face. Instantly, Mrs. Hoover turned to her visitor.

"Would you please change places and sit by the President?" she whispered.

Napkin in hand, her guest slipped around the table, catching a startled look in her daughter's eye as she passed. Seated next to Mr. Hoover, she turned with a smile,

"Well, how are the boys?" she queried.

Herbert Hoover snapped out of his reverie. He was again the

father, the friendly neighbor, completely himself, talking with relief and animation about the days that had been normal.

Unless guests were like this Californian—or some Iowa or Oregon Quaker—it was hard for the President to be "off-guard." But in the presence of old friends he could shed the solemnity of office, indulge in whimsical stories and good-natured quips—as if, for the moment, he was the companion of the Klamath campfire or the Stanford hills.

Throughout the presidential years there was one old friend from those Stanford hills on whom both Hoovers leaned for spiritual sustenance. Dr. Augustus Taber Murray was borrowed from his post as head of the Department of Classical Languages at Stanford to become Minister of the Irving Street Meeting of the Society of Friends.

Upon his election to the Presidency, Hoover and others had realized that the curious public would soon find its way to the plain little house of worship where his family had been regular attendants during their Washington years. They sensed that many would not understand the traditions of Quakerism. So far as possible, they must preserve the old-fashioned, open type of meeting; but they were wise enough to foresee that strangers would not always be guided by inner light. Crackpots could use the freedom to air their political views on social reform before the President. It would be essential to have a disciplined thinker, spiritually aware and tactful, as a leader in these gatherings. As members of the Irving Street Meeting pondered their choice of an able and prominent Friend to attend regularly, the Hoover's desire to have Dr. Murray in Washington came as the solution.

The quiet voice of the classical scholar who often journeyed across the continent, fitting his Stanford teaching responsibilities to his new religious duties, drew many listeners to these Sunday services. The Irving Street Meeting House soon became inadequate. Dr. Murray shared the concern of the Hoovers over a division of allegiance among Washington Quakers, the result of a major separation in the Society of Friends nearly a century before. Within a year after the President had called his spiritual counsellor to this leadership, the two groups had composed their differences. Then the United Friends Meeting of Washington announced their intention to build an appropriate and dignified house of worship in the nation's capital.

This project ranked high among the interests of the First Lady. Her influence drew money out of hiding; influential Quakers, well able to give, were guests at intimate White House luncheons. Generous responses justified her faith.

An attractive stone Meeting House was erected on Florida Avenue. As Lou Henry Hoover inscribed her name to start the new roll, she became officially, for the first time, a member of the Society to whose principles she had so long dedicated her loyalty. Because this was an "independent" Meeting, Herbert Hoover's signature did not nullify his unbroken affiliation with the Oregon Meeting where he had joined as a youngster under the guidance of Uncle John Minthorn.

From that time on through their remaining years in Washington, the Hoovers often walked together through the gate of the garden-surrounded Meeting House seeking surcease in its quiet from the increasing burdens of national leadership.

There were other weekends when they sought respite from the oppressively hot city. Early in the spring of 1929, they realized that there must be a Summer White House close at hand where important conferences might be held in some degree of comfort. The President was not fond of long ocean voyages. He did not expect to make much use of the Presidential yacht. But he must have some relaxation.

He discovered and purchased a camp site on the Rapidan. Here the Hoovers established a simple out-of-doors way of life consistent with their California background.

While some of the furnishings came from the Presidential yacht, Mrs. Hoover wanted the camp to conform to its rustic surroundings. She hired local artisans to build simple tables, chairs, and cabinets—incidentally, giving employment where it was needed. Indian rugs from her own collection brightened the cabins. Detachments from a nearby Marine Base helped build guest cabins in the surrounding woods. The sitting room of the main cabin soon became a Town Hall in which all phases of American policy were threshed out among well-informed visitors.

Before the camp was completed, the President had a young caller, possibly not so well informed in matters of public moment, but generous with a prized possession. A boy from nearby Dark Hollow appeared one afternoon with a gift—an opossum he had shot himself. The man, whose childhood prowess in the woods was a cherished memory, forgot affairs of state as he chatted with the young hunter. How was school? Where did he live? Thus Herbert Hoover learned to his amazement that there was no school in this backwoods community. The boy told him of his family, eight children, aged two to sixteen, living in a two-room cabin with a loft.

The Hoovers investigated their new locale. They found pioneer Americans with an average mental age of seven, still speaking the language of Elizabethan England. These people had only a crude conception of the world beyond their blue ridge.

When the Hoovers discovered that the Virginia Legislature had no funds with which to build and maintain a school for these isolated families, they determined to provide one for their Rapidan neighbors. They recognized, however, that the task of finding the right teacher was more difficult and important than letting the contract for the rustic cabin which would house both teacher and schoolroom.

Mrs. Hoover made that her business. She found her answer in a letter from President William J. Hutchins of Berea College in Kentucky. Dr. Hutchin's son, Robert, at Yale, was already famous as the youngest Dean of a Law School in the nation; the father was a man of insight and understanding. He wrote Mrs. Hoover that Christine Vest, a Berea alumna, would have a sympathetic approach. The young teacher was immediately invited to the White House.

With two of Mrs. Hoover's staff, she went to visit Dark Hollow. After a cold December night ride through Fredericksburg and the Marine camp, they were warmly welcomed around the hospitable kitchen table in the Buraker cabin, home of the lad with the 'possum. Miss Vest's report convinced the First Lady that Dr. Hutchins had sent her the right person.

The new building was ready in February. Once the frozen pipes were repaired and the linoleum thawed out sufficiently to lay over pine floors, Miss Vest's apartment adjoining the schoolroom became an object lesson in orderly housekeeping for visiting parents.

Children not only walked miles to attend day school. They also showed up eagerly on Sunday mornings for the first organized religious training they had ever known. By the second summer, the Hoovers were rewarded by signs of improving standards in the mountain homes and a hearty welcome from the grateful children.

In the meantime Rapidan had begun to fulfill its original purpose. In October, 1929, as soon as the camp was sufficiently settled, the President invited Premier Ramsay MacDonald to be his first guest. As the two sat under the trees, discussing their common aims and hopes for world peace, they reached an agreement on reduction of naval armament, a subject on which they had been carrying on diplomatic correspondence for ten months.

As a Quaker and as a practical world citizen whose inner being was seared with burning consciousness of the brutality of modern war, the President had pursued the aim of his Inaugural, building for permanent peace.

During the Harding and Coolidge administrations, he had backed their efforts to halt the race in naval armament. Thus far, only limitation of battleship building had been accomplished. When Hoover became President, his friend Hugh Gibson, now Ambassador to Belgium, was in Geneva representing the United States at the European Arms Conference. Through him the new President had offered a policy which they both hoped might lead to agreement in limiting all types of naval tonnage.

Active personal negotiations with Premier MacDonald

through Secretary of State Stimson and General Dawes, newly appointed to the Court of St. James, had followed Gibson's declaration of the policy in Geneva. The proposed program agreed upon by Great Britain and the United States had been accepted by Japan, but rejected by France and Italy.

Now, in October, as the British Premier and the President concurred in the wisdom of going ahead with Japanese participation only, they issued a joint statement. This proclaimed the establishment of British-American good will as the mutual objective of their two governments, although each would endeavor to promote world peace in radically different ways. The United States, according to this declaration would *never* consent to become entangled in European diplomacy; while England resolved to pursue a policy of active cooperation with its European neighbors. The clear assumption was that war between these three nations—Britain, Japan, and the United States—would be banished forever and that conflict between their military and naval forces could never take place.

Chapter Twenty-one

WORLD FINANCIAL CRISIS

Two weeks after this peaceful Indian Summer conference, financial earthquake rocked the world. Herbert Hoover, who would long be maligned for the aftermath of that disaster of October 24, 1929, was not taken unawares. He had long recognized the slips and faults in the economic structure of his country. As Secretary of Commerce he had been skeptical about the soundness of the "Coolidge prosperity era." Yet, all of his warnings had gone unheeded, as a tidal wave of speculation had swept hitherto conservative investors on its crest.

Even as he repeated the Presidential oath his inner ear caught portentous rumblings. He was convinced from the start that economic problems would beset his administration. And he was determined to forestall what he most feared. His first thought had been to form a council of economic advisors, similar to the Supreme Economic Council on which he had served in the Versailles period. He knew that world monetary affairs were so interrelated that he must have men on this domestic council who understood all that was happening abroad as well as at home.

The first person he had consulted was an international banker, Eugene Meyer, whom he had known in the London "Mining Syndicate" days. Meyer, an associate of the Guggenheims and Chester Beatty, was as conversant with world monetary conditions as any man in Washington. His rejection of the Economic Council idea in their February conversation had been a shock.

The banker had made an alternative suggestion. He pointed

out that as predicted at Versailles by Hoover, the Reparations imposed on Germany were upsetting the financial structure of the world. If the United States would propose cutting them by forty-five per cent it might be a major step toward stability. Germany, he said, had no great natural resources out of which to raise the $500 million levied under the Young Plan. There would never be enough manpower to earn that amount through labor alone.

"But why," the President had asked, "should this not be proposed by France?"

"Because," Meyer had replied, "such a proposal from the French Government would precipitate its fall. The United States is the only country where the President could make such a radical proposal and still remain in office."

The banker continued to predict that if Germany collapsed financially, the whole world would follow, pressing the reluctant President to make this his initial move in world leadership.

The cautious engineer had not been ready for so radical a proposition. Such a subject demanded long-range thinking and many substantiating facts. His immediate objective had been to set his own national house in order. He was determined to keep the United States solvent by balancing the budget, increasing taxes and eliminating waste. His life principle adhered to pay-as-you-go methods. He believed that future security for nations as for individuals came only through increased production and making the best possible use of natural resources.

During the ten months preceding the stock market crash, the President had continually aired these views before conferences of leaders from all walks of life, from whom he had been seeking cooperation. Throughout that summer of 1929, Secretary of the Treasury Mellon advised bond buying instead of stocks. The people, drunk with the exhilaration of rising prices, mocked the ultra-conservative Secretary.

Now the crash had come! The President recognized the fulfilled predictions of those who knew world-wide economic conditions. Nevertheless, he must curb hysteria. He tried to reassure the nation the next morning through a press conference.

"The fundamental business of the country, that is, the production and distribution of commodities, is on a sound and prosperous basis," he said, "although production and consumption are at high levels, the average price of commodities as a whole has not increased . . . there have been no appreciable increases in the stocks . . . all of which indicates a healthy condition."

The people were *not* reassured! Investors continued to liquidate their holdings at a frenzied pace. Five days after the initial shock, on October 29, the New York Stock Exchange reported the greatest volume of sales in its history. 16,410,030 shares changed hands in that one day. Such well-known stocks as Allied Chemical declined thirty-five points; American Telephone and Telegraph, twenty-eight; Santa Fe Railroad, sixteen; Dupont, thirty-four; General Electric twenty-eight. Hundreds of others plunged downward.

Attempting to cure the financial sickness at what he considered the source, the President instructed the Department of Justice to prevent "bucket shops" and market tipsters from using the mails to stimulate speculation. This was the only legal way in which the Federal Government could exert direct influence. Reports indicated that telephone calls in New York decreased by 150,000 in one day. The Better Business Bureau called this order the most effective cleanup in the history of the Stock Exchange.

The President's next step was likewise constructive. As Secretary of Commerce he had probably been the first official to suggest that useful Public Works be expanded during times of unemployment and depression. Now he urged immediate appropriation by Congress of $420-million for such purposes.

Relying upon the same voluntary cooperation from fellow citizens that had assured the success of the Food Administration and Relief programs, he called business leaders from every part of the nation to a November Conference in Washington. They were the men who must consider the growing problems of unemployment, the necessity of maintaining proper wages during hard times, the task of spreading work and increasing useful construction everywhere.

He knew, and he told them bluntly, that deflation and depression were world wide. He explained that in the period immediately ahead there would be inevitable liquidation of inflated values, debts and prices. Heavy penalties would fall on everyone. No one could, at the moment, measure the destructive forces swelling into a tidal wave.

From his intimate knowledge of European affairs, he recognized that the back-wash of war was seeping into the foundations of the American economic structure.

"You must think beyond emergency relief," he said to these chosen confidants, "and plan ahead to maintain social order and industrial peace while bringing about orderly liquidation and prevention of panic during a period of readjustment to new ideas of living more in accordance with the heritage of America's founders."

A group of outstanding labor leaders heard the same message. Their promised loyalty involved sacrifice, but convinced by the seriousness of the emergency they willingly withdrew wage demands already announced.

Fearing the effect of the Depression on farmers, the President requested Chairman Legge of the Farm Board to make loans on wheat and cotton, with the promise of later purchase. By December this cushioning of such basic staples had helped to stabilize prices of most agricultural commodities.

At the annual Gridiron Club dinner that month, the President answered critics of his multiplying Commissions and Committees, by now the butt of many editorial jibes.

"The most dangerous animal in the United States," he told this audience, "is the man with an emotion and a desire to pass a new law. He is prolific with drama from the headlines. He is not on the road to the fundamental advance of the liberty and progress of the American people at this time in our history. The greatest antidote for him is to set him upon a committee with a dozen people whose appetite is for facts. The greatest catastrophe that could come to our country is that administration policies or voluntary movements shall be encouraged or enacted upon the basis of emotion and not upon facts and reason."

This was the engineer speaking again, the man who had been honored earlier in the year as the recipient of the John Fritz Medal, the highest award of his profession. In nominating him, Michael Pupin, renowned Serbian-American inventor, quoted a conversation with a Viennese lady on a Serbian railroad in post-war relief days.

"God bless Herbert Hoover," she said, "and may engineers like him become rulers and rid the world of horrible hatreds and wars."

But the United States in December, 1929, was too emotionally unbalanced to weigh the cold facts which were so clear to the President.

His reply to increasing clamor for Federal aid for the unemployed was adamant. He would instigate a Public Works program to absorb labor which private industry could no longer afford. To make this practical, he was ready with plans for the re-building and beautification of Washington. In his thinking, "the nation's capital should be the symbol of America. Its dignity and architectural inspiration should stimulate pride in the country and elevation of thought."

Immediate objectives were a program of slum clearance in the Capitol area, building adequate additions to the House and Senate Offices, a new Supreme Court Building, and extension of the Library of Congress, a new Civic Center, and worthy headquarters for the Departments of Commerce, Labor, Justice, the Post Office, Interstate Commerce, and Archives. Throughout the States he would erect proper government buildings. He approved plans for waterway development which he claimed would be larger than the Panama Canal.

But the administration of out-and-out relief must be by States and municipalities, not the Federal Government.

Through every speech and every press release from the White House Hoover's theme was the same. The Federal Government had a responsibility toward those in distress, a duty that could be met through regulating the fundamental business of the country so that *its people could help themselves.* The American Way was predicated upon voluntary and cooperative action. Abroad, the United States should work in harmony with other nations in everything affecting world security. At home, the government would exert every effort to help prevent industrial conflict, avoid bankruptcy, and balance the budget. Above all, he repeated incessantly, the American dollar should ring true on every counter in the world!

The President sought advice from those he could trust. Since the United States was not a member of any of the international banking organizations set up after the war, he considered the feasibility of participation in current plans for a World Bank. But he received no encouragement from his former associate on the Supreme Economic Council. Henry M. Robinson was quoted in the *New York American* in late January with this observation:

"On first blush, such a plan appears desirable; but it must be remembered that for ten years the United States has been hold- thirty to thirty-five percent of the available monetary gold of the world. The World Bank will have at least six governments represented among its directors to our one—with each of these nations much more in need of gold than we are. Obviously, no one in private affairs would enter a pool where he supplies all the resources and only has one vote."

In his continual probing for reliable information on world economic conditions, the President often put incisive questions to Adolph Miller.

On March 4, he asked his secretary, George Akerson, to invite the Millers to dinner.

"I'll have to ask my wife first," Miller hesitated when the phone call came. "I think we are due at the Italian Embassy to meet Toscanini and the chief sponsor of the New York Philharmonic."

"In that case," Akerson replied, "The President said not to press the dinner part if you had an engagement, but to 'tell Miller to come direct to the White House at six oclock—not to the Executive Office, but to my own study. I will not need him for long.' "

Miller arrived a few minutes early. As he stood in the Lincoln Study watching the sunset sky across the Potomac, his eyes shifted to the evening paper on the desk. March 4! Oh, he thought, an anniversary party! We should have changed our plans.

The President walked in, saying abruptly:

"Here, I want to talk with you." And without further preliminaries, "Where do you think we are in the recession?"

Miller answered deliberately.

"It is always painful to tell unwelcome news. You mean the depression that has now begun?"

"Depression?" The president's voice was sharp. "Would you use that word advisedly?"

"Yes, I hope that I am wrong; but I feel sure we are in for a serious period."

"Still," said Hoover, "I have talked with many people who feel that the worst is over."

Two hours of discussion was interrupted by a call from Mrs. Miller, reminding her husband of the date at the Italian Embassy.

Swift-moving events of that spring began to verify Miller's worst fears. And the President, intent upon solving the accumulating problems in a way consistent with his concept of American tradition, found lack of agreement with his ideas in many circles.

Organized Veterans were insistent. The President sympathized with legitimate claims; but he vetoed an act largely increasing pensions to Spanish-American War Veterans in 1930. He was convinced that most of the proposed beneficiaries had sufficient income beyond their pensions, or had incurred disability through habits having no connection with war service. Nevertheless, Congress passed the bill over the President's veto.

Then another bill was introduced, extending the period of "World-War incurred disability." Conferences with the Director of the Veterans' Bureau and the American Medical Association convinced the President that certain features of this bill constituted a subterfuge under which the government would be paying men who had not incurred disabilities during wartime. Moreover, he objected to applying the same benefits to those who had not left this country as to the men who had fought in the Argonne.

As a counterproposal, the President instituted complete revision in Veterans' legislation to incorporate generous provision for those in real need. Aided by a Republican caucus, he secured Congressional support for a bill that made every veteran disabled through service-incurred illness eligible for hospitalization and disability allowance for the remainder of his civilian life. This helped to lift the burden of destitute unemployed veterans from State and local governments; but the President was continually criticized by economy leagues and disappointed politicians alike.

Dissatisfaction was mounting. Public debate and Congressional parleying over the President's proposal for tariff reform brought opposition from members of both parties. Old Guard Republicans, objecting to the President's moderate views on protection, had joined free-trade Democrats in blocking proposals presented to a Special Session early in the administration.

Now, in June, 1930, bitter debate threatened futility. Hoover authorized Senator Watson to re-state his desire for the first clear-cut flexible tariff based on cost of production that had ever been presented to Congress. What Hoover wanted was a bi-partisan Tariff Commission that would free the country from what he called "the orgy of greed at every legislative adjustment." Senator Grundy, leader among the Old Guard Republicans, allied himself with Democrats and Progressives to block such a Commission.

Many of the President's closest advisors warned him that the Smoot-Hawley Tariff Bill which was coming to a vote in June would hamper all that he hoped to achieve. Nevertheless, he finally accepted it as passed by both Houses, because it represented the fulfillment of pledges made by the Republican Party in the Convention which had nominated him. Platform promises, to one of his integrity, must not be empty gestures!

"No tariff bill has ever been, or ever will be enacted under the present system that will be perfect," he said in his press statement. "There are items upon which duties will prove too high, and others, too low. I have insisted, however, that there should be created a new basis for the flexible tariff which has been incorporated in this law, thereby establishing the means for objective and judicial review of these rates free from pressures inherent in legislative action."

No matter how insistent these debates on home policies were, the President, acutely aware of world interdependence, overlooked no opportunity to learn first-hand about European economic conditions. One hot July evening the Millers, with Judge and Mrs. Harlan Stone of the Supreme Court, were dining at the White House. As they were leaving, Miller remarked:

"You know we four are going to Europe this summer."

"What are you doing that for?" queried the President, "to drink beer and hear some music?"

"Yes," answered Miller, "I won't miss that; but I have a serious purpose. I want to see if I can find any facts that will correct my view that we are in for a long and deep depression."

"I know," said Hoover, "You told me that two months ago."

Making mental note of the time they planned to return, the President bade them farewell, and turned to the engrossing problems, incident to the worst drought in American history.

Beseeched on all sides to help sufferers in the Mississippi Basin, where so short a time before he had been fighting floods, Hoover appointed Secretary of Agriculture James Hyde Chairman of a National Drought Commission. He assigned the responsibility of encouraging the full participation of bankers to Henry M. Robinson. Then he instructed these men to unite Federal, State and private philanthropy in a common effort to give immediate assistance, and appealed to the railroads for help in transporting supplies.

While this Commission was seeking an answer to the drought problem, a long-anticipated report was laid on the President's desk. As he read the findings of the Hoover-Young San Francisco Bay Bridge Commission, its challenging figures and constructive prophecies lifted his mind temporarily from current distress.

This project, once the fantastic dream of San Francisco's mad "Emperor" Norton in the 1860's, had long gripped the imagination of progressive engineers. Even railroad builder Senator Stanford had voiced interest. Vociferous objection, however, had always come from both arms of the Service whenever the subject was publicly discussed. The Navy, appreciating the unique advantages of the land-locked Bay, feared interference with national defense; the Army, with commerce and navigation.

Herbert Hoover had always been one of the engineers who foretold eventual solution of both problems. In 1922, as Secretary of Commerce, he had requested an official report by Army Engineers on various proposed routes. And in 1928, the subject had been thoroughly discussed enroute to the Republican Convention. The group on that trip had included California's Governor Young, San Francisco's Mayor Rolph, *Chronicle* publisher, George Cameron, and State Highway Engineer Purcell. Cameron had ventured the suggestion that a bridge might be built high enough to allow the largest battleship to pass beneath. Hoover had promised that, should he win the nomination and election, he would seek Army and Navy support for an unbiased survey.

As soon as the bill establishing a California Toll Bridge Authority had passed the State Legislature in June, 1929, the President asked Rear Admiral William V. Pratt, Chief of Naval Operations, for advice in selecting navy engineers who would approach the subject with professional understanding. As a result, Rear Admiral William H. Standley, a native Californian, was one of the Presidential appointees when the Hoover-Young Commission was announced in August. Serving with him was Rear Admiral Luther E. Gregory. The Army was equally cooperative with the Commander-in-Chief. Their representatives, Brigadier General G. B. Pillsbury and Lieutenant Colonel E. L. Daley, brought decisive minds to the important problem of finding a feasible way to connect the growing metropolitan Bay Area. The President named his old mining associate, Mark Requa, as chairman. The Governor's nominees included Cameron, Purcell, and Hoover's former professor of Civil Engineering "Daddy" Marx from Stanford.

Acquiescence of the Service members to the safety and feasibility of the route originally suggested, from Rincon Hill just above the San Francisco water front through a tunnel in Goat Island (Yerba Buena) to Oakland, had paved the way for a recommendation to undertake "one of the greatest engineering feats ever attempted." The Engineer-President concurred in the prediction in their report that income from tolls would make it possible to pay off the investment in twenty years. He also agreed that reduced costs of transportation between Bay Area cities would contribute effectively to economic and social progress.

A less perceptive leader might have hesitated in a period of depression like that of 1930. But Hoover habitually thought into the future. His mental agenda already listed contemplated legislation which would authorize Federal loans for just such productive public works. He continued to try to muster Congressional support for measures to cure rather than alleviate depression.

As his mind focused on these distant objectives, the President became more and more isolated within the walls of the Lincoln Study. Even those who passed the guards at the outer doors were apt to feel as remote as had those friends who sat at the dinner table of the Secretary of Commerce on "S" Street, without conscious recognition of their presence on the part of the host.

The report of the Drought Commission toward the end of August added to the growing unpopularity of the overburdened President. Farmers, expecting that the Great Relief Administrator would propose liberal Federal financial aid, were disappointed. In an interview with Henry Robinson, regarded in this situation as spokesman for the Administration, one reporter quoted the banker as saying that he had no suggestions for the assistance of farmers who had no adequate security. Of course, he explained, those with good reputations, or tenants of more prosperous landholders, would probably find these men willing to vouch for their notes. But for the small farmer, unfortunately without security, the Commission offered no solution.

Simultaneously with this distress at home, Adolph Miller brought further bad news when he returned from Europe. Arriving at his Washington home past midnight, he found that the President had kept track of his travels. A note on his desk asked him to call the White House regardless of the hour. Nevertheless, he decided to wait until morning. Before he presumed to make an early call, he received a message, saying that he and Mrs. Miller were expected to dine with the President that night.

When they arrived, they found only one other guest, an Ambassador. Miller walked in with Mrs. Hoover, next to whom he was seated. The President spoke brusquely—

"No! I want Adolph Miller over here."

There was no preliminary conversation as Hoover peppered the traveler with questions, quizzing him for every fact bearing on the state of world finance. As Miller repeated each discouraging observation, he discovered that the President had changed his point of view. Now they both recognized the bitter truth that a long depression was inevitable.

The following month, September, Hoover called Eugene Meyer at his home in Mt. Kisko, New York.

"There is a vacancy on the Federal Reserve Board. I want you to take it and to become Chairman. I will not take 'no' for an answer."

Meyer, too, had accepted the finality of the gathering storm. As he assumed the difficult task, he applied all the force of his strong personality, and his experience in world-wide banking, to the fight.

Before the end of the year, there was a new crisis. The world harvest of 1930 was large; grain prices collapsed in Europe to an equivalent of about fifty cents a bushel in the American market. At the same time, the Soviets dumped many products on the market at extremely low prices. Again, the Farm Board authorized farmers' cooperatives to cushion grain and cotton markets. The President, who had promised his people peace and plenty, faced a world in financial collapse, a market glutted with surplus. Where were there any purchasers who could afford prices that would maintain American standards?

This being a Congressional election year, opposition to the administration became vociferous. The *New York World,* the paper that had carried such enthusiastic "Hoover-for-President" editorials in 1920 and 1928, ran a series of syndicated articles written by a discharged employee of the Department of Interior. In these the author charged Secretary Wilbur with disgraceful scandal in leasing oil shale lands in the West. The Attorney General's report to the President was made public and brought an apology from the *World* when the accusations were proved groundless. But the lie was effectual.

Disappointed voters, frantic over lost fortunes and jobs, blamed their misfortunes on the Republicans. The President faced a hostile Democrat-controlled Congress.

But Herbert Hoover clung to his faith that Right would triumph in the long run. The factual engineer, the humanitarian idealist, had neither time nor talent for politics. He *believed* in the ultimate good sense of the American people. He relied upon those thousands of men and women who had helped to win the war as participants in the Food Administration. He could turn to those who had rallied to save the children of stricken Europe. Surely, these same fellow citizens would follow his leadership in succoring each other in this time of domestic emergency! They would abide by the traditions of their forefathers, whose hard work, independence, and frugality had made a nation out of a wilderness.

All through that grim winter of 1930-1931 the President struggled with problems heaped on his desk in the room that had once been Lincoln's. Speaking over the radio from this study, he tried to explain why he did not approve Federal appropriations for charity.

To the Senators who were attempting to force an extra session for that purpose, he said: "This is not an issue as to whether or not people shall go hungry or cold in the United States. It is merely a question of the best method by which cold and hunger shall be prevented."

He idealized all true Americans as imbued with the spirit of those Quaker neighbors he had known on the plains of Iowa or in the wilds of Oregon. He refused to recognize the greed and selfishness that was sapping the strength from a disillusioned generation. If these appropriations were made from the national treasury, he argued, those responsible would have impaired something infinitely valuable in the life of the American people. Even the great Democrat, President Grover Cleveland, had recognized that when he said in 1887: "Although the people support the Government, the Government should not support the people."

Ironically, a man who had spent most of his life fighting hardship and starvation abroad, floods and drought at home, was now forced to answer critics who charged him with a lack of human sympathy. Quietly, Herbert Hoover reminded his listeners that in every organization with which he had been connected, it had always been possible to summon maximum self-help.

He spoke with pride of the times he had successfully sought the help of Congress for nations disorganized by war and anarchy to the extent that self-help was impossible; but he emphasized that government appropriations had been dwarfed by contributions from public charity in the United States and other countries.

Then he reminded his listeners that even in the present emergency, there was no such paralysis in the United States. He was confident that Americans of the 1930s had the resources, the initiative, the courage, stamina and kindliness to meet the situation with the same spirit with which former generations had attacked their problems. He did pledge, however, that should the time come when voluntary agencies, local and State Governments could not prevent hunger and suffering, he would invoke every resource of the Federal Government. He added that his faith in those who were listening was so strong that they would never let that day come.

Sincere as he was in this trust, he could not stem the tide of insidious opposition propaganda which had begun with the fall campaign to poison the stream of free thought in the American press. Using his vitriolic pen to spearhead this attack, Charlie Michelson, that same correspondent who had once bragged of his fine relations with the Secretary of Commerce, was leading an army of journalists determined to break down faith in the President. Millions of dollars poured into an unprecedented effort to undermine the whole structure of Hoover's program.

Nothing in his past had prepared him for this perfidy. He thought straight. He expected others to do the same. Anne O'Hare McCormick wrote in the *New York Times* in February that the President "has stiffened rather than sagged under opposition . . . showing a deep-rooted and growing impatience with the way politicians and political machinery work in times of emergency."

Her interview had convinced her that his "well-oiled thinking machine grasped too many, rather than too few details." She seemed to feel that in appraising these facts, he apparently lost track of the immediate in pursuing his findings into ultimate and remote complications. She concluded that in the field of political action, Hoover had found himself associated with such a different type of intelligence that each was irritated and confused by the other. This led to the prophecy that "if the Commission form of Government ever extended to the nation, Hoover would be the ideal business manager."

But Hoover, reared with veneration for the highest office in the land, braced his shoulders to the wheel, wrapped the burdens of his people close about him as a heavy cloak in the increasing winter chill and determined to save them all from the disaster his prescient mind foresaw. The only method he knew was hard work. Thus, he spent constantly longer hours studying beneath the portrait of the brooding Lincoln. He invited more national leaders to conference; but he did not have access to the minds of the people in the street.

Theodore Joslin, one of his secretaries, described him as "figuratively, the father protecting his family against impending troubles, shouldering their burdens for them, keeping the bad news to himself, outwardly trying to be as smiling and cheerful as possible, but behind the scenes, worrying as few other Presidents in history."

Only the early morning game of volley ball, which his physician, Admiral Joel Boone, insisted upon, gave him relaxation from mounting cares. In those half hours, shared always by Dr. Wilbur and sometimes by other Cabinet Members, he tossed aside his worries momentarily with the rebounding ball.

As weary weeks brought new problems, the President had less time for the public. No matter how intelligently he labored to help those in need, he had a physical repugnance for actual suffering. Just as he had fled, with tear-dimmed eyes, when Charlotte Kellogg had once tried to show him a room full of starving Belgian children, so now he could not face the apple vendors rubbing their cold fingers to keep them supple as they stood on street corners, mute symbol of the breakdown in the economic order he was striving so desperately to maintain.

There was no "Great Headquarters" to which he could carry his picture of innocent sufferers, no Lloyd George to convince with logic and humanitarian appeal. His own must be the ultimate word as he directed the course of American recovery from world depression which was by now enmeshing every nation in globe-circling interdependence. With stubborn conviction that he was right, he continued to recoil from every suggestion of centralizing relief control in the Federal Government.

CHAPTER TWENTY-TWO

CUMULATING CRISES

PRESIDENT HOOVER'S DETERMINATION to "hold the Gibralter of world stability" found him besieged on all sides. Overseas forces beyond his control continued to upset financial equilibrium. A Democrat-controlled Congress balked at his every attempt to find remedies. Their opposition was all the more perplexing as it contrasted with the cooperation they gave him during his Commerce years. In the beginning of that period, Harding leaned on Hoover for help at every step; Coolidge tolerantly, though often grudgingly, acknowledged his wisdom. Congress listened with respect, and usually acted in harmony with the views he presented. Now, when it was important to pull together Hoover was increasingly unheeded and directly opposed.

Constant pressure for Federal aid took on a new form when the Democrats played on public sympathy using the plight of the war veterans. In spite of the earlier Presidential veto of the bill to increase the bonus, they now proposed to loan these men fifty per cent of their regular bonus, under guise of relief. After carefully assembling facts, the President estimated that approximately twenty per cent were in actual need. He would help only those. But Congress insisted upon applying the offer to everyone—a potential drain of $1.7 billion on the treasury. Hoover protested vehemently. Such action, he said, would nullify benefits to veterans with legitimate claims; it would inflict financial injury on the whole country.

The bill passed over his veto. Accepting defeat, the President requested General Hines of the Veterans' Administration to give priority to those in real need.

He incurred deep congressional hostility when he vetoed the Muscle Shoals Bill in his constant opposition to government competition with private business. In his veto message, he cited the precedent of the successful Colorado River project and expressed conviction that the real development of Tennessee Valley could best be accomplished by the people of the valley. To this end, he suggested that the States of Alabama and Tennessee set up a commission of their own citizens to work with representatives of farm organizations and Army engineers. He would give such a commission full authority to lease the plants at Muscle Shoals in the best interests of local communities and of agriculture in general.

Although he opposed federal operation of the power business, he continually urged federal regulation of interstate electrical power as an essential function of the reorganized Federal Power Commission. But Congress refused to give the necessary regulatory authority.

During this spring of 1931 another commission, one of his first appointments, brought in a report that highlighted his disagreement not only with Congress, but also with a discouraged public, who flaunted disregard for the Prohibition law in speakeasies and hidden stills. The section on Prohibition in the "Wickersham Report on Law Enforcement" was significantly divided in opinion. Two members of the commission favored repeal of the Eighteenth Amendment. Six favored revision and three recommended further trials.

The President acknowledged their thorough study, but he added that he could not be counted on to favor the proposed revisions. Urgent letters came from friends, who remembered his statement in the Inaugural Address that if people did not approve a law it was their right to seek its repeal. If he would agree to revisions, they promised to try to eliminate this issue from the election of 1932.

In ignoring this advice, Hoover failed to sense that his attitude toward Prohibition contradicted his often repeated slogan of personal liberty. He avowed that the Government should not intrude into personal or business affairs. He upheld the dignity of the individual who should be able to choose for himself. Yet he was apparently blind to the undermining effect of a law that was being openly flouted by independent Americans, many of whom had never used liquor before, but who refused dictation in a matter so personal.

In addition to these domestic worries, his nights were made sleepless by repercussions from serious financial conditions across the Atlantic. Germany had been borrowing billions from the United States during prosperous years, using the money to pay Reparations. Thus the Allies had been able to meet their payments on War Debts. Until now the Germans had paid interest regularly. But Hitler's sweeping gains in the April elections, plus the banking collapse in Austria, had begun to shake confidence in their willingness and ability to honor these obligations.

Ambassador Sackett made a hurried trip from Berlin in May to give the President a first-hand report on the disheartened German people. He told Hoover that they seemed to feel that nothing short of a revolution such as that which had transformed Russia could keep the nation from complete disintegration. President von Hindenberg broke all diplomatic precedent in a direct letter of appeal to President Hoover to use the good offices and prestige of the United States for "the preservation of a great people."

Day after day, night after night, the American President conferred with one ambassador after another, with his cabinet advisors, and with bankers familiar with every implication of the international situation. He was convinced that stringent measures were imperative to stay the force of the financial storm. The world *must* have breathing time in which to regain economic equilibrium.

He told an Indianapolis audience in early June that he had confidence in the ability of the United States to recover, regardless of the rest of the world. Three days later he proposed a moratorium on war debts conditioned upon similar action regarding all European intergovernmental debts. This release from immediate pressure, he said, would give all countries time to build reserves in industry and to stabilize their currencies.

A grateful world breathed easier when the fifteen governments involved accepted the American proposal on July 6. Hoover pointed out in his announcement that, although the primary object was economic relief, this action would swing men's minds from fear to confidence and nations from disorder to hope for the future.

He spent the hot summer wrestling with further complications in international and domestic finance. Although the Moratorium was easing pressure on government treasuries, the Bank of International Settlements divulged that more than ten billion dollars in short-term banking bills at high interest had been issued by Germany and other Central European countries to American, British, French, and Scandinavian banks, as well as to those of other accredited countries. Interest was already in default. Billions of American depositors' dollars were jeopardized by this threatened welching.

Secretaries Mellon and Stimson hurried to London for a bankers' conference. They found European finance paralyzed. Hoover proposed another bold idea. His "Standstill Agreement," under which banks would hold these short term bills for a stipulated time while an international bankers' committee was appointed to administer them, was accepted on July 23, despite vehement protest, from the banks.

In the discussion period, bankers in America, England, and France urged their governments to loan more money to Central Europe, joined in this plea for a time by Mellon and Stimson. But Hoover was unswerving. Neither the government nor the banks of the United States should pour any more money into this bottomless bucket!

Hoover's announcement that the London Conference had laid sound foundations for the economic stability of Germany helped restore confidence everywhere. Conditions in the United States began to improve visibly. Those Americans who understood the significance of the threatened danger realized that a bad panic had been averted.

But the lull was temporary. Acutely aware of signs of trouble in unexpected places, the President had been keeping an eye on the Orient. During the summer he sent an economic mission to China to check his suspicions of a possible Bolshevik invasion. The report of the returning mission justified his worst fears. They told him of serious internal disorder and unstable conditions.

One member, Senator Tasker H. Oddie of Nevada, reported confidentially a personal incident which nearly had fatal consequences to him and Mrs. Oddie. The Senator had supported Hoover ardently in opposition to the recognition of Soviet Russia. Thus the President was not surprised when Oddie told him that on the morning of a scheduled flight over the Yangtze, they had been wakened at two o'clock by a courier from the American Embassy. This man reported that a plot had been uncovered in which a suicidal pilot had intended to wreck the plane. The Oddies canceled their flight under pretext of "sudden illness" and left Peking under Marine guard!

While the President kept alert for further evidence of Russian perfidy, the respite from world economic worries achieved by the London Conference waned. Serious unrest was again seething among Americans. In September, with world panic at new heights, the Democratic Congress proposed payment of the Veterans' Bonus in full, totalling some $3.4-billion.

The American Legion was in session in Detroit. The President made a hurried trip to explain to these men in person the serious import of this proposal. He pointed out how they could serve in peacetime toward stabilization of the economy of the nation they had so recently fought to preserve. He appealed to their pride, suggesting that while uninformed people might have lost nerve and courage, surely members of the American Legion had a particularly sacred stake in the future of their country. His audience was impressed by his confidence in their willingness to practice self-denial. Patriotically, the convention voted to repudiate the proposal.

No sooner was this catastrophe averted, when a new shock rocked the financial world. On September 21 the Bank of England discontinued gold purchases at the long-established price. This was a repercussion from the failure of Central Europe, South American and other countries to meet obligations to British banks. The Federal Reserve Board, with approval of President Hoover, immediately offered help. In addition to $125-million thus advanced, the Bank of France and private French bankers advanced equal amounts. Still the Bank of England could not carry on with its established gold purchase policy.

Black news was headlined daily. There were reports of a mutiny in the British Navy. Commodity and security markets closed in most of Europe. Heavy withdrawals of American gold and exchange began to seep abroad, thus shrinking the American credit structure. Foreign countries increased tariffs and set embargoes on imports to protect their own currencies. Immediately, cautious and fearful Americans commenced hoarding currency and gold, withdrawing several billion dollars from circulation.

The President knew that this new crisis would be more devastating than the two already met. A recurrence of the Stock Exchange debacle of 1929 had been forestalled in some degree by regulatory measures. The Moratorium and Standstill had alleviated conditions caused by the European collapse in June and July of 1931. Now, in the fall of that same year, the President realized that the Federal Reserve System was not sufficiently flexible to cope with this new shock caused by British default, complicated as it was by demands from other countries.

As the new Federal budget was assembled, it was evident that there would be a drop of over two billion dollars in government revenues from the pre-depression normal. In the face of an unprecedented budget deficit, demand for relief expenditures was reaching a high pitch of emotion.

The Senate was rife with opposition to the conservative President. The Democrat-controlled House made every move difficult. Hoover was convinced that if America failed now, all civilization might be paralyzed. After a preliminary confidential meeting with the Federal Reserve Board, Advisory Council, and Treasury officials, he invited heads of Clearing House banks and of leading insurance companies to confer with him at Andrew Mellon's home on Sunday evening, October 4. At the same time, he called a bi-partisan conference of ranking members of the Banking and Finance Committees of both houses of Congress on the sixth.

While his advisors were preparing agenda for these meetings, a new crisis broke in the Far East. Japan had taken advantage of world confusion to abandon the policy announced jointly with Britain and the United States to help maintain international peace. In Manchuria, a Japanese railroad guard was shot by a Chinese. Military leaders in Tokyo seized on this "act of banditry" as an excuse to invade that territory, in direct violation of the Nine-Power Treaty of 1921, in which all Pacific Basin countries had agreed to respect the integrity of China.

Public hatred for Japan flared. The press bristled with accusations. This invasion had also violated the Kellogg Pact and the time-honored Hayes Doctrine of the Open Door in China. The President warned his Cabinet that the United States must not become militarily involved in a situation so full of threat.

He knew first-hand the workings of the Asiatic mind. He was emphatic in branding Japanese action in Manchuria immoral, an offense against the comity of nations, an affront to the Uniteed States. But he reminded his associates that the Nine-Power Treaty and the Kellogg Pact were solely moral instruments. They could be enforced only by moral reprobation. The Covenant of the League of Nations had indeed been broken, but the United States was not a party to the League! This country could cooperate in any measure short of war; but it had no legal obligation to do anything. The United States, he reiterated, had *never set out to preserve peace among other nations by force.*

He diagnosed the case as he might have dealt with a sick mine or an analysis of a business. He pictured both sides of the problem for the Cabinet. From his knowledge of history and his personal experience in China, he explained the slow-moving tempo of Asiatic life, the cultural resistance of the Chinese to invaders. Then he recalled the long-standing friendship between the United States and Nippon, suggesting that something might be said on the side of Japan. Possibly under changed conditions Japan could no longer endure the treaties. They might offer the excuse that China had failed to maintain order, that anarchy would endanger Japanese business.

The President reminded his Cabinet again that the announced policy of the administration was to exhaust every process of peaceful negotiation. Did they consider war with Japan inevitable if other methods failed? He did not propose to sacrifice American lives for anything less than a threat to the freedom of their own people or to the future of the United States.

The Secretary of State wanted punitive action. Stimson's experience in the administration of the Philippines made him suspicious of Japanese motives. He advocated sanctions such as an economic blockade of the offending nation. Preferably, he would carry this out in collaboration with other great powers; if they refused the United States should proceed alone.

Herbert Hoover opposed this with all his will. Through personal and reliable sources he sounded out Britain's probable position and consulted his military advisors in respect to the proposed sanctions. Convinced that neither would support them, he withstood official and public pressure from those who were blind to the inevitable results.

In the meantime he commissioned Under-Secretary of State William R. Castle to do all he could with the Japanese representatives in Washington. He was also to cooperate with the American Embassy in Tokyo in an attempt to bring Japan to a more reasonable attitude. Since Castle had only recently been called home from his post as Ambassador to Japan to assume the office left vacant by the death of Joseph R. Cotton, the President relied on him to persuade the Japanese to re-assume their pledge to work for world peace.

Failure of these efforts added new perplexities. The League of Nations was in session in Geneva. Secretary Stimson incorporated the President's idea of non-recognition of territorial conquest into a note to be presented by the U.S. Consul in the Swiss Capital. Prentiss Gilbert was authorized to attend and to use every means to obtain British and French support for this "Hoover-Stimson" policy.

Both nations, however, refused to cooperate at the time in protesting what they termed "a minor incident in Manchuria." They were fearful that any interference on the part of the Great Powers might precipitate a war for which they were not prepared.

A few months later a League resolution did incorporate the Hoover-Stimson policy into a means of marshalling world opinion against an aggressor nation. But that was after Japan, encouraged by the earlier rebuff to American diplomacy, had pushed on to attack Shanghai!

CHAPTER TWENTY-THREE

STRUGGLING FOR CURES

AT THE SAME time that this threat from the Pacific was endangering world peace, European economic conditions were steadily worsening. Hoover came to the meeting in Secretary Mellon's home on the night of October 4, determined to obtain constructive help from the bankers and insurance men he had invited. He impressed on them the seriousness of the British monetary collapse. Surveys showed that at least twenty other countries were about to be forced off the gold standard. Banks in large centers of the United States were calling domestic loans to fortify themselves against foreign drains.

To counteract what he termed "senseless bankers' panics and public fear" Hoover had a working plan already approved by the Federal Reserve System. This proposed that American bankers would create a National Credit Association with a five hundred million dollar capital to be subscribed by all of them in a ratio of two percent of their deposits. With such credit available, insurance companies, working with the Farm Loan Bank, would be in a position to announce to farmers and home owners that no mortgages would be foreclosed if borrowers made an honest effort to pay.

When he met the group of bi-partisan leaders two days later, he explained the proposal to establish the National Credit Association that had been accepted by the bankers' conference in Mellon's home. Secretary Mellon and Federal Reserve Board Chairman Meyer helped explain to these thirty men the far-reaching significance of such a move in strengthening the United States to meet what could prove a more devastating crisis than that of the previous June.

Because world financial conditions were so critical, the President also told the solons that he had invited the Premier of France to come to Washington, with the hope that he and M. Laval could devise some practical method of easing these monetary crises.

Vehement discussion prolonged the meeting into early morning hours. Meyer brought up an earlier suggestion to the President that the old War Finance Corporation should be revived. This proposal brought expressions of apprehension from Republicans and Democrats alike. No one wanted to project the government into the business of lending money unless as a last resort.

With almost exasperating patience, the President listened to every argument. When they finally dispersed, he had extracted hopeful promises of support from most of them. But Senator Borah and Congressman Garner went out muttering disapproval.

The President wrote immediately to the Governor of the Federal Reserve Bank of New York, telling Mr. Harrison that he was counting on the New York banks to take the lead in setting up the capital required to establish this five hundred million dollar National Credit Association. If this could be accomplished, the President promised to seek bi-partisan support from Congress for further remedial measures, if needed.

The challenge was accepted the next day. Bankers Hoover knew and trusted served as directors of the new association. They acted promptly to avert serious banking crises in Louisiana, South Carolina, Tennessee, and California.

When Laval arrived, the President took him to Rapidan. Here, under trees bright with autumn color, the two discussed ways and means of achieving closer cooperation in combatting world depression. Their joint statement of October 24 was mostly one of good will, but behind their reiteration of mutual convictions regarding essential monetary stability was the determination to maintain the gold standard in both their countries.

The month of November was gloomy with frustrating world news. The brief respite from pressure afforded by the National Credit Association petered out in renewed fear. Bankers and public alike gave up trying private palliatives as the depression deepened.

The President again sent for the chairman of the Federal Reserve Board. He told Meyer that the time had finally come to formulate an institution along the general lines discussed at the October conference. Hoover proposed that a new agency be set up, to be called the "Reconstruction Finance Corporation." It should function in such a way that the Federal Government could make loans to various private and public bodies, supplying renewed support to business, industry, and agriculture. His idea was that the Corporation would have a capital of five hundred million dollars, with the authority to borrow up to three billion dollars from the Treasury or from private sources.

Encouraged by Meyer's concurrence, the President sent for Senate Leader Robinson and House Speaker Garner. He won assurance from them that they would work for the passage of a bill authorizing this measure at the next session, with a proviso that each would have the privilege of naming a member to the board.

The taciturn Quaker in the White House had been constantly working behind the scenes to "mobilize the gigantic strength of our country for recovery." The very fact that he was self-disciplined to control and mask emotions made it difficult, however, to cope with vociferous claimants for sympathy who continually pressed against a door closed for the sake of study. He knew, he cared, but he did not often share his feelings beyond the conference room.

When Walter Gifford, then chairman of the President's Unemployment Commission, came to tell him that this organization must be strengthened to meet an unprecedented relief load for the coming winter, the President was receptive. He knew full well the effect that the European crisis would have on American workers.

Still he turned to private charity when he could. Word of the plight of the children of unemployed miners in the Appalachian States was quickly passed on to the American Friends Service. Fellow Quakers had never failed Hoover, whether he had asked them to feed a million and a half undernourished German children in 1919 or the starving Russians in Samara in 1921-1922. Now they quickly mobilized aid for the thousands of deprived youngsters in Pennsylvania and down through the mountains to Tennessee.

In the midst of all these emergencies, Hoover found time for some of his long-range programs. He took comfort from Public Health Service statistics which revealed that community response to the finding of the White House Conference on Child Health and Protection had resulted in lower mortality rates and better general health during these years of frugal living.

The welfare, education, and proper homelife for children were fundamentals that occupied Hoover's thoughts. The residue from Belgian Relief funds had gone to educational projects. Remaining funds in the American Relief Administration coffers had been used to underwrite the White House Children's Conference. But a portion had been reserved to promote the Better Homes in America inspired by Lincoln's sage observation that "the best citizen is the man with pride in his own home." For more than a year, a committee, working under Secretary of Commerce Lamont, had been planning a national conference on Home Building and Ownership scheduled to meet in Washington on December 2, 1931.

When this group convened, the President outlined a practical program for facilitating and protecting home ownership. He told them that he was seeking Congressional approval for loans to corporations formed just for the purpose of building homes for families of low incomes, or for the reconstruction of slum areas. He explained plans for home loan banking, one of the ideas he expected to submit in his forthcoming message to Congress.

That message, pregnant with constructive reform, received scant attention from the Congress. In the face of so many critical world problems, the legislators declared a two-week holiday and left the President to ponder their solution alone. Only the arrival of Herbert, Jr., with his wife and babies from Cambridge, where he attended the Harvard Graduate School of Business, and of Allan from Stanford, gave him any pause. One snowy afternoon the Secret Service guards trailed the President to a downtown department store. There they met him, coming through the swinging glass doors after an incognito shopping tour, his arms loaded with packages of skates, dolls, and rubber toys jostling his way through the crowd like any other indulgent grandfather.

When Congress re-convened in January, the President sent another urgent message: "Our hope and confidence for the future rest on the unity of our people and of the Government in prompt and courageous action," he said in part.

Although the bill creating the Reconstruction Finance Corporation presented in the December message had been whittled down in committee and Congress, both as to capital and scope, it finally was passed on January 22, 1932. Eugene Meyer, who had prepared the draft, became chairman of the board, with General Charles G. Dawes as president. Two days later, the entire board met with the President. They were already functioning and granting loans.

While the RFC began at once to relieve economic disturbances within the country, the President faced another crisis. Decreasing gold reserves had reached a point where Federal Reserve System surveys showed that they might not last more than two or three weeks. Hoover gathered his forces to fight for the gold standard. Early in February a White House conference with Ogden Mills, who had recently replaced Andrew Mellon as Secretary of the Treasury; Eugene Meyer, Governor Harrison, and General Dawes agreed that emergency action was overdue.

With their backing the President invited Republican and Democratic majority and minority leaders, ranking members of the Senate Committee on Banking and Currency, and administration officials to breakfast the next morning. During the long session Mills, Dawes, and Meyer backed the President effectively. In the end, Senator Glass, chairman of the Banking Committee, was persuaded to accede to the President's request to use his name in proposing necessary legislation. On February 7, the Glass-Steagal Bill became law.

As the President explained its provisions to the public, he called it "in a sense a defense measure." Two vital purposes were served. By freeing large amounts of gold in the Federal Reserve System (in excess of basic legal requirement) Federal Reserve banks were in a position to meet any conceivable demands at home or abroad. It also liberalized collateral provisions to enable many banks to use sound assets which heretofore had not been available for re-discount purposes.

Now, with the RFC functioning, and banks fortified to meet demands, Hoover hoped for an upturn in business and increasing employment. But he added that every hoarder must put his dollars to work in conservative investment or on deposit in sound institutions. Hoover was insistent that all the resources of the country must become productive.

He was not reassured, however, when he asked Adolph Miller one morning in the early spring,

"Where are we in the depression?"

The former professor weighed his words.

"It is a most critical period in history, Mr. President," he replied. "If it lasts much longer, it will degenerate into a social revolution. It is now affecting the minds and reactions of people in every sphere."

Doggedly, the worried President labored on throughout the spring, hounding Congress for further reforms in banking, picking the brains of Miller and other informed associates for every shred of fact. Then, just as he was making his most heroic stand in defense of the stability of the American dollar, two more shocks unexpectedly jangled financial nerves.

In Paris, Ivar Krueger committed suicide, exposing a fantastic speculative debauch in international finance. In the Middle West, the Insull utility empire collapsed, wiping out tens of thousands of small investors in America and further discrediting public confidence in banks and investments.

Answering an early call to "come to the White House immediately upon arriving downtown," Adolph Miller hastened to the Executive offices. As he hurried along he realized that Hoover had probably been lying awake most of the night pondering some phase of the country's distress. When Miller arrived, the haggard President began pumping and arguing, a process that went on without respite for over two hours. As they parted, Hoover said, "I believe you are right. I am going along that line."

In the ante room, two impatient men looked up as the Federal Reserve Board member walked out.

"So you are the fellow," chorused Secretaries Stimson and Hurley, "who has been keeping the President from his appointments!"

After they went in, the President's secretary turned to Miller,

"I reminded the President of his appointments when he asked me to phone you," said Joslin, "but he replied, 'That doesn't matter. I want to pump Miller dry on the depression before I go any further with the day. Don't let *anyone* pass that door until we have had our conference.' "

While the President was thus shouldering its burdens, the public was beginning to discuss possible candidates for the November election. A "Hate Hoover" campaign, swept through the country like a chill wind stripping the cherry trees along the Potomac of their blossoms. The force of vehement, propaganda swept away all memory of Hoover's three years of selfless service in the White House. But the President, intently studying mounds of bank reports and business statistics on his big desk, did not seem to feel the blast. Out of his window he could see that the pink blooms were gone, but the glass kept out the cold. In much the same way his loyal and admiring staff insulated him from the vicious attacks that cluttered the mail If a clear-sighted friend came to warn him of the growing flood of abuse, he was likely to be diverted at the door.

Some of these attacks attained book stature; but the President would not use the prestige of his office for rebuttal. Rather, he concentrated his energies in a serious effort to interest the proper Congressional committees in government reorganization for economy and efficiency.

His plans were based on the completed survey begun by Walter Newton in the early months of the Administration. He recognized that it would be an unpleasant task to abolish Boards and Bureaus, to consolidate others, and to do it wisely so as not to injure the effectiveness and morale of Army, Navy and other essential services. But he appealed once more to lawmakers for executive authority to effect these changes promptly enough to afford relief for taxpayers.

When his concern for all such citizens made him veto a fiat money bill that carried with it immediate payment of the Veterans' Bonus in full, agitation throughout the country started shabby cars trekking across deserts and mountains.

The President, barricaded in his Study, was scarcely conscious of this "Bonus Army" converging upon Washington. He had no time for panaceas, regardless of popular demand. Sedatives and patent medicines were never in his kit. As a doctor of sick mines, he had made careful diagnoses of faulty methods of engineering and management. No matter how drastic a cure was indicated, he had not hesitated over purgatives or surgery. Now he sought to treat economic ills and government ailments the same way.

While he was conferring with the Directors of the RFC at Rapidan in mid-June, thousands of "bonus-marchers" were encamped along the Potomac. Congressmen who had been thwarted in their efforts to put through the fiat money bill, were visiting in the camps, exhorting the marchers to demand their rights as citizens. Newspapers raised "relief funds." Welfare organizations in the District of Columbia exhausted their resources.

With the Capital thus besieged, the Republicans were assembling in Chicago to nominate a leader for the next four years. The unanimous enthusiasm of 1928 was lacking. Some, influenced by Senator Norris of Nebraska, spoke openly of disappointment over Hoover's alleged failure to carry out his promises. Others insisted that only Hoover had the experience and judgment to guide the nation at this crucial period.

Even the California delegation was not unanimous. William H. Crocker startled Chairman Requa with a blunt declaration. If Hoover did not repudiate the Prohibition plank he and Nicholas Murray Butler of New York would bolt the Convention. Requa put through a call to the White House and was told that Ogden Mills, as the President's spokesman, would stand firm for law enforcement, consistent with the Hoover stand throughout his term. Mills made the pronouncement; Butler and Crocker took a midnight train to New York before the final vote.

Chapter Twenty-four

CANDIDATE AGAIN

When he was notified by wire that he had been re-nominated, the President telegraphed that he would continue to combat the effect of the world-wide storm still engulfing the country. Then he added that beyond the Platform was "a sacred realm of ideals and hopes and aspirations . . . With unceasing effort and faith in the Almighty God our objectives will be attained . . . If the American people shall commit to me the high trust of this great office, I pledge to them the full measure of devotion to their service."

The American people did not then know to what extent he meant "the full measure." The President had not let it be known that not one cent of taxpayers' money had ever gone to pay for those services. From the moment he closed his London office and shouldered the burden of the starving Belgians, he had vowed never to receive money for charitable nor for public service. His salary as Secretary of Commerce had gone into a special fund from which he was able to augment salaries for assistants and for other government employees who, he felt, were not sufficiently compensated. The Presidential salary had never been touched; but was in a special deposit ready to be returned to the United States Treasury at the close of his term.

The campaign did not start with the éclat of 1928. Hoover found it difficult to translate the weighty problems into terms simple enough to be understood by the public. Michelson continued to pour misinformation into the press.

The Democratic candidate, his former neighbor, Franklin

Delano Roosevelt, thrilled expectant listeners with glorious promises of a rosy dawn. The President concentrated on essential back-stage details, with scant attention to the audience beyond the footlights. He could not glamorize hard facts and cold logic into phrases warm enough to compete with the confidential tone of the man who chatted so easily with "My Friends" of his radio audiences.

In fact, the didactic monotony of Hoover's cheerless voice often repelled the very listeners who had most at stake in the struggle to preserve the fundamentals he was so determined to defend.

Troubles heaped high. The Central Bank of Chicago, founded by General Dawes, had fallen into difficulty. Having resigned from the presidency of the RFC two months earlier, Dawes felt that he should not seek help from the RFC for his former banking associates. However, Melvin Traylor, president of the First National Bank of Chicago, a leading Democrat, insisted on RFC aid for Dawes' bank.

As soon as the public learned of this, the Democratic press slanted accusing editorials at the Administration. Speaker Garner described the RFC as "Wall Street's three-billion dollar soup kitchen," ignoring the fact that Dawes, then Ambassador to Britain, was no longer on the board; and that due to Eugene Meyer's resignation in July, Democratic Senator Atlee Pomerene was now chairman.

July, 1932 proved to be the trough of the Depression. The basic law of supply and demand began to operate toward readjustment. As world inventories diminished, business curves turned upward; prices rose in every major industrial country, and each European nation showed a continuous upturn of business in spite of what happened later in the United States. While the Standard Statistics Index of 351 industrial stocks showed a low of 34 in July, this mounted steadily until it reached 56 in September. In August the Department of Labor report showed the first upturn in seasonally-adjusted indices of factory employment and payrolls since the spring of 1931. The President kept a steady hand on the wheel, watching the re-establishment of banking credit. He hoped that would bring permanent relief.

Before Congress adjourned, a vote-catching bill extending RFC loans to all kinds of enterprises, was laid on the President's desk for signature. In explaining his veto he said that it violated every principle of sound public finance and of good government, that the purpose of this expansion was no longer in the spirit of solving a major emergency. Its intention was to establish a privilege whether it served a great national end or not. Hoover wanted a relief measure; but not this!

Finally, an amended act was passed on July 16. This added over a billion dollars to the amount authorized for productive works, and $300-million for loans to States for relief; but Garner had succeeded in inserting a dangerous clause, a provision requiring monthly publication of the names of borrowers. The President appealed to the Senate. By common consent the provision was limited at that time to a confidential report to Congress.

As trouble eased in one sphere, complications of strangely unexpected character plagued the President as he worked full time on fundamental relief measures. Before Congress adjourned, he suggested that funds be appropriated to provide transportation home for the bonus marchers whose camps were becoming a menace to health and morale in the Capital.

Some six thousand men accepted. But the hoodlum elements among the remaining five thousand, composed principally of I.W.W.s and communists, soon forced a crisis that reverberated across the nation. Drama was furnished to every sensational headline writer by the picture of Chief-of-Staff General Douglas MacArthur, flanked by his aide, Dwight D. Eisenhower, at the head of five hundred "regulars" forcing rioting Americans out of their Capital. Few took pains to study the facts or to listen to the official statements of General MacArthur and Secretary of War Hurley. These explained in detail why the President of the District of Columbia Commissioners had been forced to call for Federal assistance in the same way that any

State Governor would have turned to the National Guard to quell a threatening mob that was out of hand.

Not a shot was fired, nor a single person injured as order was restored; but the flames of shacks and camps burned by evacuees before the soldiers arrived were dramatized in the minds of Administration-haters.

The President was matter-of-fact. He wrote Commissioner Reichelderfer the next day, informing him that martial law had not been declared; that the civil government of Washington was functioning uninterruptedly. But he insisted that no group, no matter what its origin, could be allowed to violate the laws of the city nor to intimidate the government.

Faced with all these disturbing problems, Herbert Hoover did not travel West for any celebration when he made his acceptance speech on August 11. From the Lincoln Study he pledged himself to uphold the ideals and the American spirit which he held inspired enterprise and built individual character.

"Not regimented mechanisms, but free men is our goal," he told his radio audience. "Herein is the fundamental issue—a representative democracy, progressive and unafraid to meet problems; but meeting them upon the foundations of experience, not upon the wave of emotion or insensate demands of a radicalism which grasps at every opportunity to exploit the sufferings of a people . . ."

Hoover was not ready, yet, to leave Washington on a campaign tour. First, he must gather representatives of important volunteer relief agencies to consider ways and means of preventing the distress that loomed with approaching winter. When Gifford's successor, Newton D. Baker, former Secretary of War in Wilson's Cabinet, introduced the President to the conference held in September, Hoover challenged them to maintain all benevolent agencies at full strength.

"A cold and distant charity which puts out its sympathy only through the tax collector yields a very meager dole of unloving and perfunctory relief," he said.

Then he revealed that, following practices he had established in his years of directing overseas relief, he had been looking ahead. Before Congress adjourned he had obtained 5,000,000 bushels of wheat, as well as 500,000 bales of cotton for the Red Cross. And he had put through an authorization for the RFC to advance $300-million to those States that could not finance relief to meet their own internal distress.

According to his tradition, the President went to Iowa to commence his campaign. In Des Moines he explained details of the battle that had been fought for the solvency of America, the skirmishes with panic which he had not dared to discuss during the critical months of its waging. Here were listeners who understood. A flood of telegrams from farm leaders and businessmen indicated that many agreed with Governor Capper of Kansas that this speech was a "stroke of genius in the method of clarifying immense issues and problems in the minds of millions of hearers." The Governor's telegram said further that this speech was bracing to hope, courage, and faith.

The sentiment of the people of Kansas was held by a minority among the voters of the United States. As the campaign progressed, it became more and more apparent that the hard-working President lacked the ability to take the people into his confidence. He could not make them understand how he had saved them from worse disaster during those years in the White House. In a way, he seemed to resent the obligation to go before the public and tell them things that seemed obvious.

It is never easy to share with those in the valley the breadth of vision that comes to one who climbs a high mountain peak. The President, who had struggled up the steep precipice, knew what lay below. He also could look far ahead and see range after range stretching out to the blue horizon. But he lacked the dramatic ability to carry his listeners on his mental journey. Nor could he understand the blindness of people who could not comprehend what had happened in the years just past. The close teamwork that had brought success in all his previous enterprises had been impossible to attain in the political arena.

Nevertheless, he went to Cleveland to discuss problems of employment, wages, and salaries, still confident that the facts spoke for themselves to people of intelligence. He told them that he had met such questions, both as a worker and as an employer, desperate to find money to meet the next week's payroll. Wherever he went throughout that month of October, he spoke as the president of a corporation, reporting to the people, its stockholders, exactly what had happened to the business of the United States in the recent difficult three-and-a-half-year period.

He confined most public appearances to places near Washington. Finally, on October 31, he stood before a surging crowd in New York City's Madison Square Garden. There he said that the campaign was more than a contest between two men, or between two philosophies of government. He objected to the proposed New Deal because it would alter the whole foundation of American life, built through generations of testing and struggle. Mastery of government could not be extended over the daily life of a people, he insisted, without somewhere making it the master of their souls and thoughts.

"Expansion of government in business means that the government, in order to protect itself from the political consequences of its errors, is driven irresistibly without peace to greater and greater control of the nation's press and platform," he warned.

As he closed with his succinctly-phrased conception of America as a land where men and women may work in ordered liberty, two friends in Washington, who had been listening for a specific paragraph amplifying that thought, looked at each other in disappointment.

The night before he left for New York, the President summoned Secretary Mills and William R. Castle to the White House.

"I want to read you something," he had said, as he took the manuscript of his intended speech out of his pocket. "I have been restudying the Constitution and the Eighteenth Amendment and have reached the conclusion that it is not contrary to the Presidential oath for the Chief Executive to make recommendations to Congress regarding changes." He began turning the pages to a marked paragraph. "One of the first things I shall urge upon the next session of Congress, will be the repeal of that experiment noble in purpose. Sometimes experiments fail. . . ."

There had been no mention of the "noble experiment" in the Madison Square Garden speech. When he returned to Washington, Castle asked, "What happened? You did not include the paragraph we all agreed was so very important!"

"I'm no politician," replied the President. "As we went up on the train, I said to Walter Newton, 'What do you think of this?' Newton replied, 'The whole country is expecting you to stand by the Prohibition plank. You cannot let them down.' "

As the campaign drew to a close, even his most enthusiastic friends could not find words strong enough to command votes. The *New York Times*, commenting on an article by William Allen White, said: "The title of this article should have been 'with all thy faults, I love thee still.' "

White had summed up his opinion of the President thus: "Conceding all his enemies say—that he is stubborn in his refusal to explain and dramatize so that the American people can understand what he is driving at; that he cannot get along with his enemies and brooks no opposition; that he is slow, moves cautiously, sometimes secretly; that he is an executive who pushes buttons and tells men to go, expecting that and impatient if they do not—still marking off all his faults at one-hundred percent, still there stands in the White House a strong, wise, honest, courageous man."

The *Times* said that Republican insistence on the speech-making tour had laid the burden on Hoover's shoulders of all the troubles against which he had fought so hard. "If he had every virtue in the world, nothing would avail against the tide of discontent." The writer concluded that Hoover had been overtaken in a poetic retribution that the Republican Party had brought on itself. To put all the blame on him was unjust "and an affront to political common sense."

As the Hoover Special boomed out of Washington on the first of November en route to California, there were clouds of confetti, whistles and bells. One enthusiast shouted, "If the worst comes and Roosevelt is elected, he'll have to hire you to run the country for him." Nevertheless, Walter Lippmann called the Hoover speeches "the language of panic" and Will Rogers said, "I wish we could get the presidential candidates to travel by plane. There'd be no back platform; but no plane is big enough to hold all the yes-men."

The train steamed on through the heart of America. Bitterness, born of uncomprehending disappointment, became vociferous; but Hoover spoke patiently from the back platform in spite of catcalls. When he stopped for the last speech at Elko, Nevada, Senator Oddie came to meet him. The Senator did not need to tell him what the Governor had said as he left Reno, "If you meet the President's train, you will not be re-elected." As rotten eggs were pelted into the train, Hoover knew that his friend had made the supreme sacrifice politically. He looked sadly at the man he had trusted so long; "I see the handwriting on the wall," he said resignedly. "It is all over."

A pleasant surprise awaited him when the train pulled into Colfax, California, at six o'clock on the next morning, Tuesday, November 8, Election Day. Two thousand people jammed the platform of the little station among the pines, to watch a delegation from Grass Valley and Nevada City present to the President an old-fashioned miner's dinner pail filled with five hundred dollars worth of gold nuggets from the North Star and seven other mines of the area. On the bucket the words, "*H. Hoover, 1895, Reward Mine, N.C. Cal.*" testified to the esteem of his first mining associates.

They were greeting him today, their spokesman said, not as the Republican candidate for re-election, but as the nation's Chief Executive. They reminded him that the last time Nevada City people had met a Chief Executive was when Theodore Roosevelt had passed through. At that time, they had presented their President with a cabinet containing gold nuggets and quartz specimens. Deeply touched, the President told the crowd that he well remembered his young days as a miner in Nevada County.

Loyal friends and leading Republicans met the train at the Oakland Mole. Riding across on the ferry, they tried to make the President feel welcome; but once the cars started up Market Street, there was no use in pretense. Hooting crowds lined the street where only a few years before he had been the proud host to the grateful King and Queen of the Belgians. In this city which only four years earlier had exulted in honoring the first President from the West, the same fickle, and obviously disappointed public, hooted and yelled epithets.

Only when the official party turned into Palm Drive at the entrance to Stanford University could Hoover escape the irate people who heaped on his weary shoulders all the blame for events he had slaved to avert. Sirens heralded the procession when Herbert Hoover came home, led by the Stanford Band and followed by motor police. Worn with the weight of his office, fatigued after a long and arduous campaign, he contrived a wistful smile for the crowd massed under the palms. Before the cloistered arches of the Quad, the President greeted fellow members of the Board of Trustees, his old friends of the faculty and chosen representatives of the student body. Then the procession moved on to San Juan Hill where his own kith and kin were waiting for him. There were now three grandchildren. Allan, too, had married; their baby stretched tiny hands toward her grandfather.

The President was welcomed, however, not only by the children dearest to his heart, but also by a large contingent of Palo Alto Girl Scouts. Their leader had planned ahead with Mrs. Hoover, who had wired, "Yes, I will be happy to see them." But when cars driven by their mothers brought these three hundred girls to the foot of the hill, a secret service man wanted to turn them back. "The President is tired," he said, "they are not at home to anyone."

The leader of the Scouts, Mrs. Charles J. Crary of Palo Alto, said, "But Mrs. Hoover is expecting us." The man was willing to carry this request to the lady on the hill. Shortly he came back, saying, "You are right."

The girls and their mothers assembled on the lawn below the swimming pool. Mrs. Hoover came out on the low roof overlooking the pool, accompanied by little Peggy Ann in a Brownie uniform. She touched her granddaughter's brown tie affectionately. "See," she said, "we are carrying on."

She accepted garden flowers from troop leaders, and made a short speech. Then the President walked out to stand beside her. At the sight of all these children, daughters of their friends and neighbors, the tension of weeks and months let go. Tears flowed unashamedly down the furrowed face.

As the children were driving home, one twelve-year-old turned to her mother, "Mommy," she said, "what do they do to a President to make a man look like Mr. Hoover does?"

The Hoovers cast their votes at the campus polling place in the Women's Club House, part of that central social quadrangle which had been built at his suggestion and with his generous help years before. Then they returned to San Juan Hill to wait with a group of close friends and pioneer faculty while the election returns poured in. As the overwhelming defeat became inevitable, the President walked with dignity among his old friends. Nothing in that homecoming was more poignant than the outstretched hands of those emeritus professors. They remembered the arrival of the shy Quaker lad, who had worked his way through their university, and then gone out into the world to bring the greatest honor possible back to those who had taught him. Hoover knew that stability of friendship such as theirs could outlive all the plaudits or bitter defeats of the changing outer world.

Across the continent in Boston a visiting British playwright, John Drinkwater, who had been in this country preparing to write his great play "Abraham Lincoln," was interviewed on the eve of sailing for England on Election Day.

"Would it be conceivable," he questioned, "if Roosevelt should be elected that Hoover would be offered a Cabinet post?

It seems a tremendous wastage of ability in this country since one party coming into power eases out the capable men of the other party. In the case of Herbert Hoover, for example, it would seem a pity that all his wise counsel might be lost when such wise counsel is so sorely needed."

At the polls the citizens of only six states: Maine, Vermont, Delaware, New Hampshire, Maryland, and Pennsylvania expressed a willingness to continue to follow this leadership. An editorial writer in the *Cleveland Plain Dealer* on November 10 said, "It is the work that has been disapproved, not the man."

This writer maintained that the country had "conceived a larger personal liking after they discovered that he was a first-class fighting man. Hoover went through a heartbreaking campaign which would have left most men exhausted. In the end, the President remained the gracious and courteous gentleman, philosophically accepting the judgment of the voters, ready to give four months more of earnest service to a nation that honored him by its call and by no means dishonored him by its decision to call another. Both in battle and in defeat, a new Hoover has come into view. He lost lots of votes, but his friends are as numerous as ever."

Chapter Twenty-five

BITTER MONTHS

HOOVER STARTED BACK to Washington to give that four more months of service. On Armistice Day he stopped in Glendale in Southern California. In an impromptu speech to the loyal friends who greeted him, he sought help in promoting the constructive measures initiated during the past three years. He told them that he was returning early, "in order that the measures and instrumentalities which have been set in motion on an entirely unpartisan basis may continue to function."

He believed strongly in the two-party system—"Only through that device can public questions be properly considered and determined." He urged Republicans to strengthen all forms of national, state, county and precinct organizations for militant action. Whether or not they were in power, he said, the party should continue to give constructive service. For, he predicted, in time it would return to power.

The Presidential train had been routed south for two reasons. It was his first visit to Southern California since he had become President. The Herbert, Jrs., had a new home in Sierra Madre to show their parents.

But another plan had crystallized before they reached Glendale. The train was re-routed at Colton for a side trip across the desert to Boulder City so that the President might see the progress on the great "Hoover Dam" so christened by Secretary Wilbur as he had turned the first shovelful of earth the previous June. Now, one year after work had commenced, they were in time to ride the busses through one of the cavernous tunnels which one day would receive torrents held in check by the coffer dam. Standing on this temporary structure, Hoover could envision the day when water and power should transform the desert over which their train had just brought them, into homelands for new generations of Americans.

During his campus visit, he had observed experiments in long-distance transmission at the Harris J. Ryan Laboratory which would make possible the use of energy generated at Hoover Dam in cities far removed from the great Colorado. He knew that the personal energy that had gone into resolving the differences between the States that now would be benefited, had been directed toward an achievement that no vote-changing could obliterate.

As the Presidential train rolled on across the Arizona desert, Hoover and his close advisors—Mark Requa, Secretary Wilbur, and Henry M. Robinson—worked together to draft a telegram to the President-elect. Specifically it invited the President-elect to meet Hoover in Washington with any Democratic leaders or advisors he wished to bring. They would discuss the approaching close of the moratorium and the appointment of delegates to the world economic conference scheduled for early winter.

Hoover returned to Washington freed from his most uncongenial task—that of trying to explain himself and his actions to an uncomprehending public. Now he could work uninterruptedly in an attempt to leave the country in the best condition that circumstances would permit. Judging others by his own attitude, he felt that the President-elect surely would cooperate on matters that could not wait for attention until March 4. But it soon became apparent that Franklin Roosevelt had no intention of following that course.

The telegram that waited for the President in Washington said that the Governor would be delighted to stop over for what he hoped would be "an entirely informal and impersonal conference." Eight days later Governor Roosevelt with his adviser, Professor Raymond Moley, talked for an hour at the White House with President Hoover and Secretary of the

Treasury Mills. After their advisors left, the two principals spent seventeen minutes alone!

Although the President had expected to recommend resumption of debt negotiations with Congressional leaders the next morning and the support of Governor Roosevelt in a promised press statement, he was disappointed to find vigorous opposition. The Governor indicated his attitude in a joking remark to a press conference as he referred to a conference on international affairs—"That's not my baby!"

Hoover issued his own statement.

"If our civilization is to be perpetuated," he said, "the great causes of world peace, world disarmament and world recovery must prevail. Peace and honest friendship with all nations have been cardinal principles by which we have ever guided our foreign relations. They are the stars by which the world must today guide its course—a world in which our country must assume its share of leadership and responsibility."

The Governor also refused to deny insistent rumors that the new administration planned to tamper with currency. The American public was jittery. Reports to *Bradstreet's Weekly* from fifty-five key cities, published in their trade review on December 3, indicated that business was at a standstill and showed little definite promise of early improvement. Wholesale trade volume was slightly below the year previous. Orders were small. Everyone was cautious. Collections were slow, and outstanding accounts of leading department stores were equal to three or four months' volume of sales.

Repeated requests to the President-elect brought no response, even when Hoover sent a draft of the special message to Congress he proposed to send during the first week of the Lame Duck Session.

Hoover had worked unceasingly for the success of this London Conference. He had confidential information from Germans he knew and trusted that Hitler, the frustrated Munich demagogue, would be no danger in a stabilized Germany. Thus, he aimed to bring together those who could evolve a program that would put Germany back on its feet. He felt certain if this could be accomplished, Hitler would have no chance to be elected.

Regardless of Roosevelt's public statement that he was keeping hands off, it was apparent that through his close touch with Democratic leaders, he was backing what became an informal "standstill" on Capitol Hill. The only major measure passed before the Christmas holidays was a vote to grant Philippine independence.

New problems began in January. Speaker Garner introduced a bill in the House insisting upon the RFC publicity clause. In spite of protests that publication of the names of all banks that received aid would precipitate runs, Garner put through his bill.

Failures immediately jumped to fifty-four per week. Senators Robinson and Byrnes wired Roosevelt, urging a repeal of the Garner publicity laws. This appeal was likewise ignored. Secretary Mills had obtained Garner's pledge to push through the program for balancing the budget as had been proposed in the President's Message; this promise was also repudiated. The panicky fears of the country were further inflamed when Henry Wallace, a recent recruit to the New Deal, was quoted from Warm Springs as saying, "the smart thing would be to go off the gold standard a little farther than England has!"

As fear gripped the shaky public, Adolph Miller confided to Hoover that Roosevelt had told him at Hyde Park soon after the election that he intended to take the country off the gold standard. It was apparent early in the year that the President-elect had let his secret purpose leak. Thus, by the time he made a public statement to the effect that when he entered the White House every bank would be closed and he would re-open them, any remaining shred of public condence vanished.

By February, a bank holiday was declared in Michigan. Again Hoover disagreed with the Chairman of the Federal Reserve Board. The President urged a scrip plan until the Michigan banks could find relief. Meyer and Governor Harrison of the New York Federal Reserve Bank opposed him. They felt that it would reflect on the flexibility and adequacy of the system. Senator Vandenberg tried to steer an emergency resolution through the Senate, giving the Secretary of the Treasury control of the currency in his discretion, and opportunity to act in a crisis. Secretary Mills enlisted Speaker Garner's pledge to its prompt passage in the House. Their agreement was reached on February 15.

Two days later, the seventeenth, President Hoover wrote a long-hand letter to Roosevelt. In this he urged the President-elect to make a reassuring statement outlining his major fiscal policies. The secret service messenger delivered the letter in person to Roosevelt, just back from Miami, at a newspaper banquet in New York. He accepted the letter, glanced through it hurriedly, and with a hearty laugh over the handwriting, passed it among his dinner companions. They, in turn, read that the President, desiring to inform his successor-to-be confidentially on the serious situation, had sent the letter through secret service because its misplacement would only feed the fire and increase the danger. In it, Hoover asked if Roosevelt were ready to announce the name of the incoming Secretary of the Treasury so that Mills could confer and thus assure some continuity.

No word came back from Roosevelt. The next night Senator Dill of Washington, spokesman for the Democratic silver bloc, broadcast his views on increased use of silver and inflation. The President-elect conferred with Professors Raymond Moley and Rexford Tugwell on national banking issues. Melvin Traylor told the Senate Finance Committee in executive session in strong language, that unless a firm statement against inflation came from the President-elect, there would be a national panic. When the committee reported this to the White House, they were told confidentially of the letter that had gone to Roosevelt two days before.

Morning papers on February 21 announced that Carter Glass had refused the Treasury post. The Federal Advisory Council, bankers from the twelve Federal Reserve Districts, met at the Treasury in the afternoon. They also urged Roosevelt to clarify his position.

On the same day, Roosevelt announced William H. Woodin as the new Secretary of the Treasury. Ogden Mills started at once for New York, hoping that the legal holiday on Washington's Birthday would give them an opportunity to confer. Woodin had only one hour for him on the evening of the twenty-second, and another the next morning.

No reply to the President's letter came from Roosevelt until March 1. Then the Governor explained that he had been dismayed to find that a letter which had been written in New York the previous week had not gone forward because his secretary had assumed that it was only a draft. In the enclosed undated note, he told the President that he had definitely had a refusal from Senator Glass to accept the Treasury post and that he was asking Mr. Woodin to take it. He expressed hope that his announcement of that appointment, along with Senator Cordell Hull as Secretary of State might have some reassuring effect on the banking situation; but, frankly, he doubted if anything short of a fairly general withdrawal of deposits could be prevented at that time.

Hoover refused to give up. In conference with his various banking associates, he tried to the last moment to avert disaster. Even Dr. Wilbur could not dissuade him from working overtime. Chatting informally with the President on the Thursday before the inauguration, the Secretary of the Interior said that everything humanly possible had been done. Since the Inauguration was only forty-eight hours ahead, there appeared little possibility that the President could accomplish anything.

Hoover looked sternly at his old friend, answering, "We will fight until 10:49 in the morning of March 4 when I leave for the capital. We must try everything, not once, but a dozen times."

As late as the evening of March 3, the President offered to join with the President-elect in a proclamation against excessive currency withdrawals, or to promulgate any plan submitted by Roosevelt with the approval of Senator Glass and the Federal Reserve Board. Roosevelt called the White House from his suite in the Mayflower to ask what the President thought of a national bank holiday. That, to Hoover, seemed unnecessarily drastic, even dangerous. He remained insistent that a joint proclamation against excessive withdrawals of currency and gold, with added control of gold reserves, would tide over until Saturday (Inauguration Day). The President-elect asked time to hold a telephone conference with Governor Lehman in New York.

Throughout the evening the White House phone rang incessantly. Federal Reserve Governors, Harrison in New York, Meyer at the Treasury, were equally sure that a bank holiday *must* be declared. It was nearly midnight when Hoover finally called Roosevelt again. What had he decided? The President-elect reported that Lehman had informed him that his advisors saw no need for a general suspension. Nor would Roosevelt join the President in the suggested control proclamation. He wished to study the whole situation and perfect his own plan *after* the Inauguration.

Asking Roosevelt to hold the telephone, Hoover, in a voice loud enough to carry over the wire to the Mayflower, repeated the conversation to Secretary Mills, Attorney General Mitchell, and Henry M. Robinson, who were seated around his desk. As the clock struck twelve, he hung up the phone, finally convinced that Roosevelt would not join in any relief action. At four o'clock on Inauguration morning, New York and Chicago completed arrangements for State bank holiday proclamations to govern that day.

And so, with their minds functioning on completely different planes, the two men rode together down Pennsylvania Avenue on the morning of March 4. Hoover's face, drawn and worried, revealed the deep anxiety he felt for the men and women who now looked at him in stoney silence. Roosevelt, smiling on the people who had swept him into office, gave promise of a glowing future in every gesture of his waving hand.

Up in the Senate Gallery where the wives of members were permitted to view the Inaugural ceremony, the Roosevelt family were seated in the third row, chatting gaily. Lou Henry Hoover walked in unobtrusively to join her friend and former neighbor, Mrs. David Reed, wife of the Pennsylvania Senator, and Mrs. Tasker Oddie.

Her steady blue eyes searched for her husband about to take his seat on the rostrum. In a few moments, the voice of Franklin Delano Roosevelt repeating the oath of office, made her once more a private citizen. At last she could return, with the companion whose career had taken them on so many far treks, to those hills of which Stanford students sing as ". . . where the Coast Range lies in the sunset fire."

Part Three

FRUITFUL RETIREMENT

CHAPTER TWENTY-SIX

AT HOME ON SAN JUAN HILL

HEDGES HAD GROWN high on the curving hillside, hiding the entrance to the house on the Stanford campus that now offered seclusion to the homing Hoovers. Its front door opened on a winding graveled drive ascending inconspicuously from a road that seemed to lead to the back entrances of a group of faculty houses surrounded by lush California gardens.

Visible only from certain vantage points, known to fraternity men on "The Row" below, the flat-roofed stucco house evaded tourists who plagued students with daily requests for guidance to the "Hoover House." The time had finally come when the neatly-lettered signs, "Private—No Trespassing" could mean that once more Hoover hospitality could be reserved for those who had personal significance in their lives.

Until now, this house had been like all the others in Herbert Hoover's life of wandering, a place where his family lived and where he could spend a few weeks between important assignments. During the years when he had led the campaign for "Better Homes in America," he had poured his strength into efforts to stabilize the economy of a nation of "23 million families," he had paid relatively little attention to his own "seven-room house on the Stanford hills." From the day in 1918 when Lou Henry Hoover selected this hilltop for their permanent home, the project had been hers. He stipulated three things, he must have his view, the roof space must be useable, and the building must be fireproof.

As chairman of Buildings and Grounds during his early years

on the Stanford Board of Trustees, he had proposed use of these hills for faculty homes. He had even fathered a generous borrowing scheme that enabled professors to finance comfortable dwellings close to the campus; but beyond being sure that his family had the site they wanted, he left details to his wife.

The first architect she consulted was a distinguished San Franciscan who had just completed a "President's House" for the Wilburs on a hill overlooking Lake Lagunita. When his sketches of an elaborate home were published in a San Francisco paper, together with a news story of a mansion being erected by the Hoovers at Stanford University, he was quietly paid off. The Hoovers announced that plans for a post-war home were being abandoned.

After a decent interval, Mrs. Hoover went to her longtime friend and neighbor, Arthur Bridgman Clark, head of the Stanford art department. He had occasionally practiced architecture down the years, designing several fraternity houses and professors' homes during summer vacations. Clark had been her instructor during undergraduate years when her mother had insisted that she include one art course among her scientific studies. The professor had listened sympathetically to her dream of materializing lifetime memories in wood and stone. He agreed to draw preliminary plans, with the proviso that Mrs. Hoover herself would act as architect, with his son Birge (soon to return from service with the Army of Occupation in Germany) as her assistant.

Now that they could begin to feel permanent on the campus, the Hoovers were grateful to the elder Clark, who had been lenient with their unorthodox ideas of planning a house to look "as if a child had piled up some blocks." Every leaded glass window framed a special view because, before they had even broken ground, Clark had erected a scaffold and runway where he and his former pupil could climb together, selecting the exact height for each window and flat roof. Those unprotected roof-sitting-rooms, reminiscent of some stopover in North Africa where they had once spent happy days, already had their Stanford memories, too. In spite of the spring wind that sometimes sweeps up from the lower end of the Bay against the Stanford hills, there had been many neighborhood gatherings around the fireplace on the house-top. From one of these outdoor sitting rooms, the Hoover family had received the cheering crowds in 1928. Yes, the Algerian roofs had been a good idea.

Inside, the English influence contrasted as completely with those roofs as if one had crossed an ocean instead of walking through a front door in California. Even here the effect was personal rather than conventional. The young draftsman Clark engaged to draw up the original specifications had studiously steeped himself in traditional English interiors, only to find that all Mrs. Hoover wanted was to make the rooms as much like Red House as possible.

She had even sent for the mantel and fireplace bricks from Horton Street when she heard that the new owners were planning to remodel it. When the sections arrived, she was dismayed that they did not look at all as she remembered them. They certainly would not fit the semi-octagonal corner already prepared for the fireplace at one end of the large room.

"I'm not even sure this is the right fireplace," was her first reaction; but she soon realized that moving the fireplace to California without its English setting just did not work. The fireplace from Red House was still stored in the basement when the Hoovers finally came home.

To her husband's insistence that the house be fireproof, Mrs. Hoover brought an equal determination that it be flexible. She had been charmed with English homes which down the years had been remodeled to suit varying generations, and felt sure that she would want to build an added room here, or a bay window there. Hollow tile curtain walls with reinforced concrete columns, floors and roofs were the answer. Indeed, at one stage, the home looked much like a modern office building.

Somewhat dismaying to Birge Clark and his father was Hoover's idea of applying this flexibility to letting contracts as well as to design; for the Secretary of Commerce had insisted that spiralling costs were a post-war phenomenon. Each phase had to be separately contracted, because Hoover assured him that in 1920 costs would surely be lower!

Thus, with post-war shortages, it had taken years to finish the details of construction. Even in 1928 the house had not been completely ready to welcome the Republican nominee when he came home to make his acceptance speech. There was still no light fixture in the ceiling of the study. The temporary shade, fashioned by an obliging Palo Alto craftsman on a Saturday morning, was still reflecting indirect light from the cream-colored ceiling. Mrs. Hoover had handed Birge Clark a large brass Turkish tray, saying, "see what you can do with this." The lamp shade was the result.

That, like the plate glass window, had been a concession to the practical engineer. He never wholly approved of the dark ceiling in the living room, where three hundred little light bulbs were concealed in the burnished gold to give the effect of "cove lighting." The first time he saw this room during a brief visit to California, he wounded Mrs. Hoover's pride in her artistic accomplishment by saying, "It looks like early Pullman to me." Then he remarked with a smile, on the "antique plaster" effect being painstakingly achieved by a decorator, and that he had seen better looking basements in Belgium. The antiquing was promptly discontinued, but the cove in the living room had progressed too far to be changed.

By the spring of 1933, the home that welcomed its returning owners was filled with treasures and happy memories of growing grandchildren, friends, and relatives. Like all such well-used dwellings, it had known days of sorrow as well as joy. Here, Mrs. Henry had spent her last days, and once Herbert Hoover was called from his study by his frantic niece who found her younger brother floating face down in the swimming pool in the lower garden. His secretary, Bill Mullendore, tried to revive the little boy with artificial respiration, but the uncle stood with tear-drenched cheeks as Dr. Wilbur pronounced the effort futile.

Now the Hoovers had returned from the chill of a Washington winter to California, bright with fragrant acacia, to their own garden where early daffodils and pungent hyacinths invited them to days of leisure and companionship. But his study was the magnet for the man who could not easily throw off the burdens he had carried so long. Through the great plate glass window on clear days he could enjoy the full sweep of the Bay and Peninsula. When spring winds blew fog veils away from the crest of Mt. Tamalpais, he could see that sentinel across the Golden Gate above San Francisco. Mt. Diablo, silhouetted against the sky back of Oakland, sometimes gleamed white in the morning sun, its flanks snow-covered after a late March storm. If he turned to the east another window showed a myriad of blossoms bursting out in the prune orchards of the Santa Clara Valley.

But his inner vision swept far beyond this familiar landscape to encompass the whole world, most of which was equally vivid in his memory. His had been a lifetime of unremitting work. He could not change the pattern now. On this campus where he had once struggled so hard to meet the requirements of English I-B, this man of vast experience now sat at his desk to share his thoughts with posterity. In speeches and in magazine articles, he expressed anxiety over fundamental changes that were altering the American pattern as New Dealers tampered with tradition.

Finally, in the autumn of 1934, Scribners published his "Challenge to Liberty." In two-hundred pages of stern writing he intended to awaken America to dangers inherent in making permanent encroachments on the principles of liberty that had been introduced as emergency measures only. His faith in the ultimate triumph of individualism was reflected when he wrote: "The spark of liberty in the mind and spirit of man cannot be long extinguished; it will break into flames that will destroy every coercion which seeks to limit it."

The publication of this book brought invitations to speak in many parts of the country. Hoover was soon on trek again, explaining to those who would listen what had actually happened to cause the bank panic of 1933; debating national policies, which he described as "the buffeting of those in distress from one alphabetical agency to another—a sort of rainmaking cabalistic dance. When they are all buried, their spirit will live on as IOU."

As the Democratic press busied itself with the Congressional elections of that autumn, the Hoover administration was accused of accomplishing nothing at the same time that it was stigmatized as "little brothers of the rich, devoted to the bankers." "One would think," wrote Hoover to a friend, "that it might occur to somebody that in the most difficult part of the Depression—that is, the descending part—we managed by some device to maintain complete industrial peace."

The letter continued to point out that in his administration, "not a single soldier was called upon in an industrial conflict. Now the country is torn to pieces and militia are being called out in all directions to preserve public order."

He also reminded his friend that, in spite of the fact that his policies had helped to turn the tide of depression in July, 1932, when the United States, together with the rest of the world, was on the way up, this country had been the only one to stop enroute.

It was, however, among friends and neighbors on the Stanford Campus that he spoke his mind most freely. Dean J. Hugh Jackson, who had succeeded Hotchkiss in the Graduate School of Business, craved some of this first-hand information for his students. He would sometimes call the Hoover home to request the privilege of a question period for these leaders-in-training.

"Bring them up," the former President of the United States would answer. And a group of young men preparing to shoulder some of the tasks of a new era, sat informally around the great fireplace listening to his analyses of world conditions and his advice on their possible contribution to a better future.

Graduate students in business were not the only ones to profit from the years of Hoover's campus residence. Theodore Hoover had become Dean of the School of Engineering. His students, too, could learn from the brother who had given so many fruitful years to their profession. And if Herbert Hoover wished to stop as he walked from the engineering corner to Dr.

Wilbur's administration offices on the Outer Quad, he could discuss world food conditions with Alonzo Taylor in the Carnegie Food Research Headquarters.

Stanford women were also welcomed to the flat roofs overlooking their campus. An old friend of the Hoovers, widow of Gerrit J. Diekema, who had been Minister to the Netherlands during the Hoover Administration, was now Director of Roble Hall, the freshmen women's dormitory.

Often Mrs. Hoover would telephone her saying, "It is a beautiful evening. Will you bring some of the girls up to enjoy the terrace? I have sixty-five coffee cups."

Members of Cap and Gown, the Senior women's honor society, grew accustomed to Lou Henry Hoover's presence at their informal meetings, sometimes held on that same terrace, or in winter around the hospitable fireplace. And the local Girl Scouts shared the enthusiasm of their former national director in camp at Big Basin in the Santa Cruz mountains.

With release from major public service, Hoover was turning to some phases of his own chosen profession. The quicksilver mines, at New Idria in Central California were close enough to command frequent personal inspection. One lovely spring day the Hoovers asked Mrs. Diekema to join them on a trip to San Benito to visit these mines. En route the car stalled. The chauffeur was having difficulty when the former President, bending over the engine with him said, "Let me try." The practical hands of the son of an Iowa blacksmith had lost none of their skill. A few minutes of tinkering and the party was on its way.

That spring of 1935 Herbert Hoover was the Stanford Commencement speaker. He understood the problems of the students who were graduating into a world where jobs were scarce and poorly paid. He, too, had graduated into a depression era.

"White collar possibilities having been eliminated," he told them, "my first serious entrance into the economic world was by manual labor; but, somehow, both in the stages of manual labor and of professional work, I missed the discovery that I was a wage slave . . . I found a cheery and helpful lot of folks who took an enormous interest in helping young people to get a start and to get along in life. You will find that the case today. Human helpfulness has improved rather than deteriorated in this generation . . . If your course is wrongly directed," he said with marked emphasis, "civilization can go as deeply into eclipse as it did in the Middle Ages, despite all our gas and electricity and our knowledge of atoms and microbe organisms!"

Deep concern over the trend of American political life was reflected when he said: "Permanent social growth cannot be had by hot house methods. The soil of human nature requires infinite patience in search of useful plants, and equally in search for methods of elimination of weeds and pests. It requires experiments to develop the plants and to poison the pests. The essence of experiment is not to transform the whole field, but to try with a small part. Social security must be builded upon a cult of work—not a cult of leisure."

The former President assured the black-gowned students seated before him on the turf that "none of these attainments is beyond American capacity to realize. They can be achieved in the pure air of orderly liberty, nurtured through sacrifice in our generation—through faith, courage, and a steady will."

During that summer the Hoovers were invited to spend the Fourth of July weekend at a celebration in Grass Valley. Hoover replied that he would be glad to come, but that he did not need the services of a motorcycle escort nor a reception committee. He would prefer to watch rather than to participate in the parade.

Accompanied by Mr. and Mrs. Ben Allen of Palo Alto (invited because this former Food Administration aide and lifelong associate had been born at Ophir Hill near Grass Valley), the Hoovers motored up the hot valley to the Mother Lode country in the Sierra foothills. When they arrived, Hoover returned the greetings of old friends by saying that in mining circles, it was always a good recommendation to say that you came from Grass Valley. He felt that it was even better to come back, and that was why he was glad that he could accept the invitations of the citizens with whom he had worked in the mines.

The Hoovers were entertained in the home of Mr. and Mrs. Fred Nobs, the Stanford engineer who had represented his Nicaraguan interests long ago. Perhaps the Nobs persuaded their guests to change their minds about the parade. The next morning as it swung by the Bret Harte Inn, the Hoover car took its place behind the color guard and the Grass Valley concert band. In a friendly reminiscent mood, the former President rode the fifteen blocks receiving and returning hearty greetings.

After the Fourth of July ovation, Hoover was presented by Superior Judge Raglan Tuttle. His talk, spontaneous and from his heart, had been mapped out earlier that morning as he sat at Mrs. Nob's desk. He said that as they met to commemorate the signing of the Declaration of Independence, the courage of that act and the great human achievements which flowed from it should lift spirits above the tangles of the day. With whimsical humor he referred to his pleasure in returning to the scene of his first mining job, remarking that the prosperity of these two camps since he had left to go to Australia seemed to prove that his labors had not produced all the gold from those mines. He referred also to the visit that George Starr had made to him in Kalgoorlie, expressing appreciation for the sage advice the older man had given about sticking to a chosen job, regardless of early difficulties.

After the parade a group of the men, whose acquaintance he had made as fellow miners forty-one years before, sat with him at luncheon in the Bret Harte Inn. As the editor of the *Nevada City Morning Union* remarked, it was probably a gathering with no comparable precedent in American history. Gassoway, Ninnis, and others who had shared his days of mucking, laughingly called the former President "Bert" and "Fatty," joking with him about the time he had been sent laboriously to the surface, "to secure the key to the sump."

Contact with professional friends of earlier years began to lure him further from the Stanford hilltop. Invitations to reenter the business world roused his active mind. With Julius

Barnes, former president of the Grain Corporation, and others of his eastern associates, he formed the Inter-Continental Development Company. He also crossed the continent regularly to attend meetings of the Board of Directors of the New York Life Insurance Company.

These trips, too, meant that he did not lose touch with old friends and their interests. On one trip he learned that Vernon Kellogg's daughter, recently graduated from Yale Art School, was to have her first "one-man show." Walking through the door into the flower-filled New York studio where Jean and her mother were supervising the hanging, he greeted the artist by her childhood pet name.

"Hello, Rabbit," he said. "I came to see the pictures. You show them to me yourself."

Then he turned to his companions, one of whom carried a camera.

"Meet my friends," he said, introducing reporters from the *New York Times*. He posed with Jean looking at an oil of the Monterey Coast. The next morning the picture was published with the caption—"Two Californians look at a familiar scene."

Chapter Twenty-seven

TRAVELER WITHOUT PORTFOLIO

During these years of comparative leisure, Hoover received invitations from scattered former associates in far places, urging him to visit and observe what was happening on the international scene. Then, one day late in 1937, a distinguished caller arrived at the Stanford home. He was Count Robert van der Straten-Ponthoz, Belgian Ambassador to the United States. He brought an official invitation, requesting that the "Friend of the Belgian People and Honorary Citizen of Belgium" return to his "foster country" for a twentieth reunion of former members of the Comité National de Secours et Alimentation. The idea of assembling these former associates to honor the chairman of the C.R.B. had been the inspiration of M. Felicien Cattier, who had succeeded the late Emile Francqui as president of the Fondation Universitaire.

Hoover was convinced that the time had come to re-visit Europe as a private citizen, with no compulsions beyond his own desires as to what he should see or say. Accompanied by Paul Smith, young editor of the *San Francisco Chronicle*, and Perrin Galpin, executive director of the Belgian American Education Foundation, he sailed from New York in February, 1938.

The party was met in Le Havre by Captain Tracy Kittredge, then on the staff of the Rockefeller Foundation, who had assisted in planning the itinerary.

His old associates and newer admirers gathered in a *Séance Solonele* at the University of Brussels. Le Baron Carton de Wiart and Edgar Sengier greeted the former chairman of the

C.R.B., reminding him of the days of 1914 when they worked together daily to save the Belgian people. Firmin von Bree was there, too, his black eyes twinkling above a waist-long, wavy beard. Von Bree, now president of the Hoover Foundation for the University of Louvain, talked about the Centre of Pisciculture he planned to establish in the nearby village of Linkebeck and predicted important results from scientific fish culture.

Louis Solvay, the Belgian philanthropist who had first called a relief committee to aid refugees during the earliest days of the German invasion, was present, as was M. Edmond Labbé of the Committee for Northern France, recently Commissioner for the Paris Exposition of 1937. His response on behalf of the people of France closed with a tribute to The Chief as the apostle of Peace.

A bust of Francqui draped with Belgian and American flags looked down from the mantel, seeming to bring that vital personality into the midst of the meeting of the group he had commanded so long ago.

Hoover's reply to salutations at another dinner noted the progress of Belgium in the years since he had last sat with these friends. "It is one of the only countries where production and well-béing progress regularly . . . Here is written one of the most moving chapters in the history of human liberty." On this occasion he received the Vermeil Medal of Honor, a distinction shared with only one other living person—King Leopold.

On the cover of the weekly *Pourquoi Pas* was a smiling Herbert Hoover, who would have been unrecognizable to most of his compatriots at home. Perhaps it would have been more familiar to his underground companions of Nevada City, who had seen that crinkling smile spread over his face when they told their "Cousin Jack" stories. Several columns of the leading article reviewed the career of Belgium's famous guest and enumerated the many causes for gratitude they owed this man from across the sea.

In Liége he dined with the Minister of Foreign Affairs, Paul Spaak, and received an honorary M.S. from the University of Liége. Hoover combined a call on Madame Francqui with his reception at the University of Ghent where he received an honorary Ph.D. His plan to limit his visits to the Universities sharing the C.R.B. Educational Fund was altered only for a pause in the city of Namur to sign the Golden Book.

Before he left Belgium he had an invitation to confer with Hitler in Berlin. Their forty-minute interview bristled with clashing viewpoints. The former President informed Hitler that the United States would never become reconciled to Nazism as a political and national creed. He added his personal doubts as to whether the system would endure within Germany itself, because no political structure could be practical without intellectual freedom.

Hitler replied with ironic bitterness that such liberty could be afforded only in a country with great natural resources. "You may be able to indulge in cooperation," he snapped. "I just order."

Then Hitler confided to the former American President that it was essential to find more food for starving Germany; that he planned to take the Ukraine, not only for that purpose, but also to show Russia the might of the German Army.

Later Hoover was the luncheon guest of United States Ambassador Wilson. Here he discussed current world problems with Baron Konstantin von Neurath, chairman of the German Council on Foreign Policy, Dr. Hjalmar Schacht, president of the Reichsbank, and the British, French, and Polish Ambassadors.

During the dinner at the Carl Schurz Foundation, Dr. Schacht toasted Herbert Hoover as "the protagonist of conscience, humanitarianism and international understanding. . . There is a certain tragic element in the fact that the man who had the noblest ideas and the most humanitarian thoughts was unable to bring his ideals to full success because of the mistakes and consequences of post-war times. . . But we may yet expect great things from the man who is our guest tonight."

Such words of appreciation, sometimes accompanied by gifts, highlighted all those days. The German secret police were always on guard. When they ripped the wrappings from one large package (fearing a bomb) they found a picture of the late Czarina, the tribute of a grateful White Russian. Hoover, too, had a gift to bestow. When he learned that seven-year-old Axel *Hoover* Gebhard had been born on the day that Hoover had proposed the Debt Moratorium, June 20, 1931, the former President gave the lad a piece of silver ore studded with garnets. The boy could only say "Hello" and "Good-bye" in English, but his radiant smile was thanks enough.

Even Goering offered hospitality. During a dinner at his country estate, Hoover was startled to see a gold bust of the late Frau Goering in the center of the dining table, presided over by Goering's current wife. But Hoover was alerted by the boastful tales of naval and air strength with which his host monopolized the conversation.

The threat of strength seemed so menacing that Hoover decided he must stop long enough in London to confide his information to important British leaders. He must advise them that if Hitler started to march on Poland, it would be wise not to try to stop him. Hitler's objective lay East, not West!

Before he crossed the Channel, however, there were many other calls to make. Perhaps the most touching of all the receptions in Europe was during his trip through Poland. Young men and women who were alive only because his Mission had come to succor them in their extremity pressed his hand in gratitude. Probably among them were some he had last seen chasing the rabbit across Mokolowski Park in 1919.

Everywhere homage was paid. The French welcomed The Chief at Lille Dormitory, where students presented a *beret d'honneur*—designating him a "citizen of honor" among them. Crowds and officials greeted him wherever he stopped in Paris, Zurich, Vienna, Prague, Cracow, Riga. At Helsinki he was the first foreigner in ninety-nine years to receive an honorary degree from their University. Although he had been Commander-in-Chief of the United States Army, he had never owned a sword. The gold-handled blade presented at this ceremony caused much embarrassment and almost upset the solemnity. Since Hoover wore suspenders and no belt, the official who presented it fumbled in great confusion until he hit upon the idea of hooking the handle through a suspender fastener. Then the long scabbard became so entangled in the recipient's legs that he nearly lost his balance!

That celebration safely over, the Hoover party went on to London via Stockholm. Having imparted his Berlin fears to proper British officials, he returned to America. Here he was forthright in warnings of what he foresaw in the disturbed countries he had visited. He shared with his closest friends deep-rooted forebodings over the new ideology rising in Germany. He felt that this fanatic Nazi dictatorship was pregnant with danger for the whole world.

In San Francisco he told a reporter that if the world was to keep the peace, the United States must learn to get along with dictators, as well as with popular governments, that the form of other governments was not the business of the United States.

"We can never herd the world into paths of righteousness with the dogs of war," he said. "Our watchword should be absolute independence of political action and at the same time, adequate preparedness. . . Our national mission is to keep alight the lamp of true liberalism, *but it is in the United States that we must keep it alight.*"

Chapter Twenty-eight

SPURNED ADVISOR

THROUGHOUT THE INTERVENING years Hoover never swerved from his self-appointed task as keeper of ". . . the lamp of true liberalism." But his determination to tend the light in person sometimes caused concern among members of his party. Three years before, in the summer of 1935, the country was still smarting under what was dubbed by his political opponents "The Hoover Depression." Some of his Washington associates proposed that if he would keep in the background politically in the coming campaign, he would probably emerge in 1940 as the Elder Statesman. He might even become the Republican nominee.

Hoover was adamant in refusing such a course. He was determined to bend every effort toward defeating the Roosevelt philosophy, which he maintained was contrary to fundamental American tradition. He questioned the strength of the favored Republican candidate, Governor Alfred Landon of Kansas, in a contest with the popular New Dealer. Then, in an attempt to infuse the Party with new determination, he invited a few leaders to be his house guests on the Stanford campus. Colonel Frank Knox, Ogden Mills, Governor Nice of Maryland, and a few others accepted. Governor Landon sent his regrets because of pressing gubernatorial duties. Those who came spent hours devising plans to defeat Roosevelt.

When his guests departed Hoover took to the road again. From Oregon to Indiana, from Ohio to Colorado he talked earnestly about "The Confused State of the Union." As titular head of the Party he tried to rouse Republicans everywhere to their patriotic duty. As he met these people he could not be insensible to a "Draft Hoover" movement among thousands of loyal supporters who were trying to pledge delegates for the nomination he insisted that he did not want. Almost up to the time of the Cleveland Convention he told his associates that he would not attend.

Privately, Hoover distrusted forces pushing the nomination of Landon, especially when the Hearst papers took up the cause in California. But he had confidence in his own Kansas friend, William Allen White, editor of the *Emporia Gazette,* who was enthusiastically working for Governor Landon. White's insistence that for the sake of larger issues Hoover should add endorsement to the Landon boom, brought the former President to Cleveland.

Here he was rewarded by a standing ovation on the first night when the keynoter, Senator William Stiewer of Oregon, reminded the country of Roosevelt's failure to cooperate in Hoover's efforts to avert the bank panic of 1933. In spite of rumors that men like Colonel Knox and Senators Borah and Vandenburgh were behind a "Stop Landon" movement the Kansas sunflower banners dominated the convention and Governor Landon remained the favorite. Behind the scenes loyal Hooverites still hoped that some eventuality would force their reluctant candidate to change his mind.

On the second day Hoover came to the platform. He assailed the Administration's attempts to solve the nation's business problems with "Mother Hubbard economics." He left the stage in a din of acclaim, still turning deaf ears to its implication. Later one of his closest friends sought him out at his hotel to voice the refrain heard repeatedly during the recess following his speech: "If Herbert Hoover as much as sets foot in the Convention Hall again tonight, he will be nominated." Hoover was unmoved.

"I do not want the nomination," he replied. "My only concern is that the Party be strong and wise enough to choose a man who can lead America back to fundamentals."

He was probably the only man who could have accomplished that purpose then, but he boarded a train at two o'clock in the morning to sleep a few hours en route to New York. In Cleveland the men who might have urged him back into office were smoking on through interminable committee meetings.

The next day Chester Rowell, Chairman of the California Delegation, had a telegram from Hoover, advising him on the wording of a currency plank in the party platform. It was evident that his brain would be in the fight even if his person had been decisively removed from the emotional scene. He wired to Rowell that all Presidential powers over currency should be repealed. He insisted that the plank should guarantee no further devaluation, should seek international agreement to stabilize currencies and should resolutely determine to restore gold convertibility as soon as it should become wise and practicable.

In spite of his personal doubts as to Landon's effectiveness, once the Kansan was chosen by the Convention, Hoover got behind the campaign. He believed that unless Roosevelt was ousted the nation would face repeated crises as crucial as the depression from which he refused Hoover's offer to help lead the nation.

Beaten, but not discouraged, by the 1936 election, he continued his educational tours, speaking out vehemently in February when Roosevelt tried to pack the Supreme Court. The Union League Club of Chicago heard strong words when he spoke to them on the theme, "Hands Off the Supreme Court."

Before the 1940 election year the war that Hoover could see brewing in Europe during his tour had erupted and was raging. He was filled with anxiety over the plight of the countries invaded by the German "blitzkrieg." In Poughkeepsie, he stirred his audience with prophecies of famine in "The Five Little Democracies"—Belgium, Holland, Norway, Finland, and Central Poland.

"Whoever is right or wrong," he said, "these little nations are ground between two millstones, German requisitions and

British blockade. . . . The operation required in those countries is Food Administration, not individual relief in the ordinary sense. . . . When one speaks of war to me, I do not see the glorious parade of troops marching to gay music . . . I cannot forget the faces of the hungry, despairing, and terrorized women and little children, who are the real victims of modern war. . . ."

Hoover words, as usual, were backed with action. He knew that a few hours after Hitler's invasion of Poland his former aide, Maurice Pate, had left the New York investment firm he had joined in 1935 to volunteer whatever assistance he could give to that "adopted country." Hoover was quick to help form a commission for Polish Relief, using his influence to have Pate named president of this private organization. In Pate's capable hands he knew that food stuffs and relief supplies of all kinds would soon be moving from America and Scandinavia to mutual friends who were struggling for life.

Thoughts were divided now between the plight of the millions of famine-threatened European children and what seemed to Hoover disastrous trends in American political life. He approached the 1940 election year more than ever determined to "save America for free men." Wendell Wilkie, another impassioned exponent of free enterprise, had come out of the Middle West. In Philadelphia, Wilkie had a gallery full of cheering supporters, reminding Hoover of 1920. When this untried candidate, who had changed from Democrat to Republican, won the nomination on the sixth ballot, Hoover and his Old Guard associates were baffled and alarmed. Something in the emotional fervor of this "Dark Horse" candidate seemed to arouse suspicion. Hoover told a dinner companion that he doubted Wilkie's sincerity; but as the campaign progressed, he was on the trains again, speeding from one great city to another as he fought vehemently against Roosevelt's campaign for a third term.

"We are almost the last stand in this world today of representative government under which only limited powers rest in any man's hand," he told an audience in Columbus, Ohio,

"If we are to make sure that kind of government is not to perish, we must do it here and now by the election of Wendell Wilkie."

But Hoover's logic and choruses singing "God Bless America" under the evangelistic direction of Wilkie with his tireless smile and fervent energy, could not rouse enough votes to change the country's leadership. Roosevelt remained in Washington, and Hoover returned to his Stanford hilltop to read, listen, and think ever more seriously about his country.

Although Roosevelt had invited Hoover's Secretary of State, Henry L. Stimson, and Colonel Frank Knox into his Cabinet, he still disregarded the experienced voice of his predecessor. Hoover urged repeal of the Neutrality Act. He wrote to Sol Bloom, chairman of the House Committee on Foreign Affairs, regarding possible dangers in lend-lease. He spoke somberly of America's unpreparedness; of disunity within the country. He traveled from coast to coast speaking at college commencements.

On June 19, 1941 he addressed a Symposium at the fiftieth anniversary of the founding of Stanford University. The following day he participated in the dedication of a lasting tribute to his prophetic vision, the Hoover Institution on War, Revolution and Peace. That monumental Library, with its tower dominating the Stanford landscape, had been built with funds raised by associates in every period of Hoover's varied career. Its stacks were filled with irreplacable documents gathered from governments and organizations all over the world. Its use was dedicated to the great motivating ideal that kept its founder unceasingly at work.

"Surely," said that founder, "from these records, there can be help to mankind in its confusions and perplexities, and its yearnings for peace."

Hoover's dynamic mind was never content with a *fait accompli*. He was soon on his way again, broadcasting from Chicago a week later what he termed a "Call to American Reason." Fearful lest insistent demands to join the war against Hitler should sweep the country into battles for which it was not ready, he answered arguments, one by one.

To the people who said that the United States could aid their British friends better on the firing line than as an arsenal, he maintained that essential production was more necessary than fighting. He warned, too, that should America enter the war, Japan would be drawn in. To those who said that Hitler intended to attack and that this nation should gain the advantage of being the first in offensive action, Hoover insisted that entry of the United States into such a war would only increase moral and economic wastage. If the United States stayed out, here at least would be preserved much that could be used for reconstruction of a war-damaged world.

Aid to Stalin and his militant communism, said Hoover, would be a conspiracy against all democratic ideals. He reminded listeners that on August 22, 1939, Stalin and Hitler had agreed upon a joint onslaught against the democracies of the world. Nine days after that, their attack on the Poles had destroyed the freedom of this great democratic people. Fourteen days later, Latvia, Lithuania, and Esthonia had met similar fate. And two months later Russia invaded Finland.

"If we go further and join this war and we win," Hoover warned, "then we will have won for Stalin the grip of communism on Russia and a greater opportunity for it to extend in the world. We should at least cease to tell our sons that they will be giving their lives to restore democracy and freedom."

By October, he was worrying again about the fate of the children of Europe. Senator Butler of Nebraska, a staunch friend who still appreciated Hoover wisdom, asked that part of Hoover's radio speech from New York, entitled, "Can Europe's Children be Saved?" should be written into the Congressional Record as "one of the greatest speeches made to the American people in our day."

In this speech the former President had revealed that with some of his colleagues he had directed a small stream of relief to fifty thousand children in Poland since the present war began. He added that daily appeals from the people of the little democracies were constant reminders that helpless people cannot eat morals and international laws.

Pearl Harbor changed the focus. Visions of "terrorized women and children who are the real victims" were transposed from Belgian and French faces to possible American ones. Hoover was in New York. On December 8, 1941, he exhorted his fellow citizens to fight with all they had. He had opposed the foreign policy of the Administration. He believed better alternatives could have been devised. Now, whatever differences had existed would have to be threshed out by history. He was ready to offer any assistance his preparation fitted him for. The ears in the White House were still deaf!

Throughout America, however, there were thousands who still turned to Hoover for guidance. Close friends knew that the desk on San Juan Hill held many pages of personal memoirs of World War I. As America faced new threats and new responsibilities, the public should have the benefit of his accumulated wisdom. Finally, they persuaded him that the portion dealing with the Treaty of Versailles should be published.

Appearing first in the *Saturday Evening Post,* "America's First Crusade" was later brought out in book form by Scribners. Step by step, he traced the contribution of America to the defeat of one system of despotism and militarism. At the same time he pointed poignantly to the failure to achieve a peace based on justice, or the farseeing statesmanship that replaces conflict with cooperation.

"North America," he wrote, "is the only nation since the Crusades that has fought the battles of other people at her own gigantic loss. We may be proud of this Crusade, even if it largely failed, for some help and light did come to mankind and valuable experience to America."

Shortly after America's entry into World War II, Hoover asked Hugh Gibson to join him in enlarging this book into a longer volume whose purpose should help guide toward victory beyond that of the battlefield. The introduction to "The Problems of Lasting Peace" outlined the "single purpose now uniting all Americans—to achieve victory and thereafter to build a world where we can hope to live in peace and security."

Hoover was convinced that "only from lasting peace can we hope to save our civilization." He was dedicated to the faith that by sharing some of his own disillusioning experiences he could inspire leaders now locked in desperate struggle to grasp the significance of the opportunity that could be theirs in eventual victory.

The book warned of the necessity to be wide awake. Ideas might shift, but human nature would not be greatly changed. Unless the forces of fear, hate, and revenge could be turned aside, the authors predicted that the ceaseless treadmill of war would go on and on. With all the fervor of his maternal inheritance, Herbert Hoover concluded that "moral concepts are far more important than police if there is to be a peace. . . despite all that has happened in nineteen hundred years, the Sermon on the Mount has thundered down the ages and now it thunders anew."

The book was hard, brain-testing reading; but the public seemed hungry for substantial mental food. In October, Hoover wrote to William Allen White that sales were holding up astonishingly well for a serious book in times of public bewilderment. He confided to his friend, too, that he was planning to have some twenty thousand copies distributed free to high schools in order that young debaters might have authentic material.

Colliers for November 28 and December 5 carried the Hoover warning, "We'll Have to Feed the World Again." He reviewed for the American public the details of his long experience in feeding post-war Europe, both the liberated countries and the former enemy territory. He reminded them, too, that had the blockade been lifted immediately the course of history might have been different. He pointed out, as he had done in 1918, that such steps should be taken at once when the Second World War ended. Then statesmen could take time to settle the details of reconstruction and retribution during a period of provisional peace.

No rebuffs from the White House could silence the one man who knew more than anyone in the world of ways to meet such crises. Early in January, the National Broadcasting Company offered radio time to the former Food Administrator for his comments on the proposed rationing of food. He recalled the loyal army of housewives and school children in 1917-1918 as he reminded his listeners that "the American people are the most cooperative in the world and the hardest to drive. . ." Production, and more production, he insisted, would be the surest way to avoid rationing. He also counselled that agriculture should be placed in the first rank of war effort, along with planes and ships.

Now that America was fighting on the side of the Allies, the responsibility for feeding starving women, children, and unemployed men in German-invaded democracies was even more insistent than it had been when Hoover had first pleaded for the *Five Little Democracies*. He accepted the invitation of *The Christian Advocate* to use their pages.

"In the Name of Humanity" he wrote as one who had dealt with famine among millions of war victims. He had hoped that such starvation as he had seen would never afflict mankind again; but now that war had come, he would be untrue to himself and his country if he did not fight to the end to ameliorate these new conditions.

Still the President did not call on the experienced humanitarian to help formulate relief policies. Many others recognized the practical answer to Hoover's plans. General Pershing urged that the United States adopt the Hoover proposals. Admiral Pratt said publicly that: "Taking the long view, it is of vital importance to America that Mr. Hoover's plans be carried through."

But they were still studiously ignored by President Roosevelt!

CHAPTER TWENTY-NINE

OCCASIONAL CONSULTANT

EARLY IN FEBRUARY 1943 the Senate Committee on Appropriations sought Hoover's advice on the American manpower problem. He arrived in Washington promptly to testify freely and constructively, withholding any criticism of the Administration. At last there were some who were waking to the fact that a wise counsellor was available.

Next, the Conference of Mid-West Governors invited the former President to Des Moines. He brought current data from the Carnegie Food Institute to add to his own wide knowledge of world conditions. He told these men that when war ceased there would be millions to feed in Europe and Asia, a burden that America would have to assume not only out of compassion, but also in self-defense.

Although he still had no official responsibility, Hoover devoted full time to the cause of winning the war and planning the peace. He was in and out of Pullmans, composing speeches to the accompaniment of clicking wheels, carrying him from one part of the country to another, making what he called "Addresses On The American Road." For a few brief weekends he relaxed under the redwoods of the Bohemian Grove or enjoyed fishing trips to the Klamath. Otherwise he was constantly writing article after article.

In November, 1943, he was the speaker at the opening of the United Church canvas in New York. He pointed out that for the first time in history sixteen creeds and denominations, Christian and Jewish, were speaking with a single voice to the people of America. The fact that all were uniting in an effort to raise funds to assuage suffering abroad was to him proof that the world was hungering for spiritual strength.

Then, suddenly the calm life-partner whose spiritual strength had buoyed him in every undertaking, succumbed to a heart attack. The Hoovers were living in the Waldorf Towers most of the year, for the Stanford Campus had proved too far from his pressing interests. Cheerfully, with no outward sign of regret, Lou Henry Hoover had once more closed the door of her dream house and crossed the continent to remain at the side of the man who needed her most when others misinterpreted and misunderstood his ideals and motives.

Although his first granddaughter was now a freshman at Stanford, and Dr. Wilbur (recently retired) was readily accessible in his new office in the Hoover Tower, Hoover did not remain to seek solace among family and old friends after the California funeral. He gave his key to the house on San Juan Hill to the new President of the University, Donald Tresidder and his wife, who preferred not to live in the forbidding presidential mansion overlooking Lake Lagunita. Then he departed for New York.

There he quietly took up his pen again, writing for the people who must save America from inroads on their heritage of freedom—inroads that he feared were causing a breakdown of national character.

With a purpose that was deeper than the title indicated, he tried out some typical Hoover philosophy in an article in *Colliers,* entitled, "Let's Go Fishing"—advice that probably would be followed more readily than his many treatises on government duties!

"The reason for a fishing trip," he wrote, "is the chance to wash one's soul with pure air, with the rush of the brook or the shimmer of the sun on blue waters. It brings meekness and inspiration from the decency of nature, charity towards tacklemakers, patience towards fish, a mockery of profits and egos, the quieting of hate, a rejoicing that you do not have to decide a darned thing until next week. And it is discipline as to the equality of men, for all men are equal before fish."

This was 1944, another Presidential election year. Hoover retained confidence that the time must have come for the Republicans to take over the affairs of the troubled nation. He went to Chicago to challenge another convention with the necessity of devoting the best they had to remove personal power diplomacy from America. He spoke fervently to the youth who were there. They should go forth again as crusaders—crusaders for a freedom that alone could come under a Constitutional Republic, a Constitutional America."

Again, voice and pen were used unstintedly for a losing cause. Governor Dewey, as had Landon and Wilkie, went down before the stranglehold of the Roosevelt regime on American politics.

War dragged into a fourth year of sorrow and sacrifice. The man who had borne so many burdens for America still stubbornly gave unsought advice. Even as plans were formulated for a meeting of the United Nations in San Francisco, no one in high place remembered that Herbert Hoover was the one man whose experience had encompassed the whole world. They seemed to forget that the English economist, John Maynard Keynes, had written of him after Versailles as one of two men who came out of that conference with an enhanced reputation.

Planners of the conference ignored all of Hoover's years of thought and service, all of his books, his articles, his speeches devoted to programs for peace and world cooperation. Nevertheless, as the time approached for the meeting, Hoover published four more articles, suggesting additions to the Dumbarton Oaks proposals being considered at the time as a basis for the United Nations Charter.

His first criticism was that the great principles of political rights of nations and men were wholly absent from the original proposals. He warned that the world was in danger of setting up a purely mechanistic body, without spiritual inspiration.

Hoover felt, too, that the Dumbarton Oaks plan was inadequate. It included the creation of one world committee to promote economic welfare and another to promote social justice. He suggested the creation of a third world committee to promote political rights. This carried out an idea that he and Hugh Gibson had incorporated in their book when he outlined a more definite regional organization. Groups in the Western Hemisphere, Europe and Asia should deal first with all controversies that might lead to war in their respective areas. If these groups should fail to secure settlement, only then should the World Security Council intervene.

He was insistent that the United Nations Charter, or a separate agreement, should be based upon continued and total disarmament of the enemy; but he said that the United Nations should keep a force of 100,000 men in Germany and the same number in Japan for a generation at least. He drew on his own experience in working for limitation of armaments through the League of Nations, when he warned that there should be a much more definite program for limitation of size of military establishments among the members of the United Nations than that which was then planned. He closed with a plea that plenty of time be taken in formulating the eventual shape of a world organization because its purpose must be to create a regime of law and justice in the world, not regencies of hate.

When the United Nations Conference in San Francisco opened, Hoover was not even in California. He spoke from Philadelphia at a meeting of the Foreign Policy Association on April 17, saying that he knew he expressed the sorrow of the American people that President Roosevelt had not been spared to guide the San Francisco Conference. He added that since problems remained as they were, the nation must rally behind the new President in his gigantic task.

The main burden of this talk was to point out that the primary weakness of the Holy Alliance, the League of Nations, and Dumbarton Oaks proposals had been the failure to face facts as to the real causes of war. He outlined suggested remedies, concluding with his familiar refrain, "truly peace is a matter of spirit resting upon moral forces, upon the building of good will among mankind."

Hoover stayed in the East until after VE Day. On May 16 he urged that the U.S. Army take over the problem of feeding the peoples of the liberated countries of Western Europe until harvest time three months hence. During this time, he said, it would be possible to organize a better method of dealing with rehabilitation. As one who had administered post-war relief all over the world, he knew from experience that supplying food was as urgent as preserving order.

He returned to California while the United Nations meeting in San Francisco was still in session. After the Charter was signed, so many people asked for his opinion that he broadcast his answer on July 18. He conceded that the Charter was better than the Dumbarton Oaks version, and probably as good as could be obtained under existing emotions. He recommended that it should be ratified by the Senate promptly; but he warned that it did not contain the basis for lasting peace. He pointed out that it did not recover the principles of the Atlantic Charter which had been whittled away at Teheran and after Yalta.

He predicted that peace could come only if the leaders of the victorious nations would differentiate between the militarists and the common people in the defeated countries. Stern justice to war criminals must not be transformed into vengeance. Although he believed in total disarmament for defeated people, he urged that those nations be assisted to restore their productivity as a contribution to the economic recovery of the entire world. While he saw faults in some of the decisions in San Francisco, he said that he felt the Preamble to the Charter was an expression of hope. If its ideas could be carried out in the political and economic settlements of the war, then there was hope that lasting peace might be achieved.

The day after his seventy-first birthday, Hoover was in Long Beach attending a reunion of the Iowa Association of Southern California. The following day the streets were wild with excitement of Japanese surrender. Hoover spoke solemnly as he answered requests for a public statement. With deep thankfulness to God that this most hideous war of all history was ended, he warned that the era just ahead would demand high statesmanship.

With undiminished energy he kept on the road. A month later, his old associate General Dawes introduced him to the Executives' Club in Chicago. There he spoke to men who understood his blunt language. He told them that never in human history had there been such a demand for wisdom and imagination in facing the common problems of mankind. He was sure that faith might be restored if leaders approached their solution with generosity and tolerance; but he cautioned that idealism must be guided by men with feet planted firmly on the ground. He believed that the United States should not expect much, if any, repayment of the $40-billion of lend-lease; that there should be a world-wide moratorium on all intergovernmental war debts for five years, during which time all weapons furnished under lend-lease should be destroyed.

On the economic level, he reminded them that there were certain commodities in all nations in which there was a surplus. The United States had an abundance of wheat, cotton, machinery, and some metals, while the British had rubber and tin; the Russians manganese and wood pulp, and the Dutch more tin and rubber. The exchange of such surpluses immediately could be undertaken with mutual benefit. The former President made a strong plea that America should help to the limit of what taxpayers could afford, organizing aid in a way that would minimize any possible ill will.

As an engineer and as a statesman, Hoover was seriously concerned with future use of the atom bomb. But he was not consulted. Through the press he suggested methods of control of this most terrible and barbaric weapon. He reminded readers that all international agreements not to use poison gas in war had been adhered to because each nation was fearful of reprisals should they break this promise. Although such an agreement regarding the A-Bomb would not guarantee against its use in war, it still might put some brake on the intention to use it.

As a geologist Hoover proposed that if the control of uranium ore were placed under the Security Council, the use of atomic energy might be limited to peaceful arts. In the interest of civilization, he hoped that the United States and Great Britain would not share the secrets of A-Bomb manufacture with any other nation.

He had other words of warning. The age-old Palestine problem was the subject of an article in the *New York Herald Tribune.* "Why not," he wrote, "finance Iraq as a home for Arabs and clear Palestine for large Jewish emigration and colonization?"

He described the broad extent and fertile soil of ancient lands bordering on the Tigris and the Euphrates, the traditional Garden of Eden. This he could picture from personal knowledge. As for the Arabs, he wrote, they would be among others of their own race and religion; the land they would be given would be vastly superior to the bare brown hills of Palestine; Iraq would gain agriculture population needed to restore their valleys to the state attained centuries ago before Mongol invaders destroyed their irrigation works and caused the population to shrink from ten to three-and-a-half million. He offered this challenge to the statesmanship of the Great Powers and to the good will of the countries involved.

Washington still spurned his ideas and programs. But educational institutions from one side of the continent to the other were listening as he prompted from the wings of the public stage. Those new actors about to play parts on a confused world platform listened to one who knew that every line would need to be spoken with courage and sensitivity to moral wrong. Wise leaders continued to hang bright hoods denoting honorary degrees upon his aging shoulders, thus showing recognition that transcended temporary repudiation in government circles.

Once more he came back to the campus he knew and loved best to make a gift overshadowing every other in tender significance. Returning the rent money from the San Juan Hill house to the Board of Trustees, he deeded his home to the university as a permament residence for the president. Over the door a simple bronze plaque memoralized it as "The Lou Henry Hoover House."

Chapter Thirty

OFFICIAL WELCOME BACK TO PUBLIC SERVICE

In 1946 when leaden skies closed in on wintry Manhattan and snow flurries swirled down Park Avenue, Herbert Hoover took his own advice and went fishing off the sunny Florida Keys. But he did not stay long.

Just before he left New York he talked with reporters about various current subjects. Senator Fullbright had consulted him on the pending bill involving educational exchanges. This had delighted Hoover as the chairman of the Belgian-American Educational Foundation, and he saw an opportunity for the United States to take the lead in providing a broader base for world understanding.

However, his Florida vacation was interrupted by the more immediate urgency in his other published comments on President Truman's appeal to the people of America to help avert threatened world famine.

"Peace and progress will not be restored," Hoover wrote, "if those who survive are to be infected by a generation of men and women stunted in body and distorted in mind."

In the White House the worried President must have pondered Hoover's warnings as he read of infant mortality in some areas on the continent as well over fifty percent; and was reminded of the voluntary cooperation of housewives, restaurants and the food trade in 1917. Hoover contended that the facts would prove that food consumption per capita had been no more, and was probably less, under the voluntary food administration than under the recent rationing.

On the last day of February 1946 in response to an S.O.S. from President Truman, the former President, tanned and fit, alighted from a Navy plane at the Washington airport. Accustomed to the familiar Hoover blue serge suit and high white collar, that was almost a uniform during his long years in public life, the reporters remarked on the becoming brown tweed and soft shirt.

When Herbert Hoover stepped across the threshold of the White House for the first time since he had left in March 1933 he was welcomed by a man humbled in the face of unexpected responsibilities for which he was not prepared. Harry Truman recognized the vast store of knowledge on which he could draw and turned to the man of experience.

The President told his caller that he had asked him to come to Washington to assume the honorary chairmanship of a famine emergency committee, to which he had invited twelve outstanding national leaders. In his public acceptance of this appointment Hoover repeated his conviction that Americans should voluntarily eat less food, reduce waste and use substitute food. Europeans, he said, were accustomed to wheat. As an Iowan he extolled the merits of corn bread.

The press responded quickly. Attractive pictures of crisp corn muffins appeared on women's pages, with recipes for appetizing variations. Housewives were urged to substitute oatmeal for toast at breakfast, and potatoes for bread at dinner.

This was a propitious beginning, but the President realized that more first-hand data would be necessary to further popularize the food saving program. He turned to the honorary chairman of the emergency committee. Would Mr. Hoover be willing to gather an appropriate staff who could accompany him on a quick world food survey? Hoover agreed and the President immediately designated Dr. D. A. Fitzgerald, food allocation officer of the Department of Agriculture, as government representative on such a trip.

The Chief knew exactly where to turn for experienced aides in this undertaking. He also was sure that while he and his selected group were making the survey, they must have the home backing of an enlarged National Emergency Famine Committee. One-hundred and twenty-five telegrams went across the country, inviting key persons to serve under Chester A. Davis, a St. Louis banker who agreed to be chairman. For vice chairman Hoover suggested Eugene Meyer, then owner of the *Washington Post.* He knew that the rugged former chairman of the Federal Reserve Board would help to vitalize this program. Among the group who accepted the challenge were men like James W. Young, of the New York Advertising Council; the famed director of public opinion polls Dr. George H. Gallup, and Anna Lord Strauss, president of the National League of Women Voters.

On the eve of the departure of the survey team the emergency committee gathered in Washington. Their honorary chairman outlined what he felt was a legitimate appeal to the American people. He predicted that by a voluntary decrease in consumption of forty per cent in wheat products and twenty per cent of fats in the coming four months in the U.S.A., famine could be averted in less fortunate countries. Once more, he challenged fellow citizens to don their overalls and grow victory gardens.

"Guns," he said, "speak the first word of victory; but only food can speak the last."

Before leaving America he broadcast a nation-wide appeal, asking that every family imagine that they had invited an invisible guest to their table. Surely no right-thinking citizen would let a neighbor go hungry. The starving women and children across the seas must be considered neighbors in the shrinking world. With a touch of irony he reminded listeners of his repeated warnings and recommendations during the past five years when he had known that the effective organization of world supplies should have been made against this inevitable after-war famine. The time had now come for cooperation, not controversy. Their purpose now must be to feed the last starving person. It was not too late to prevent mass starvation.

The next day, March 17, 1946, Herbert Hoover climbed into an Army transport plane equipped for long distance continuous travel on the start of a journey significant in humanitarian history. As the plane whirred across the Atlantic, The Chief assigned specific duties to each of the former welfare associates he had chosen to fly with him.

Ambassador Hugh Gibson, the experienced diplomat, would be at his side to plan and carry through the approach to top level leaders in the countries that needed extra food or had a surplus to share. Perrin Galpin, who knew Hoover's ways from their nearly lifetime association, would coordinate their schedules, send advances cables, and make necessary arrangements. As publc relations officer he was fortunate in enlisting the former president of the International News Service, Colonel Frank E. Mason, a man thoroughly familiar with the press in foreign countries.

At Mason's suggestion Hoover invited Maurice Pate to join the group. Pate had a wide knowledge of the needs of children throughout the world, he understood the Poles among whom he lived many years, and was fluent in their language. Charles Dalzell, who was equally well informed on Italy, would guide their research in the "Boot of Europe." When they reached Paris, Hallam Tuck of C.R.B. experience would join them to handle industrial and transportation problems involving food.

The first night out the group listened to Dr. Fitzgerald's account of world food problems, each relating newly-acquired knowledge to his specific duty. They learned that the task on which all must concentrate would be to meet the immediate crisis of finding and moving food to critical areas in time to tide over the population until the next harvest. Since that season differed according to climate, their travel must be oriented accordingly.

Their C-54-E plane was dubbed "The Faithful Cow" by Hoover because of the "moo" sound of its hydraulic system when it landed. It was equipped with offices ready for the heavy load-schedule of study and report writing between stops. Hugo

Meier, who was loaned by Edgar Rickard to substitute on this all male trip for Bernice ("Bunny") Miller, Mr. Hoover's long-time secretary, was prepared to type the reports that would emerge from the intensive weeks ahead.

Each evening passengers and crew shed cares for a refreshing half-hour before dinner, when The Chief put away his pencil and enjoyed his strict limit of one and one-half Martinis. In their first casual conversation Major MacOdrum, the captain of the plane, assured them of special protection, because his Quaker mother had sent him off with a blessing as he had left home "to pilot the greatest Quaker."

Thus it was that this picked group of qualified men spent eighty-two days covering 50,000 miles surveying or visiting thirty-eight stricken countries and returned confident in the fulfillment of their Chief's prediction at every stop that "The Wolf of Famine will go away from the door on September first."

As they traveled and met leaders of nations, great and small, Hoover faith brought "a breath of fresh hope, not only in matters of food, but in elevated constructive human thinking to the heads of these countries groping for guidance in a bewildered world, as well as to American diplomats and military leaders abroad." So recorded Maurice Pate in his diary. The recommended equitable flow of food all over the world in that critical spring and summer, averted the threat of world hunger and the calamitous hoarding of food.

Out of this experience, too, came an eventual result undreamed of when the anxious President sought the advice of his predecessor. A permanent international organization to save and care for the needy children of the world was conceived during brief conversations in "The Faithful Cow." Sometimes Pate would step to the door of The Chief's "office aloft" for a quick decision on a child-care plan for Poland or Iraq, and would hear, "Come, sit down, Maurice, I want to relax and smoke my pipe awhile." Relaxation was not easy. As smoke rings rose, they would find the conversation reverting to the subject nearest their hearts. Then they would dream together of ways to save children like those Pate had seen in Berlin, where the annual infant death rate was 723 per 1,000 or fourteen times the pre-war rate.

Specific plans for feeding children were crystallized after they reached Bagdad, where Hoover received a cable from Lowell Thomas asking for a five-thousand-word article for *Life Magazine* upon his return. Hoover asked Frank Mason to "telegraph Lowell Thomas and tell him if *Life* would pay $5,000 to the Boys' School in Bagdad, between us we'll work up an article." Knowing how busy The Chief was and would be, Pate volunteered to draft a story on food needs of children throughout the world. With Hoover's "go ahead" this project filled moments between reports for the rest of the journey. Eventually, that undertaking opened a new career for Pate, and new hope for the future of the world; but in that spring of 1946 there were many other duties to claim the full attention of all the men aboard.

The reference to the American Boys' School in Bagdad was typical of the interwoven interests of the remarkable men who made up the Hoover Mission. Ambassador Gibson and Frank Mason were both directors of this school. They had taken The Chief with pride to see where hundreds of boys from little farms all over the country had been educated during the past twenty years. The practical Hoover mind quickly grasped the significance of the special agriculture training these boys were getting to enable them to return to form new centers of development in their home communities.

Flying in from Cairo, Hoover had asked his pilot to head in the direction that would bring them to the Tigris River about one-hundred miles above Bagdad. As they flew above fertile plains on each side of the river, the engineer ex-President sat in the cockpit sizing up the possibilities if the flow of the river could be controlled. He could envision the abundant food resources below if this land, from which thousands of families had been flooded, could only be brought into constant and safe production!

Such observations, and the Chief's retentive memory, constantly amazed his companions. In Greece he astonished them, as well as the offical hosts, by replying to the Prime Minister's plea for food with a speech of hope that included a recounting of the glory of Athens and of what Greek civilization had given to the world. Even the Greeks in the audience sat in rapt attention as he quoted names and dates with meticulous accuracy. His staff remarked on the unbelievable amount of work any group working under his leadership can turn out in a day, because we all know where we are going, and that what we are doing is coordinated on the highest plane."

Hoover's interest in Greece was rewarded in two ceremonies. Each took but a few minutes of his one-day stay; yet he went on to Cairo with an Honorary degree from the University of Athens, and a scroll designating him an honorary citizen of Athens.

Egyptians, too, were impressed with Hoover's understanding of their antiquities when he found a free hour to visit the Cairo Musuem. Here Hoover's geological knowledge came to the surface. As the museum director showed him the remarkable recoveries from the tomb of King Tutankhammun, the Egyptian scholar pointed out some iron tools made before the Bronze Age, and preserved because of enclosure within dry, rock constructions. This, said his host, reminded him of a statement made by Hoover long ago, contrary to the opinion of most archaelogists, he had been certain that the world must have possessed iron tools prior to theso-called Bronze Age, but that most iron tools must have corroded and disappeared while bronze endured.

This was one country where Hugh Gibson's tact could not fend off the large social gathering which The Chief usually wished to avoid. Hallam Tuck's brother, H. Pickney Tuck, was the American Ambassador to Egypt. At the embassy reception more than seven hundred people shook the hand of the American ex-President in the hour-and-a-half he spared from his world mission of mercy. The Land of the Pharaohs did not honor Hoover academically as had Greece. However, a hundred-foot, horseshoe-shaped table banked with thousands of "Herbert Hoover" roses at King Farouk's luncheon opened the way to a relaxing conversation while the monarch told him of his gardening hobby.

A cable from President Truman suggested that before going to the Far East it might be wise to come home from Cairo, report findings in order to arouse more favorable public response to food-saving proposals. The Chief was certain that this would appear to slight expectant nations now so near. He telephoned the President. His presentation was so promptly convincing that, after he had explained the situation to the President, received his approval and hung up, the operator called back to say that he had used only two-and-a-half of his alloted three minutes.

In lieu of the President's suggestion that they return home to report, Frank Mason was able to arrange with an American broadcasting company for a fifteen-minute interview with Hoover from the Egyptian capital. This broadcast carried to world listeners news of the dire needs the mission had uncovered in its first month of travel. In it Hoover asserted that to avoid starvation at least 150,000,000 people must have contributions of food supplies within the next four months. He pointed out that the only possible substantial sources were in Canada, the U.S.A., Britain, The Argentine, Australia, Siam, and Russia.

Part of his talk was directed to the Soviets, reminding them of the relief he had organized and directed in 1922-3. He recalled that then America's gift of over three million tons of food had saved Russians during their worst famine. He spoke, too, of the sacrificial giving of many millions of the more fortunate Soviet citizens for their starving neighbors, and referred to the untold hardships their nation had endured during the war just passed. But he said that recent grain exports to France seemed to indicate improvement in Russia's food production. Could he hope, perhaps, for the contribution of at least 300,000 tons per month from them to the general food pool?

As the members of the Mission had collaborated with their Chief in putting together data for this broadcast, they took stock of what they had seen in the seventeen countries visited thus far. And they recalled Hoover's remark at a luncheon given by the French Minister of Foreign Affairs, who had referred to their association a quarter of a century earlier.

"I was young in years at that time," The Chief said, "but today I find myself like the old family doctor called out of retirement to consult again in a most grave illness of the world. I have indeed been called in late in the crisis."

How late had been revealed when they looked over the reports in Italy. Here, in another land famed for food, they had found decreased production, exhausted stocks, only enough cereal on hand and en route to assure the ration of about seven ounces per person per day for another month. Black market prices were high. Those who had money could eat luxuriously at restaurants; but skilled workers, with average earnings of about forty dollars a month, and clerical workers with fifty, could scarcely buy four meals a month for their families at these black market rates.

The stop in Rome had included a significant audience with the Holy Father, one of the many instances when Ambassador Gibson's presence had been helpful, although Herbert Hoover was not himself a stranger to Pope Pius XI. Many years before, when the Prelate was Papal Nuncio to Poland, he had been photographed with Hoover and Paderewski in Warsaw. Now the official call of the former American President had a poignant meaning. The appeal to the Vatican was to enlist the Head of the Roman Catholic Church in persuading his flock all over the world, and especially in Latin America, to join in the self-sacrifice needed to avert famine. When Ambassador Gibson suggested that the Pope send a broadcast to Latin America with the request that it be re-broadcast there on their standard wave lengths, Pope Pius responded with gracious understanding, saying "You write it. I'll send it."

Feelings had been most stirred in Warsaw. Historic reasons for the mutual bond of respect and gratitude between their two nations underlay their conversation as Hoover and other members of the mission dined with President Bierut. They spoke of General Kosciuszko, who came from Poland to help America in the Revolutionary War, became adjutant to General Washington, and later engineer in charge of the construction of West Point. Hoover described the Pulaski Skyway in New Jersey, approaching New York City. This had been dedicated during his Presidency to honor Count Casimir Pulaski, another Polish citizen who rose through the ranks to become a general in Washington's army and who had given his life in the struggle for American independence. Ironically, on this day in 1946, the former American President, possibly the world's most outstanding exponent of private enterprise, was being honored by hosts representing a Communist government!

Hoover's reply to the long speech by the Polish President reminded his hosts that one-fifth of the world's people of Polish origin were now citizens of the United States. He also mentioned that several of his colleagues on the present journey had worked for the survival of Poland in 1919. His toast to the head of the provisional government of Poland spoke of the gallantry, hope, and courage of his people. The interpreter, Mrs. Winnecka, a pleasant, friendly woman, told Hoover that she was alive because of the children's kitchens provided by his relief mission after World War I. Then she turned to Vice-Prime Minister Gomulka and said, "You, too, were one of these beneficiaries. You should tell Mr. Hoover how much that meant to us."

All these experiences and conclusions had entered into the Cairo broadcast. At the same time The Chief had been generous in credit to the voluntary agencies seeking to cope with post-war problems—the International Red Cross, and various religious organizations from America, Britain, Switzerland, and Sweden. But his findings indicated that all of these voluntary organizations, plus UNRRA, official relief agency of the U.N. were able to meet the needs of less than one-third of the undernourished children and hungry adults from the English Channel to the Russian border.

And even that portion dependent on UNRRA seemed to be on a tenuous basis. Letters and news clippings from home indicated grass roots dissatisfaction in America with this organization, in which Russia was demanding more power and at the same time failing to meet it financial commitments. When word came of former Governor Lehman's resignation as Director of UNRRA, members of the Food Mission suspected that New York's ex-Mayor LaGuardia was appointed expressly to wind up its widespread activities.

To avoid the political wrangling in which UNRRA had become involved, the Hoover group took every opportunity to make the public image of their survey clear. They were circling the world with a definite purpose. They were searching for surplus food, seeking the cooperation of people in lands of plenty to eliminate waste, and finding means of transporting available food to the nearest deficit areas with a minimum of cross-hauling at the lowest possible cost.

By the time the party reached Bombay on May 24, Hoover was ready to beam an international radio plea in a new direction. This time he sought the ears of his old associates in Australia. After three days in India, which included a visit with the Viceroy and Lady Wavell, conferences with Gandhi and Nehru, and a hundred-mile auto drive into drought territory, Hoover punctuated his message with urgency as he asked Australian ranchers to speed help to nearby India.

When *The Faithful Cow* lifted its weary passengers from Bangalore for a refreshing eight-hour flight above the blue waters of the Bay of Bengal, the Survey party was ready for some relaxation. Hoover, comfortable in the light tropical suit made quickly by Lord Wavell's tailor, went forward to share the view from the cockpit. After the "Moo" sound ceased and they were safely landed at the Bangkok airport, a welcome sight greeted them on the long ride into the city. The firm brown bodies of Siamese children, mostly naked in the tropical heat, told them that at last they were in a "food surplus country" where malnutrition was not a spectre.

After an eighteen-hour visit in this city of bamboo, canals (klongs) lined with banana palms, and fantastic gold-leafed temples, The Chief actually took a half-hour off to enjoy Siamese classical dancers. His usual preliminary request for simplicity in eating and entertainment had seemingly never reached the Prime Minster's chef. After an eleven-course dinner of exotically-flavored food this relaxation was essential.

Hoover left Bangkok with an idea that came to fruition in Manila. Here he found Filipinos in dire need of rice, a commodity going to waste in Siam for lack of transportation facilities. Why not, he proposed, exchange surplus Army transportation equipment in The Philippines for Siamese rice? The plan was favored by officials of both countries, and the Mission flew on to Shanghai. There Hoover, Hugh Gibson, an American Consul-General Davis lunched with T. V. Soong to discuss the intricacies of the political and economic picture in China. Then General Claire Lee Chennault called to offer his Flying Tigers for transporting food from Shanghai's bulging warehouses to interior famine areas. This gesture was an offer characteristic of the impetuous general, but too costly for acceptance.

On their second day The Chief accepted an invitation from Chiang Kai-shek to visit him in Nanking. *The Faithful Cow* carried Hoover, Hugh Gibson, Dr. Fitzgerald, and Frank Mason to the new capital for an intensive five-hour stop, in which they lunched with the Foreign Minister, visited General Marshall and had tea with the Generalissimo and Madame Chiang Kai-shek.

The next day they flew on to Seoul, Korea, encouraged by the good news as they left Shanghai that the first Navy L.S.M. had successfully negotiated the difficult rapids of the Yangtze. Now they knew that there would be at least a small contribution toward the solution of the inland food problem in China.

On this leg of the flight Maurice Pate found an opportunity to show The Chief his draft of the child-feeding article proposed in Bagdad. In this he incorporated the seeds of a plan that a year hence would blossom into an organization dedicated to permanent life-saving. Now all he had were the facts, a blueprint of possible operation, and a suggestion for action that would involve several hundred million dollars. He left it, hoping that it would be implemented with pungent Hoover words after they had tackled new problems waiting in Korea and Japan.

A few hours after they landed in Seoul the men of the mission were seated around a large table, participating in a meeting called by General John R. Hodge, commander of the U.S. Forces. Some fifty or sixty U.S. Army Officers and Korean leaders were there with a clear-cut food picture, ready to outline the difficulties of American-Russian occupation and the many problems of re-assimilating displaced persons. Hoover's own familiarity with the region, gained during his early mining days there, was helpful to the discussion.

The final foreign stop was Tokyo. General MacArthur welcomed Hoover with a warm handshake as he exclaimed, "Chief." Dinner that night at the embassy compound was gracious and informal. Then, while Mrs. MacArthur served coffee, the two old friends disappeared for two hours. Dr. Rey, the flight surgeon, was worried. He had expected The Chief to wind up his evening early, because he had been complaining all day of the traditional curse of Far Eastern travelers. When Hoover finally re-entered the room smiling, the physician remarked:

"Well, I guess The Chief got his mind off his troubles. Sometimes that is better than medicine!"

In Tokyo, as in several of the cities visited, an interest remote from food problems briefly diverted Hoover's thoughts from the immediate task. In the Tokyo branch of the Hoover War Library the travelers found a group of Stanford alumni, American military men and Japanese, waiting to greet The Chief. As they sipped tea together three short speeches were made and a rare book was presented to the library by one of the Japanese alumni. Then the group hurried on to more food conferences.

Four full days in Nippon filled notebooks with facts and plans. Poignant memories of Versailles and its aftermath flooded Hoover's mind as he discussed MacArthur's constructive thoughts on Japanese reparations. The two agreed with

Hallam Tuck's report on his own intensive study in Tokyo that enough tools must be left in Japan so that this country would not become a bottomless pit consuming products from the rest of the world.

Now the Hoover Mission was ready to carry their findings home. While the plane was serviced in Honolulu, Hoover, in response to a radiogram from President Truman, had a long conference with Special Envoy Edwin Pauley.

That first night on home territory, Hoover refused all proferred hospitality and sat as dinner host with the men who had circled the world with him. He relegated his closest friends to the far end of the table and gathered officers and crew of the accompanying maintenance plane near him, because he had less chance to get to know them. Each member of the staff and crew was given a diploma, hurriedly printed by the *Honolulu Advertiser,* as a souvenir. Then for an hour after dinner Mr. Hoover enjoyed a long black cigar as he regaled them with tales from his earlier experiences.

The next morning the shining C-54 was ready at the Honolulu airfield. On its nose was a newly-lettered sign "The Faithfull Cow" the work of an enlisted man at the field. In his exuberance he had added the extra "L"—which everyone agreed was symbolic.

Homecoming in San Francisco was marred by news of a coal strike, with threats of a railroad and shipping tie-up to follow. No words were minced in the Hoover press conference. He drew a vivid picture of a world faced with the worst potential famine in history, so iminent that if the coal strike continued thousands would die because of delayed food shipments; the railroad strike could mean death to millions; the shipping strike, a holocaust. He reminded the men who were threatening these strikes that many of them were descended from people who had migrated from the countries most vulnerable.

A bee-line route across the U.S.A., with full moon glistening on the snow-white peaks of the Rockies, brought the mission back to Washington on a Sunday morning. At the traditional church hour of eleven, these men stepped out of that big plane ready to preach a "sermon." The President heard it first, in private; then the nation heard it over the radio on a national hookup. Hoover next carried his concern for the millions he would save to the United Nations, suggesting a World Food Administration under the Security Council.

With less than a week's breathing spell, the mission was in the air again, flying south this time across the volcanic mountains of Mexico. In the ornate council rooms of Chapultepec Castle, he told President Camacho and his ministers how greatly the world needed Mexico's moral support with other Latin American countries in a general movement for food conservation. Camacho agreed and even volunteered to use his good services with Peron to cooperate in the food crises. On through Panama, Columbia, and Ecuador to Peru the tragic story of hunger was repeated with varying responses. Quito headlines said: "Ecuador Offers Hoover 650,000 Sacks of Rice at $10.25 f.o.b. Guayaquil!" At Lima airport black-clad old ladies and eager children held out bouquets of exotic flowers.

In Santiago, Chile, Ambassador Bowers invited Hoover to speak at a luncheon for cabinet ministers and other leading Chileans. Again he used the words that had echoed like a refrain across the air waves of the world: "the saving of these human lives is far more than an economic necessity to the recovery of this world. . . Such action marks the return of the lamp of compassion . . . part of the moral and spiritual reconstruction of the world."

Once more he crossed the Andes into the breadbasket of The Argentine. This time they were safely piloted by Major MacOldrum; but memory brought back the miles of pampas and the threats of wrecks as their train crawled across the miles in 1928. Entreé into this and other countries of the Catholic World had been prepared through the radio broadcast by Pope Pius XII after Quaker and the Pontiff had conferred in Rome with Ambassador Gibson's tactful help. And it was not only the Pope, but also the Mexican Ambassador to Argentina who had paved the way with Peron. In spite of unfortunate timing (two days after inauguration) Hugh Gibson was able to arrange enough conferences with various high officials to send the group on their way with promises of full cooperation from Peron.

Traditional Uruguayan admiration for the U.S.A. highlighted the short stop-over in Montevideo. Even the head waiter of the Hotel de Parc remembered the reception to the then President-elect eighteen years before. The man carried out a promise to himself that on his table Mr. Hoover should now have the best breakfast and the most beautiful flowers of the entire South American visit.

By comparison, the opposition of the Communist press in Brazil made the days in Rio dramatic. A Saturday conference with Brazillian and foreign press representatives offered an opportunity for the head of the mission to speak bluntly about the Communist intrigue against constructive efforts to solve the food problem. Lack of Soviet cooperation had been noted throughout their journey. Now the Communist-controlled newspapers in parts of Latin America were accusing the Hoover Survey of using food as a political weapon, The Chief unleashed the facts, including documents from the highest officials of the Soviet Government expressing thanks for his help to the workers of Russia in 1922-23. And he re-emphasized the intention of his present mission: That food should be made available for hungry working people everywhere without regard to political, racial, or religious differences.

After productive conferences in Caracas and Havana the Survey party arrived back in Washington on June 19. The report to President Truman indicated that increased food exports promised from some South American countries and decreased imports to others should result in a net addition of 800,000 tons for food deficit areas around the world.

But it was in the final report of the Food Mission, made in Ottawa at the request of the Canadian Government, that a "Call to Action" was formulated. Eventually the closing words of Herbert Hoover's broadcast of June 28, 1946, brought to fruition seeds planted as he and Maurice Pate let their thoughts fly into the future while they soared above the suffering countries of the war-scarred world.

"I would like to suggest that the redemption of these children be organized at once," he challenged, "and that all nations be called upon to contribute to its cost. The job could be done with three or four hundred million dollars, a charge beyond the reach of any organized private charity, but not a great sum from the world as a whole."

Other voices answered the call. In one of the final sessions of the UNRRA Council, the experienced Polish delegate, Dr. Ludwik Rajchman, a man who had earlier served in the League of Nations, rose to propose a recommendation creating an international children's fund as the residuary legatee of the assets of the organization which was then winding up its general relief work. In September Director LaGuardia presented the accepted recommendation to the Economic and Social Council of the United Nations. From then until December, when the General Assembly passed Resolution 57(1), no member of any delegation could withstand the impassioned pleas for affirmative votes from white-haired Dr. Rajchman.

Once the United Nations International Children's Emergency Fund (UNICEF) was officially established, there was no question among the twenty-four nations represented on its Board as to who should be its Director. In January at the first official meeting of UNICEF, Maurice Pate, who had worked in every one of the many Hoover-directed organizations to aid children, was introduced as its new head. He was the recent appointee of the first U.N. Secretary-General Trygve Lie.

With the help of a secretary, Pate set up a small office in Washington and wrote letters to governments and private donors, seeking funds to supplement the UNRRA residue. Four years later, in 1950, another U.N. General Assembly resolution deleted "emergency" as well as "international," but left the familiar initials intact. Thus UNICEF became a permanent agency of the world organization.

When the United Nations complex rose on the bank of the

East River in mid-Manhattan, Pate and his enlarged staff were settled on the eighteenth floor of the tall, glass Secretariat Building. Within walking distance of the Hoover Suite in the Waldorf Towers, this office was always in touch with The Chief, who might well have been called "The Chairman of the Board" of the institution that grew from his vision.

While Pate struggled with the beginnings of UNICEF, Herbert Hoover was making still another survey for President Truman. This time the Chief Executive asked the former relief administrator to investigate conditions in Germany and Austria after the termination of UNRRA.

In late February 1947 Hoover laid on the President's desk careful estimates of needs and the means for meeting them. He reported in person to the House Committee on Foreign Affairs. Hoover's picture of conditions in the two countries was bleak, in spite of the brave struggle of Austrians to rise out of the rubble to preserve what they could of Western civilization from their broken-down economy. The Russian military zone now occupied the bread basket of Europe. Nature added to the bitterness of winter completely frozen canals. Rail transportation was impeded due to the lack of equipment. The coal shortage was acute. He noted a loss of vitality and a lessened ability to work everywhere. Children and adolescents were in great need of extra nourishment. Again, his words reflected his pioneer American heritage when he urged the United States to send fertilizer and seeds to enable these people to help themselves.

Then he suggested that important savings could be made if German-employed crews could be used on at least seventy-five Liberty ships to transport these supplies. Such men could be paid in marks and save the American and British taxpayers a considerable amount of money. Further savings could be effected if American Army equipment could have full holds on return voyages.

He would also add to the German fishing fleet so that more of this protein food could be made available. Altogether, he said that by increasing the food supply to health levels and helping Germany to become economically self-supporting, it would be possible to lessen by $150-million the cost to Britain and America for immediate emergency help. The balance would not be irrecoverable because it should be so arranged that it could be repaid from future net exports. In support of this, he reminded his listeners that at his insistence German civilian relief expenditures following World War I were repaid from liquid assets, ranking ahead of reparations.

He injected a new idea into the American conscience. In this generation, he said, the conqueror had an obligation to undertake relief of the vanquished, not alone from compassion, but also for self-protection. If Western civilization would survive, Germany *must* become self-supporting.

Chapter Thirty-one

TOWARD REALIZED DREAMS

THAT SUMMER NEW public service with permanent potentialities was offered. President Truman invited Herbert Hoover to chairman a commission which embodied the life-long dream of the Quaker engineer. Nearly twenty years earlier he had entered the White House with a careful blueprint for more efficiency in the executive branch of the government he was about to administer. This was based on observation and experience during his eight years in the Cabinet. But he had not reckoned with antagonistic forces that would hamper him continually in Congress.

Now, in 1947, a Democratic Congress and a Democratic President seeing eye to eye recognized the long overdue need. And they turned to the man whose patience had outlived opposition. At seventy-three Herbert Hoover accepted the new task with zest and preparedness. In the Commission for the Reorganization of the Executive Branch of the Government of the U.S.A. he had eleven associates. Three others, like himself, were appointed by the President; four by the Senate; and the other four, by the House.

Again the way was not easy. His first ideas on methods of organizing research, met opposition from the vice chairman, Secretary of State Dean Acheson. Acheson wanted to use Civil Service personnel. Hoover with his roster of informed persons in all walks of life had a list of reliable co-workers available.

He won the argument and soon divided research among twenty "task forces," each to examine and compile facts pertinent to their assigned branch. Then he turned to a former member of the Food Administration staff, Sidney A. Mitchell, a retired New York banker, to act as liaison between the forces.

Just as he had spoken to the groups about to feed the Belgians thirty-four years before, Hoover called his key men together, outlined for them his aims, and put it up to each leader to work out his own program. Then while his associates were organizing, his mind was cleared for other thoughts.

The work of food relief was not completed. Another grim winter loomed ahead. Agriculture had failed to recover in Europe and Asia. Drought had seared many promising fields, even in the corn belt of America.

In September, Hoover again spoke to a large audience in Madison Square Garden in behalf of hunger sufferers abroad. With the zeal of his Quaker mother, he preached against speculation, hoarding and waste. His message was basically the same as hers, "the fundamental law of civilization is based on compassion and charity . . . a law that does not inquire into the personal morals of a sufferer, nor as to the cause of his ill being, whether from his own fault or from forces beyond his control.

"We cannot forget," he said, "that our consciences were forged by tender women and strong men, who have built for themselves a world to their liking, always setting aside a mite for the charity they knew God enjoined upon a good people. . . I hope that the day never comes in this country when all our good works are done through taxes, for then the moral strength that comes through compassion and charity is lost to us."

His advice was no longer spurned. Nor was official gratitude lacking. President Truman issued a proclamation restoring the name *Hoover* to the spectacular dam on the Colorado River, which Secretary of Interior Ickes had changed to *Boulder* during the Roosevelt era.

National leaders continued to probe Hoover wisdom as they formulated world relief programs. In January, Senator Arthur Vandenburg brought him a draft of the proposed Marshall Plan before submitting it to the Senate Committee on Foreign Affairs. The underlying purpose, aid to sixteen European countries, was in line with Hoover thinking. He concurred emphatically with the general plan for the Economic Cooperation Administration (as the Marshall Plan was technically designated); but he proposed certain modifications and safeguards.

Christian Herter, whose own public service had begun under Hoover, was now Republican Congressman from Massachusetts. He, too, had ideas to discuss with The Chief. Hoover agreed with his proposal that this new relief organization should be directed by a group which would include not only Government department heads, but also non-official citizens.

Moreover, Hoover felt that the plan should not be confined to sixteen West-European nations; it should be offered to any country in which Communism was making inroads. Latin America and Asia were equally important to world stability. And he was convinced that there should be specific stipulations: The nations helped must balance their budgets, check inflation, stabilize foreign exchange. He felt, too, that even a moral commitment to a four-year program would be unwise. Help given according to need should be subject to withdrawal without recrimination if conditions changed. And with his consistent concern over increasing burdens on coming generations, he also suggested practical methods of relieving taxpayers.

Many of his ideas were adopted or incorporated in part. Then he wrote to the Speaker of the House, outlining further recommendations. Other Western Hemisphere nations might share the burden, if they would extend credit to Marshall Plan countries for ten years, guaranteed up to seventy percent by the United States. His letter ended with the prophecy that if this plan could produce economic, political, and self-defense unity in Western Europe and thus become a dam against Russian aggression, it would stem the tide running so strongly against civilization and peace.

American leaders had finally wakened to a realization that their former President was one of the best informed and most experienced men in the world. Invitations to speak flooded his mail. Few were accepted with more anticipation than those from his old neighbors in West Branch, who planned to celebrate his seventy-fourth birthday in the home of his childhood.

There, on August 10, 1948, he spoke from a heart nostalgic with boyhood memories as he expressed what was to him, "The Meaning of America," a phrase indelibly implanted in his being by that ever-honored early teacher. Humbly, he recounted experiences that had made that meaning personal as he had moved from the country village to the pioneer home of his uncle in Oregon, "always among those to whom hard work was the price of existence."

Then he recalled his treks to the far places of the world in days when the word "America" was hallowed by the masses who regarded it as symbolic of hope. And his home-comings when "each time my soul was washed by relief from the grinding poverty of other nations, by the kindliness and frankness which comes from the acceptance of equality and belief in wide open opportunity for all who want a chance." This revealing of his inmost thoughts was, he said, a "streamlined autobiography recounted so that in Quaker terms, I can give my own testimony."

But his talk was more than personal testimony. In it, he contrasted the agnosticism of European philosophers who insisted that man's rights come from the state, with the innate individudualism, the self-reliance and sense of service which are the underlying intangibles in the word "American."

"The greatness of America," he said, "comes from one philosophy; the despair of Europe from the other."

Back at his desk high in the Waldorf Towers he applied all of his energy to the stupendous task of what had come to be known as The Hoover Commission. On the fifth of February 1949 the monumental report was submitted to Congress, embodying in its two and a half million words, data which its chairman described as "basic to the very strength and vitality of democracy itself."

Not all sections of the report reflected unanimity. Suggested reform in the administration of the six government functions involving natural resources, commerce and industry, social welfare, business enterprises, foreign affairs and national defense had come out of long debate. Proposed reduction of the number of agencies from seventy-four to about twenty was touchy and full of human dynamite. Following the time-honored precedent of the Supreme Court, dissenting opinions had been included in the final draft.

Sometimes the chairman disagreed with findings of his task forces, even though they came from close and trusted friends. From time to time as the work progressed he invited key members of different groups to frequent and early breakfasts at the Waldorf. Listening to their diverse views, he would then try to reconcile them in the light of his own world-wide experience.

For instance, former Governor Leslie Miller of Wyoming, chairman of the Natural Resources group, and Horace Albright, former Director of National Parks, agreed with their associates that agencies dealing with agriculture, natural resources and public works should be consolidated into one organization and suggested transfer to the Department of Interior. Others wanted all in the Department of Agriculture. Hoover convinced them that, no matter how logical, neither plan would work. He recalled tough experiences with the Department of Agriculture. He knew that should they try to transfer the Forest Service to Interior, opposition would be insurmountable. In fact, President Truman had already told him so.

But now that the report was printed, bound and delivered, Hoover had harder months ahead. Throughout the spring of 1949, he became a constant commuter between New York and Washington, as he appeared in person before Congress to explain the details in its pages.

Fired by his own passion for orderly administrative procedures, Chairman Hoover startled Congressional listeners with the conclusion of the Report that some $4-billion of taxpayers' money was wasted annually in avoidable expenditure. As in the days when he had earned his engineering fame, so now he was ready with the first complete diagnosis of the American body politic. He offered effective prescriptions for the cure of disorders in top management.

Hope for the patient's eventual recovery was inherent in the Reorganization Act, passed early in 1949, an Act that laid the foundation on which to build effective structural changes in government.

Out of his own baffling experience as Chief Executive, Hoover insisted that many restrictions be removed from the organization of the President's own office. Here management practices inaugurated in George Washington's day had been incorporated into law that would not even allow the head of the nation to delegate a power of attorney!

With the thoroughness that had made him master of organization since he had first jotted down ideas for student government on those long summer evenings in the California Sierra, Hoover pointed out faults in existing practices and indicated remedies. Archaic fiscal procedures had irked him since his first entry into Federal affairs. Now he argued, with pride in his task forces' accomplishments, for a "Performance Budget" that would enable any congressman to understand what the government was doing and what each project would cost.

As soon as Congress began to act on commission recommendations, Hoover's diligence was rewarded. Potential savings of more than $25-million were indicated with the first reform, establishment of a General Services Administration to coordinate government housekeeping.

While all of the Report reflected the experience of its head, there were certain phases most typically "Hoover." As an engineer and businessman he saw potential savings in consolidating the Army Engineering Corps and the Reclamation Service. Both were engaged in flood control, river and harbor improvement. With a Board of Impartial Review in the President's office, every waterworks project in the future could be assigned to men best qualified to accomplish the public good at least cost. His idea was to "take the pork barrel off the President's doorstep."

When it came to the reorganization of the Department of Commerce, Hoover was emphatic in saying that overlapping agencies controlling modern means of communication, must be coordinated. "Federal agents from many bureaus descend upon an incoming ship like a swarm of locusts," he said, as he urged reduction of agencies controlling U.S. shipping.

Because he had participated in intergovernmental relations in such varied capacities—as a private citizen doing business abroad, as the representative of his country in unprecedented relief work, as a diplomatic advisor at Versailles, and finally as Chief Executive—he *knew* the possibilities of reorganizing the Foreign Service. He was convinced that the President was not properly staffed in this field. The report proposed a corps of trained diplomats, whose assignments would be on a flexible basis so that their services would be used wherever their experience fitted. He dreamed of a future when the United States would be represented everywhere by men and women especially educated to promote the cause of world peace.

When the Commission studied national defense, they discovered that more than one out of every three dollars was spent in this department, with the proportion continually rising. Contrasting the $2.25 per person before World War I, with the one-hundred dollars for every man, woman and child in the current era, he found no difficulty in persuading Congress to pass the recommendation calling for a unified command to make those necessary dollars go further.

On through the long pages of recommendations, Hoover came prepared to answer every question. When they reached the Bureau of Indian Affairs, plans bore a typically Hoover stamp. He who had fished and hunted beside young Indians in his youth respected the potential capability of descendants of the "first Americans." He would have them all eventually integrated into the citizenry of the country. Pending the achievement of this goal, the commission proposed that the administration of social and educational programs should be transferred from national to state control, with appropriate recompense to the states from federal funds until Indian taxes would help carry the load. For he said that one-hundred years of "Welfare State" treatment had left Indians worse off than when they started, despite "one Federal employee nurturing every Indian."

The completed report represented sixteen months of effort on the part of widely-informed, objectively-minded citizens. Their findings were supported by facts organized in easily-accessible form. Congress and the public now had the task of digesting all the data.

But the chairman would not leave this to chance. Every ounce of his energy must be used toward convincing national legislators of the vital necessity of incorporating *all* the recommendations into law. The days grew longer and hotter. In California his oldest granddaughter was planning her wedding. Of course her grandfather must be there. But he could not leave Washington.

Patiently, day by day, the seventy-four year old patriot worked on, doggedly answering questions before Congressional committees, helping to set up citizen groups to educate the public. He was determined that America should profit immediately from savings inherent in the great report, an ambition gratified when the 81st Congress took action later, approving twenty new public laws and twenty-six Presidential re-organizational plans. These included the unified military control and the Reorganization Act of 1949, which straightened lines of authority and responsibilities of seventeen major agencies.

The State Department had been re-organized to clarify staff responsibilities, expedite action and improve communications. A modern budgeting and accounting system, which would pave the way to the greatest Federal fiscal advance in many decades, had been installed. The Labor Department had been rebuilt to restore its true Cabinet stature. The Post Office accounting procedures had been modernized, with the result that much delay and duplication were eliminated.

Chapter Thirty-two

ELDER STATESMAN

GOVERNOR DEWEY OF New York had a new idea for Herbert Hoover's public service. He would like to appoint him to fill out the unexpired term of Senator Wagner. But the former President declined the honor. He had vowed never again to hold public office. He had become in fact as well as in age America's Elder Statesman. He had one fundamental objective for such remaining years as he should be allotted, to contribute all he had of time, talent, and experience toward insurance of a better future for America.

At the same time his closest friends were conspiring to pay him honor in a more intimate way. The previous year, on his seventy-fourth birthday, a group inspired by Frederick A. Wickett of Palo Alto had raised a fund of $70,000 for the Hoover Library. Now, with the approach of his seventy-fifth anniversary, this movement had greater emphasis. Dr. Wilbur, Jeremiah Milbank of New York, Arch Shaw of Chicago, Senator Hawkes of New Jersey, Bert Mattei of San Francisco and numerous other friends began to circulate letters that eventually brought more than 25,000 birthday greetings.

Not suspecting what his friends were doing, Herbert Hoover arrived on the Stanford Campus on August 8. He found the Lou Henry Hoover House teeming with young life again. The voices of children echoing from the garden, and the splashing figures in the swimming pool belonged to the family of the new president of the university. Dr. Wallace Sterling, who had come to the post following Don Tressider's untimely death, was well known to Hoover as the former director of the Huntington Library. The Sterlings welcomed the donor of the house on San Juan Hill to a family atmosphere reminiscent of its original purpose.

There were younger Hoovers on the campus ready to personalize the celebration. A grandson Herbert Hoover, III was among the many post-war married students enrolled at Stanford. The Junior Herbert Hoovers and their youngest daughter Joan had come from Southern California with the Allan Hoovers.

Three pre-birthday celebrations were held on August 9 in the Hoover office high in the Library Tower. In the morning his campmate, J. Pearce Mitchell, registrar-emeritus, presented a parchment certificate from the local chapter of the Red Cross expressing appreciation for his services. Ray Lyman Wilbur's grandson, now president of the Associated Students of Summer Quarter, brought a framed certificate naming Herbert Hoover a permanent member of the Stanford Student Body. As he accepted this token, poignant memories seemed to bring his closest Stanford friend into the room where they had conferred so often. Dr. Wilbur had not lived to welcome Herbert Hoover home. He succumbed to a heart attack less than two months before the event he had helped to plan.

A huge cake baked in the shape of an open book was inscribed in icing on the title page:

A MEMORABLE CAREER

CHAPTER 75

HERBERT HOOVER BIRTHDAY GREETINGS

SAN FRANCISCO JUNIOR CHAMBER OF COMMERCE

The next afternoon, August 10, just twenty-one years less a day from the time he had made his acceptance speech in the Stanford Stadium, Herbert Hoover walked out onto the grassy platform of the Lawrence Frost Memorial Amphitheatre. Assembled friends and students rose as a carillon presented to the Hoover Library by the Belgian-American Educational Foundation rang out "Hail to the Chief."

Despite his seventy-five years his shoulders were unstooped, his head held high. His face radiated smiles as student voices sang "Happy Birthday to You." The refrain drifting down from upper rows of trees edging the amphitheatre was picked up by most of the thousands who had gathered there in late afternoon sunshine.

Before Dr. Sterling introduced him as speaker, Herbert Hoover received an imposing gift from his friend, Frederick A. Wickett. This was a red-lettered, white leather volume that contained greetings from thousands of friends and admirers who had enclosed checks and bills which added over $170,000 to the endowment of the institution.

As he accepted the gift in the name of the University, Dr. Sterling expressed pride in its most famous alumnus. Then he chose a letter from "a humble ranch hand." It read, "I have always agreed with you and have read many articles about you and some you have written. I am sending a dollar. I cannot send more, because I am caring for my aged mother. She is not on a pension and don't want one and I don't want one either when I get to be an old man. I wish there was more like you."

It was for men like the writer of that letter, as well as for students training for leadership that Herbert Hoover chose the title, "Think of the Next Generation" for his remarks. While the rays of the setting sun streamed into the eyes of those who sat behind him on the rostrum, he drew on the concentrated work of his past two years for a speech that dealt with the whole future of the nation to which he had dedicated his life.

"If America is to be run by the people," he told his audience, "it is the people who must think. And we do not have to put on sack cloth and ashes to think; nor should our minds think like a sun dial which records only sunshine. Our thinking must square against some lessons of history, some principles of government and morals if we would preserve the rights and dignity of men to which this nation is dedicated."

In trenchant words the chairman of the Hoover Commission gave his audience food for serious thought. He reminded them that the average working citizen labored sixty-one days of every year to earn enough to pay taxes; that proposed further spending would take another twenty days. "You might want to work for your family instead of paying for a gigantic bureaucracy," he added.

Solemnly that great crowd found their way up the grassy slopes and down through the leafy trees of this man-made amphitheatre, thinking over the challenge of his closing words: "The founding fathers dedicated the structure of government to secure the blessings of liberty for ourselves and our posterity. We of this generation inherited this precious blessing; yet, as spendthrifts, we are on our way to rob posterity of its inheritance. The American people have solved great difficulties in national life . . . the qualities of self-restraint, of conscience and courage still live in our people. It is not too late to summon these qualities into action."

Across the fields in the Hoover Institution, and around the corner in the university library, staffs had prepared exhibits of papers and photographs covering all of the activities of Hoover's long life. A banner flung out of the window of Encina Hall blazoned in large letters a typical student tribute—"Herbert Hoover Slept Here."

When the public celebration was finally over, the family and a few close friends gathered for dinner with the Sterling household. At the close of the meal, Boris came in with the huge birthday cake. (This was the same Kosta Boris who had come with Captain Gregory to serve The Chief in Paris during the days of the American Relief Administration. He was living in his own small cottage on the grounds of the Lou Henry Hoover House, continuing to minister to the needs of the former President whenever Mr. Hoover visited the campus, as well as to the comfort of those who occupy that house.)

The three youngest Hoovers hung over their grandfather's shoulder on one side; the three Sterling children on the other, all helping to blow out the candles. Most of the guests departed soon after. The children went to bed. Herbert Hoover sat with an intimate friend in the study; he was turning the pages of the big volume of letters.

"This," he said, pointing to a page meticulously printed in a childish hand, "means more to me than all the rest." That letter was signed by his youngest grandson, Allan's Andy. It said, "I have earned this dollar myself. I am sending it to the Library because you will know what to do with it."

The chairman of the Hoover Commission could not linger to enjoy these children, nor to become acquainted with the scholars who were taking advantage of the storehouse of books and documents in the Library. He left the birthday gift to be applied toward further usefulness of the Institution and boarded an east-bound train again. He must be at hand to guide the efforts of the recently-formed Citizens' Committee for the Hoover Report.

Headed by Chairman Robert L. Johnson, president of Temple University in Philadelphia, these men and women were infiltrating the minds of thinking Americans everywhere with the urgency of immediate adoption of recommendations embodied in the report. Leading magazines devoted columns to condensed summaries. Short digests were being prepared for inclusion in house organs and other periodicals that would reach the mass of American workers.

As the year drew to a close, Hoover was speaking on many platforms for this "crusade to clear the tracks for competency, a non-partisan crusade, a job for citizenship rather than partisanship." As in the days of the Food Administration, he had mobilized thousands of loyal men and women responsive to the challenge that he had shifted from the commission "to the citizens themselves, who must undertake a real and continuing responsibility." He was "The Chief" again, in a wider sense than ever before.

Chapter Thirty-three

GRANDFATHER TO AMERICAN BOYS

THE FINAL RESULTS of the Commission For The Reorganization of The Executive Branch of The Government will be a lasting monument to Hoover sagacity and relentless work. But since the early 'thirties another vital outlet for his American dreams claimed increasing attention. He became chairman of the board of The Boy's Clubs of America in 1936. From then until his death he considered increasing numbers of his country's younger citizens as his personal responsibility.

Each summer as he journeyed home to the West Coast for his weeks at the Bohemian Grove, he fulfilled a promise made to the associate director of field service of the Pacific Coast Division of the Boys' Clubs, E.L. McKenzie: "I will try to do one special thing to help publicize the work each year when I am in California."

Thus it was that campfire leisure was often interrupted by drives back to the Bay Area. From time to time the boys of the six clubs in San Francisco, as well as of the twenty-one in surrounding communities, were able to see the former President in person. He would turn the spade for a ground-breaking, cut the ribbon at a dedication, or speak for an anniversary, always reminding these youngsters of their privilege in being born in America and of the opportunities for future leadership to be gained through participation in club activities.

Sometimes he would take part in two affairs if they were held close together. But he needed to puff his pipe in between for relaxation. One day he found himself out of matches as they were leaving to cross the Bay Bridge, the great span that was one of his deepest personal satisfactions. He would use no other than the old fashioned kitchen variety reminiscent of his Iowa farm days. There weren't any available near the downtown headquarters of the regional director.

As it was time to start, Mr. McKenzie said, "Never mind. I'm sure we'll find a corner grocery in Alameda before we go on to San Leandro."

They did. The regional director came out with six large boxes. Hoover greeted the gift with eyes sparkling like those of a small boy with a favorite toy. He tore one box open and stuffed the pockets of his coat with matches. Contented, he sank back composing his thoughts as they drove on to the San Leandro groundbreaking to be the speaker of the day.

Herbert Hoover called these younger friends of the Boys' Clubs "Our Pavement Youth" whenever he spoke or wrote about them from the time of his first article on the subject that appeared in a syndicated Sunday supplement under that title. As he wrote he shared memories of his own youth spent in days ". . . before civilization became so perfect . . . before it was paved with cement and made of bricks."

When he talked at those club affairs he won the attention of the boys and their sponsors by recounting adventures in the Iowa woods when prairie chickens and pigeons were hunted by his gang with homemade bows and arrows and sling-shots. Their mouths watered at his descriptions of cooking and eating fish of their own catching. He told them how he and his brother Tad had perfected a method of catching rabbits in a figure four trap made of cracker boxes that they read about in *The Youth's Companion.* Then he reminded his listeners that his youth had not been all adventure and highliving; that there had been school, tiresome farm chores, and the strict discipline of a Quaker family.

His adult listeners heard him say that he felt that one of the saddest things in the world was that boys must grow up into the land of realities. He proposed a special bill of rights for boys as boys. This should insure to every boy the right to the kind of play that would expand his imagination, tax his ingenuity, sharpen his wits, challenge his prowess, and keep his self-starter going. A boy, he said, should have the right to satisfy his thirst for adventure, the right to friendship, and the sense of security that comes from belonging to a group. He should also have the special right to health that should make him an inch taller than his dad. Most of all, every boy had a right to education and training that would fit him for a job that would be congenial to his manhood.

Pictures of these California occasions and Hoover's own accounts of the rewarding contacts with Boys' Club members began to filter through to other communities. No matter what demands were made on his time and energy as Chairman of the Boys' Clubs he rarely declined an invitation to travel from one side of the continent to the other to dedicate a new building; and much of the money for these buildings came from persuasive conversations with people able to give. He always reminded such men and women that ". . . the way to stop crime is to stop the manufacture of criminals;" and he would say, as he did in San Francisco, that "the normal boy is a primitive animal and takes to competition and battle . . . If he doesn't contend with nature, he is likely to take on contention with a policeman . . . This is a marginal problem. It concerns only a minority of boys. And I may state generally that if the American people would only realize that our national problems are all marginal problems of eliminating evil, correcting abuse and building up the weak, rather than the legerdemain of Utopia, we would make more progress."

He often cited an experience in Chicago that illustrated the effectiveness of the clubs he sponsored. At one time the magistrate of one of the worst slum areas in the Windy City asked for a Boys' Club in his ward, citing the delinquency rate of over eighty percent where that percentage of all the boys came into the hands of the police for some offense in a year. Generous citizens provided the club headquarters. Three years later the delinquency rate dropped to fifteen percent and the official credited it all to the Boys' Club.

Back of that achievement was a speech by Herbert Hoover in Chicago in which he said, "there are millions more of these pavement boys and girls for whom we should reach . . . their dynamic instincts of energy, play, and glee, and their gregariousness can be directed to channels of prevention far more effectively than by punishment . . . Our problem is that of creating a place in which his curiosity as to what make the wheels of the world go round may be turned into learning how to make some of the wheels himself . . . In these Clubs boys are taught the spirit of sportsmanship, cooperative living, and responsibility in citizenship . . . taught the rules of life and given opportunities in this great land of ours."

Through all the later years of his life Herbert Hoover had growing satisfaction in his close personal contacts with young men who had had the advantages of these clubs in an increasing number of cities. He took real pride in calling attention to the "alumni" who had credited their membership as preparation for their own life work. Often he remarked that "a leading columnist, a leading sculptor, and five members of major league teams got their inspiration from Boys' Clubs."

In all of his talks and the innumerable articles he wrote for papers and magazines extolling the importance of such clubs Hoover expressed the conviction that "the fabric of American life is woven around our tens of thousands of voluntary associations . . . our churches, our professional societies, our women's organizations, our businesses, our labor and farmers' associations, and not the least our charitable institutions . . . The inspirations of progress spring from these voluntary agencies, not from bureaucracy. If these were to be absorbed by government bureaus, this civilization would be over. Something neither free nor noble would take its place." Then he would apply this to the Boys' Clubs, concluding that "the taxpayer should understand that the cure of a gangster is many times more expensive than the diversion of a boy from a gang. The latter costs forty dollars apiece; the former, $10,000."

When he addressed the national convention of the Boys' Clubs in Washington in 1950 he spoke of the institution as

"The University of the Pavements." At that time there were 325 branches with between 300 and 350 thousand boys enrolled, owning equipment valued at $60-million and an annual budget of seven million dollars.

"Here there is no discrimination as to religion or race," Hoover told his audience. "The greatest moral training, except for religious faith, comes from training these boys in team work and sportsmanship . . . a boy is an illuminated interrogation point . . . our first problem is to find him constructive joy instead of destructive glee . . . the world of streets is a distorted and dangerous world, which parents cannot make or unmake. So, it becomes a job of public relations."

Herbert Hoover did not interpret public relations as the task of a professional. His own adherence to the conviction that "the gift without the giver is bare" colored his relationship with staff and volunteer alike. In the early days President W.E. Hall and Executive Director David W. Armstrong never found The Chief too busy to listen to their problems and plans. He set a record of attendance at board meetings, never missing one except when he was in Europe on the Presidential Food Mission. Whenever he arrived he sought as his seatmate one of the most prominent of Democratic leaders, James A. Farley. In all the subsequent years their friendship crossed party lines, based solidly on their mutual concern for the success of the Boys' Clubs.

As long as his health allowed, Herbert Hoover looked forward to these board meetings. In later years, he was glad to greet as the new President of the Boys' Clubs of America, a member of one of the task forces on The Hoover Commission, Albert Cole, business manager of *The Readers' Digest.* He knew Cole as a man whose ideals and aspirations for the movement matched his own.

Long after the Hoover Tower rose on the Pacific Coast, symbolizing his scholarly approach to the ultimate goal of man's search for lasting peace through knowledge, Herbert Hoover had the gratifying experience of watching the construction of another building bearing his name clear across the continent.

Here, facing the fountains on the United Nations Plaza, the Herbert Hoover Building houses the national headquarters of The Boys' Clubs of America. It stands in lasting tribute to the faith he placed in boys who have been and will be trained in cooperative effort by dedicated leaders. In such human beings he sensed the possibility of a more peaceful world.

He lived to read a brochure published in his honor, taking pleasure in the history of this movement that almost spanned his life. Starting in 1860 with small boys' clubs in New England factory towns, it had grown in 1960 to 655 Clubs in 410 cities, 45 states and the District of Columbia, owning property valued at over 150 million dollars. On one of his last California trips as he and Mr. McKenzie reviewed this fine record of progress, he remarked, "As I near ninety years of age, I am beginning to drop some of my many responsibilities; but I will die with my boots on as far as the Boys' Clubs are concerned." His ambition to have 1000 clubs serving one million deserving boys became his legacy. By 1968 the goal was in sight—750 clubs serving 800,000 boys.

That day in 1960 he was making one of his last dedicatory speeches. This was at the new Boys' Club at Hunters' Point near the Navy Shipyards in San Francisco where the crime rate is high and racial tension acute. His body was frail; but his memory was alert. As he stood waiting to cut the ribbon he caught sight of Director Daughtery of the San Francisco Boys' Clubs.

"Son, I believe I know you," said Hoover, holding out his hand with a smile. "Didn't I see you standing in the rain at the New York dedication?"

Remembered incidents like this tell as much about The Chief as the memorabilia that fill the cases in Hoover Rooms in the tower at Stanford, the Presidential Library in West Branch, Iowa, and in the Hoover Memorial Room on the ground floor of the Boys' Clubs Headquarters in New York, where a unique collection reveals to the public many facets of this dedicated American's life.

CHAPTER THIRTY-FOUR

SATISFYING RETROSPECT AND CONTINUING CHORES

LONGEVITY ENABLED HERBERT HOOVER to indulge in satisfied retrospect nearly always denied to men in public office. In modern times only the long career of Winston Churchill could compare with Hoover's, as both men experienced the crests and troughs of waves of public favor.

Because his life encompassed so much history which he felt only he could interpret accurately from a personal standpoint, the American Elder Statesman had finally listened to the urging of many friends to set down his own record in the several volumes of "Hoover Memoirs." Writing these became the driving force that enabled him to rise above physical ailments and to devote almost a decade and a half to their preparation. Through many years he had been writing these life-experiences, presumably for the benefit of his family and as a record for posterity. Now he had opened the doors of that inner sanctuary which had been closed to public and press, often at the expense of warmer understanding between a leader and his people. In the introduction to a series of excerpts which began to appear in *Colliers* he unveiled his thinking: "An autobiography inclusive of an individual and an American family in itself furnishes a background of the times that might have interest and perhaps value."

Writing of the past Herbert Hoover continued to live vitally in the present. He never failed to let "The Voice of World Experience" (as he titled one speech) be heard in national emergency. Through the tumult of the 'fifties he suspected that "history had been abandoned as a guide . . . The greatest world need is a definite mobilization of the nations who believe in God against the tide of Red agnosticism." His highest hopes for the Hoover Institution at Stanford, where he kept an office with bulging files, were that scholars of the future might learn there how to bring that mobilization into action.

When the United States became involved in the Korean conflict his worst fears were aroused and he expressed his opinion forcefully at the dedication of a memorial to William Allen White in Emporia, Kansas. There he said that the non-Communist world was faced with three possible alternatives if it would have peace. To the first, war to wipe communism from the face of the earth, he repeated his consistent "no." He reminded thoughtful persons of the futility of hoping for a change of heart in the men in the Kremlin that would lead them to work for world peace through the United Nations. The only logical procedure, in his thinking, was to build the United Nations in a way that would confine that ideology to people already enslaved, stop military aggression, and trust to time for the abatement of this evil.

A new cry for help from India where starvation threatened the masses whose crops had been destroyed by locusts, floods, and drought caused President Truman to turn again to the experienced humanitarian. Hoover's graphic picture of the needs of this densely-populated country brought quick response to the President's emergency message to Congress urging a food gift of one-million tons of grain. His long-time friend, Republican Senator H. Alexander Smith of New Jersey, who had served on the Board of the Belgian-American Educational Foundation since its inception in 1920, prepared a bill authorizing this gift; but Congress dallied. Recalcitrant members of both Houses cited Nehru's criticism of United States' policy in Korea. While they debated, Soviet Russia and Red China rushed into headlines with dramatic offers to supply some of the needed grain, actually a small part, but enough to serve as active propaganda in India. Hoover and Smith were backed in the pleas for American action by President Black of the International Bank for Reconstruction and Development, who said, "Perhaps the most powerful single force in shaping history in our time is the awakening consciousness among the underprivileged masses that the condition of poverty, ill health and ignorance in which they live is not preordained, but can be changed. The Communists are using this for the purpose of revolution and thus adding to the miseries of the people. It is the duty of the free world to try to help these masses to help themselves in peace and freedom."

Although the deadline for effective help was set as April 1, it was the sixth of June before Senator Smith saw his India Grain Bill pass both Houses and go to the President for signature. In the end, it bore a proviso that reflected the far-seeing influence of Herbert Hoover. Repayment of the loan which assured the needed grain should be made in the form of scholarships for future leaders among qualified Indian youth!

Thus it was that as Hoover sat at his desk looking over diaries and notes that were shaping into his volumes of "Memoirs," dreams of new faces were added to those from familiar lands. He rejoiced in the hope that the teeming populace of India might someday be leavened by potential leaders who would have been exposed to the best this country could offer.

By now nearly a thousand Belgians and Americans had crossed and re-crossed the Atlantic as "exchange fellows," not only students, but also professors and scientists from both countries. Among those who studied in universities across the ocean are Paul Van Zeeland and Gaston Eyskens, Prime Ministers of Belgium, and Frances Willis, first woman to attain the rank of ambassador through the career service of the American State Department. Nobel Prize Winners Ernest O. Lawrence and Robert A. Millikan were numbered among C.R.B. exchange scientists and professors. These are only a few of the hundreds who have become educators, scientists, political leaders, authors and industrialists with a better grasp of the world because

Herbert Hoover and Emile Francqui met in the midst of war and decided upon one approach to lasting peace through education.

His mental roll-call brought up other faces. They had come from Poland, from Finland, from Czechoslovakia. Each of them had returned to inject what they had learned of America into their struggling democracies.

Satisfaction in the accomplishments of these world-scattered leaders whose opportunities had come through his foresight must have contrasted poignantly with his memories of his own frustrated political career; but, as he was well on the way to four-score years, ringing applause finally justified his unswerving faith in the return of his party to national leadership. The spontaneous acclaim that greeted Herbert Hoover on the platform of the Republican National Convention on July 8, 1952, should have erased the drabness of that silent ride down Pennsylvania Avenue on March 4, 1933, with F.D.R. Then, even though he had relinquished hope of leading his nation out of the depression, he had gone home to battle unceasingly against New Deal inroads on traditional Americanism.

Now, in 1952, his voice rang with new assurance. His recital of Republican achievements woke fresh admiration among those who were determined to win in the coming election.

He sat on the inaugural platform again on January 20, 1953. Once more the former President silently re-dedicated his life experience to the causes espoused by Dwight David Eisenhower, who had come, as Hoover had so long ago, from world service to lead the nation both idealized.

Seven months later, Hoover interrupted his annual summer relaxation in California to fly to Washington on summons from President Eisenhower. There was more work for him—a new opportunity to continue the task begun a quarter of a century before in his Secretary of Commerce years. Without hesitation he prepared to head a second Commission for the Reorganization of the Executive Branch of the Government.

On his seventy-ninth birthday in August, he commented that "unending public chores seem to have become my privilege in life." Then he entered his eightieth year intent upon making his main chore that of lessening the "staggering economic burdens" described by President Eisenhower.

By the latter part of August the membership of the Commission was complete. On September 29, Herbert Hoover presided at the first meeting. Among the twelve men seated around that conference table were four who had served on the earlier Commission, Joseph P. Kennedy, former Ambassador to Great Britain, Arthur S. Flemming, currently Director of the Office of Defense Mobilization, Senator John F. McClellan of Arkansas, and Representative Clarence M. Brown, House sponsor of legislation by which both commissions were established. Among the others was Sidney A. Mitchell, the New York banker who had been executive director of the first commission.

Their decision to follow the successful precedent of the 1947-1949 commission in dividing research among task forces brought acceptance from one-hundred and forty professional and businessmen and women. All were in responsible positions outside of government. To them, to quote Hoover, "government spending and taxes are no academic abstraction. They cause them acute grief."

The first Commission had removed "most of the road blocks against self-organization within the departments." The new group started with more freedom. Where limited authority handicapped the first effort, they now had free rein to inquire and to recommend, so long as the Judiciary and the Congress were not explored.

This time Congress strengthened the commission by granting the right to subpoena documents and persons, as well as by requiring that all recommendations be expressed in the form of draft bills. The cooperative spirit of the commission encouraged its chairman to place on the agenda controversial questions barred from the Truman assignment. They worked with determination to save billions of taxpayers' dollars without injury to the necessary functions of government.

During these demanding days of his eightieth year, Herbert Hoover rarely interrupted his work schedule. But he did break in long enough to come to the TV screen on a nation-wide hook-up when the Freedom Foundation presented him with a gold medal on the 248th anniversary of Benjamin Franklin's birth. Introduced as "the world's most outstanding citizen of 1954," this modern disciple of the wise and frugal Franklin praised the thrift and integrity that had motivated the early American. He stressed particularly that Franklin's principles and his habit of hard work are too often neglected by the security-conscious peoples of the twentieth century.

Citations and honors continued to attest that the voice from the wings was being heard on the world stage. Although ninety honorary university degrees were added to that hard-earned A.B. Stanford, '95, the aging Iowa farm boy really took his greatest pleasure in tabulating the number of public schools that bore his name across the land; there were forty-three in all.

As he entered his eighth decade, Clarence Buddington Kelland wrote: "By your courage in adversity and your modesty in triumph, you have erected in our hearts a monument more enduring than granite." This tribute, phrased in polished English, summed up the affectionate regard of those intimates who know the real Hoover. But the earthy words of a Negro laundress were equally descriptive.

"Herbert Hoover's got America in his bones," she remarked to her Virginia mistress.

In 1958, forty years after he had received the gold medal of the National Institute of Social Sciences, Herbert Hoover was awarded the same honor for the second time, making him the only person in the fifty-year history of that organization to be so recognized. In that same year the Rotary Club of New York presented their 1958 Citation to Herbert Clark Hoover in salute to his twenty years as chairman of the Boys Clubs of America, as well as numerous other contributions, saying in part, "not content with his own tremendous contribution to the national welfare, he has somehow found time to underwrite the future of America with a substantial group of enlightened leaders of tomorrow."

A few days after this presentation, Hoover was flying across the Atlantic again, to render still another high service to his country and to the world. On July 4, 1958, he crowned his eighty-fourth year by being spokesman for his country on United States Day at the Brussels World Fair. Where only eight years earlier he had sent his proxy to the C.R.B. reunion in that city, then part of a Europe suspicious of his negative attitude about sending troops overseas in a tense war-fearing era, this summer he was welcomed with all the acclaim King Albert could have wished when he pronounced Herbert Hoover "Friend of the Belgian People and Honorary Citizen of Belgium" in 1917.

From the flag-draped platform of the American pavilion, the voice of Herbert Hoover, its strength undiminished by his ordeal of major surgery only a few months before, rang across the air waves of the world. His was the privilege of refuting what he termed "the false legends, misrepresentations, and vicious propaganda which haunt the free world."

"Mine has been a long life," he said. "In that time, I have lived and worked among more than fifty nations. I have not visited them as a tourist; I have had some part in the lives of their peoples. And I can claim some understanding of their problems, their ideals and their aspirations . . . but today it is fitting that the representative of a particular nation should interpret here the ideals, the aspirations and the way of life of his own people. . . . Such discussion adds to this Exposition's panorama of mankind's progress. . . ."

With these words Herbert Hoover squared again the sturdy shoulders that had borne so much of the world's sorrow and care since as a six-year-old he lost his beloved father and five years later became an orphan. Today he was shouldering the concern of his countrymen, distressed because in a strangely fickle world, America was now being reviled and mocked as a "land of spies" by some of the very people he had persuaded his fellow citizens to succor.

"I would be proud if on this occasion I could contribute a mite to the better understanding of my people," he said, "and I would be especially happy if I could help the thinking of the on-coming youth in the world who are today groping as to the future."

July 5 was, by proclamation, "Hoover Day" in Belgium. Firmin von Bree presided at a reunion of the original Directors of the C.N. and the C.R.B., again meeting in the board room where the bust of Emile Francqui looked down on the nine remaining members of the comission he had helped to found.

Herbert Hoover, the man who for four decades had been a legend among the people who might have died except for him, was no longer a mere marble bust in their library at Louvain. He was a dynamic person sharing their pride in a re-vitalized Belgium, an independent, self-sustaining nation.

Undefeated American and world citizen, he was still speaking and believing the ideals learned in the Iowa schoolroom, tested and refined in the crucible of experience, and shining now in world acclaim.

But the acclaim that really mattered was satisfaction in the accomplishments of those nearest to him. He had watched his sons grow to constructive manhood, passing on their inherited ideals to still another generation, his grandchildren. He had seen Herbert, Jr. step into the international scene with his diplomatic approach to the Iranian oil strife, with the subsequent formation of the consortium to assure continued production under cooperative administration. He had heard this son take the oath of office as Under Secretary of State. Allan's career in handling vast mining interests had brought equal gratification, as the second son had prolonged the Hoover professional continuity.

"Herbert Hoover's boys" are not limited to those who bear his name. Secretaries and assistants during his many years on stage have played roles of importance in their own eras. To mention only a few, he could take pride in the scientific contribution of Vernon Kellogg, as head of the National Research Council; the political careers of Robert Taft, Republican Senate Leader and near-nominee for President, and of Christian Herter, Governor of Massachusetts, successor to Herbert Hoover, Jr., as Under Secretary of State and later Secretary after the death of John Foster Dulles. Others are Admiral Lewis Strauss, Chairman of the Atomic Energy Commission; Bill Mullendore, president and later chairman of the Board of Southern California Edison Company, one of the nation's large utility corporations, whose annual reports often had a Hoover flavor; also Perrin Galpin of the Belgian-American Educational Foundation; and many of his C.R.B. Rhodes Scholars including Emile Holman, honored heart surgeon; and Floyd Bryant, vice president of Standard Oil Company of California, and later, Assistant Secretary of Defense.

But in his last years it was, perhaps, the work directed by Maurice Pate in the nearby U.N. Secretariat Building that was among Herbert Hoover's deepest satisfactions. Reports of the expanding program of UNICEF reached the Waldorf Towers office with the regularity The Chief had always expected from any enterprise. He knew that citizens of the future in more than a hundred countries were receiving not only physical sustenance, but also proper education, vocational guidance, and needed social services because his younger associate was guiding their joint dream to maturity.

The underlying philosophy of "the father of UNICEF" seemed to shine through the quoted words of Maurice Pate in the conclusion of a Profile—"At the Heart of UNICEF"—published in *The New Yorker* for December 2, 1961, "I realize," said the Director, "that UNICEF has only begun its job. Today we are giving children a chance to grow up, to get enough to eat, to be healthy. . . My biggest hope is that the day will come when so many people everywhere will be gainfully employed that they themselves will be able to feed and protect their children and provide them with education. Then there will be no need for UNICEF."

The engineer-President could derive equal satisfaction in watching contributions to the national welfare of projects first blueprinted by him: Hoover Dam transforming the desert of the Southwest; the San Franisco Bay Bridge and New Jersey's Pulaski Skyway channeling increasing traffic on both sides of the continent; radio, and later TV, making communication instanteous because they operate over orderly air waves that he had originally assigned; well-regulated airplane routes providing transportation for millions of cross-continent travelers; the Central Valley Project serving the great farms of California; the St. Lawrence Waterway finally opening the mid-continent to interocean trade.

In 1960 he had seen the reins of Federal Government pass from the hands of his party again with the defeat by a narrow margin of Richard Nixon, a fellow Quaker. But this time he was consulted on matters of vital import by the youthful President, John F. Kennedy, son of one of his associates on the "Hoover Commissions." As the senior member of the experienced "Triumvirate," Hoover, Truman, and Eisenhower, he was now an appreciated advisor whenever President Kennedy paid a visit to the Waldorf Towers.

After Kennedy's assassination, Hoover had one more opportunity to alert his fellow Republicans to their duty to "assure the American people . . . that Republicans will not fail them in the protection of their liberties." His succinct statement read to the 1964 Republican Convention proved indeed to be his last. On October 20, 1964, two and a half months after his ninetieth birthday in August the life of the nation's most respected Elder Statesman ebbed away.

Memorial services in St. Bartholomew's Episcopal Church in New York, in the Stanford Memorial Church in California, and in the rotunda of the nation's Capitol preceded burial on a grassy knoll in West Branch, Iowa.

Late on that autumn afternoon the Hoover family and a few invited guests stood silently on the hilltop selected for the last resting place of the orphaned Quaker boy who had gone into all the world in the service of humanity. Slightly apart from this intimate group forty thousand Iowa farmers and their families had gathered. A multi-racial Honor Guard bore the flag-draped casket slowly to the open grave, where warm, freshly-turned earth waited to receive the body of the son of toiling pioneers.

The two Hoover sons, bowed with grief, stood bareheaded

in the afternoon sun as the words and melody of a hymn selected by their father floated on the breeze that tossed a field of tasselled corn nearby and kept a distant windmill whirring.

Then the incisive, measured words of David Elton Trueblood, former chaplain of Stanford University, fixed attention on the long constructive career of the man they were eulogizing today.

"This man *endured*," said Hoover's long-time Quaker friend —who interrupted a world cruise to be present in West Branch in answer to a cable. "He did not speak too much; but he *wrote* unceasingly with care and precision that the record should be left correct. . . Now, at last, these facts have crystallized in the public mind, letting us say farewell with universal gratitude for all he did for his country and for the world."

A bronze sun was setting in the red western sky. The last beautiful day in the Indian Summer of 1964 came to a close. A uniformed aide folded the silken flag and handed it to Herbert Hoover, Jr. For a moment utter stillness permeated the November air. Across the fields the windmill ceased to turn. Then the intimate group moved wordlessly to waiting cars. Behind them the Iowa neighbors formed a solemn procession, walking reverently past the casket that waited to be lowered into the grave.

Herbert Hoover's "unending public chores" were done. His image would remain forever clear above the white farm house in the village where once his six-year-old eyes had danced with the red sparks flying from his father's anvil. Now the forge had long been silent. The man who had struck that anvil with rhythmic strokes lay beneath the same sod that received his son.

APPENDIX

Extract from the List of the Public Positions and Distinctions Conferred on HERBERT HOOVER

As compiled by the Hoover Institution on War, Revolution and Peace and published as probably incomplete in 1957

OFFICIAL POSITIONS *in the* AMERICAN GOVERNMENT

1929-1933	President of the United States
1917	Chairman—Committee on Food Council of National Defense
1917-1920	The United States Food Administrator
1917-1919	Chairman—United States Grain Corporation
1917-1920	Member—United States War Trade Council
1918-1919	Chairman—United States Sugar Equalization Board
1918-1919	Member—The President's Committee of Economic Advisers at the Treaty Making in Paris
1918-1920	Director General—American Relief Administration (official organization)
1919-1920	Vice-Chairman—President Wilson's Second Industrial Conference
1921	Member—Advisory Committee, Limitation of Armaments Conference in Washington
1921-1922	Member—Cabinet Committee on Organization of the Executive Department
1921	Member—Federal Board for Vocational Education
1921	Member—Federal Narcotics Control Board
1921-1928	Secretary of Commerce
1921-1928	Chairman—Colorado River Commission
1922	Chairman—President's Conference on Unemployment
1922	Director—Relief of Russian Famine
1922-1925	Chairman—National Radio Conferences
1922-1926	Chairman—Annual Aviation Conferences
1922-1927	Member—World War Foreign Debt Commission
1923-1929	Member of Executive Committee—American National Red Cross. Honorary President 1929-1933
1923-1928	Chairman—Rio Grande River Commission
1924-1928	Member—Federal Oil Conservation Board
1924-1928	Chairman—Committee on Coordination of Rail and Water Facilities
1924-1928	Chairman—Annual National Conferences Street and Highway Safety

1924-1928 Chairman—St. Lawrence Waterway Commission

1926 Member—Cabinet Committee on Reorganization of Government Departments

1927 Chairman—International Radio-Telegraph Conference

1927 Director—Mississippi Flood Relief

1929 Honorary President—Pan-American Union

1929 Chairman—George Washington Bi-Centennial Celebration

1946-1947 Coordinator of Food Supply for World Famine of 1946-1947 for 39 Nations

1947 The President's Special Mission to Investigate the Economy of Germany and Austria

1947-1949 Chairman—Commission on Organization of the Executive Branch of the Government

1947 Member—Advisory Council, International Bank for Reconstruction and Development

1953-1955 Chairman—Commission on Organization of the Executive Branch of the Government

1954 Mission to Germany at Request of President Eisenhower and Chancellor Adenauer

AGENCIES FOUNDED BY MR. HOOVER FOR SERVICE TO CHILDREN

1914-1920 Canteen system of rehabilitation of 2,000,000 children in Belgium and Northern France

1919-1924 Canteen system of rehabilitation of 14,000,000 children in 20 countries of Central and Eastern Europe and Russia

1920-1935 Chairman of the American Child Health Association

1921-1940 Chairman of the American Children's Fund

1938 The White House Conference on Child Welfare

1946-1947 Canteen system of rehabilitation of 5,000,000 children in Germany

1946-1947 Jointly with others, established the United Nations International Children's Emergency Fund

OFFICIAL AND HONORARY POSITIONS IN CHILDREN'S SERVICE ASSOCIATIONS

1919-1922 Chairman—European Children's Fund

1920-1921 Chairman—European Relief Council (For Children)

1920-1924 Vice President—National Child Welfare Association

1921 President—American Child Hygiene Association

1921 Honorary Member—The Polish Society of the Red Cross

1922-1935 Chairman—American Child Health Association

1929-1933 Honorary President–Boy Scouts of America
1929 Honorary President–Camp Fire Girls
1931 Honorary President–Indiana Council Boy Scouts of America
1931 Honorary President–Boy Rangers of America
1936-19– Chairman–Boys' Clubs of America
1952 Honorary Membership–American Boys' Clubs Associates
1954 Honorary Director–Convalescent Home for Children, Des Moines, Iowa

SCHOOLS NAMED FOR MR. HOOVER

CALIFORNIA: Albany–Herbert Hoover Junior High School; Burlingame–Herbert Hoover School (elementary); Glendale–Herbert Hoover High School; Indio–Herbert Hoover School; Long Beach–Herbert Hoover Senior High School; Los Angeles–Hoover Street Elementary School; Merced City–Herbert Hoover Intermediate School; Oakland–Herbert Hoover Junior High School; Palo Alto–Herbert Hoover Elementary School; San Diego–Herbert Hoover Senior High School; San Francisco–Herbert Hoover School; San Jose–Herbert Hoover Junior High School; Santa Ana–Herbert Hoover Elementary School; Stockton–Herbert Hoover School; Westminster–Herbert Hoover Elementary School.

ILLINOIS: Calumet City–Hoover School.

IOWA: Cedar Rapids–Herbert C. Hoover Elementary School; Council Bluffs–Herbert Hoover Grade School; Iowa City–The Herbert Hoover School (elementary); Mason City–Herbert Hoover School (elementary); West Branch–The Hoover School.

MICHIGAN: Lincoln Park–Herbert Hoover School; Port Huron–Hoover Public School.

NEW JERSEY: Bergenfield–Herbert Hoover School; Ventnor City–Hoover School.

NEW YORK: Kenmore–Herbert Hoover School.

OKLAHOMA: Enid–Herbert Hoover School; Tulsa–Herbert Hoover Public School.

OREGON: Salem–Herbert Hoover School.

PENNSYLVANIA: Camp Hill–Herbert Hoover Elementary School.

WASHINGTON: Yakima–Hoover School.

WEST VIRGINIA: Upshur County–Hoover School.

WISCONSIN: Neenah–The Hoover Elementary School.

GERMANY: Berlin–Herbert Hoover Schule.

HONORARY CLUB MEMBERSHIPS

Alaska

Alaska Yukon Pioneers

California

Army and Navy Club, San Francisco
Bohemian Club, San Francisco
University Club, San Francisco
Family Club of San Francisco
Pacific Union Club, San Francisco
The Tuna Club, Santa Catalina Island
Union League Club, San Francisco
University Club, Los Angeles
California Club of Los Angeles
University Club, Palo Alto

Colorado

Denver Press Club

Florida

Key Largo Anglers Club
Key Fishing Club
Sailfish Club

Illinois

Chicago Club
Engineers Club
Executive Club of Chicago
Sportsman's Club of America
Union League Club
University Club
80 Club of Clay County

Maryland

Engineers Club of Baltimore

Massachusetts

Union League, Boston
University Club, Boston

New York City

Advertising Club
Anglers Club
Boys' Clubs Association
Brook Club
Burforcom Club
Circumnavigators Club
City Club
Explorers Club
Harvard Club
Lawyers Club
Links Club
Lotos Club
Madison Square Boys Club
Metropolitan Club
Mining Club
National Republican Club
Overseas Press Club
Players Club
Civic Societies
Sons of American Revolution,
Union League
University Club

Oklahoma

Engineers Club, Tulsa

Pennsylvania

Engineers Club, Philadelphia
Sons of American Revolution
Pennsylvania Society, Pittsburgh
Union League, Philadelphia
Larrys Creek Fish and Game Club, Williamsport

Texas

Headliners Club

Virginia

Fishing Club, Madison County,

Washington, D.C.

Army & Navy Club
Capitol Hill Club
Chevy Chase Club
Metropolitan Club
University Club
Columbia County Club
Congressional Country Club

Canada

Montreal Press Club

DEGREES FROM AMERICAN UNIVERSITIES

1895 STANFORD UNIVERSITY, California. A.B.
1916 BROWN UNIVERSITY, Rhode Island. Honorary LLD
1917 HARVARD UNIVERSITY, Massachusetts. Honorary LLD
1917 OBERLIN COLLEGE, OHIO. Honorary LLD
1917 UNIVERSITY OF PENNSYLVANIA. Honorary LLD (Honorary Juris Doctor 1940)
1917 PRINCETON UNIVERSITY, New Jersey. Honorary LLD
1917 WILLIAMS COLLEGE, Massachusetts. Honorary LLD
1918 UNIVERSITY OF ALABAMA. Honorary LLD
1918 YALE UNIVERSITY, Connecticut. Honorary LLD
1920 COLUMBIA UNIVERSITY, New York. Honorary LLD
1920 DARTMOUTH COLLEGE, New Hampshire. Honorary LLD
1920 GEORGE WASHINGTON UNIVERSITY, Washington, D. C. Honorary LLD
1920 JOHNS HOPKINS UNIVERSITY, Maryland. Honorary LLD
1920 RENSSELAER POLYTECHNIC INSTITUTE, New York. Honorary Doctor of Engineering
1920 RUTGERS UNIVERSITY, New Jersey. Honorary LLD
1920 SWARTHMORE COLLEGE, Pennsylvania. Honorary LLD
1920 TUFTS COLLEGE, Massachusetts. Honorary Doctor of Science
1925 PENN COLLEGE, Iowa. Honorary LLD
1926 GEORGETOWN UNIVERSITY, Washington, D.C. Honorary LLD
1927 CORNELL COLLEGE, Iowa. Honorary LLD
1927 WASHINGTON COLLEGE, Maryland. Honorary LLD
1928 SOUTHWESTERN UNIVERSITY, Tennessee. Honorary LLD
1931 GETTYSBURG COLLEGE, Pennsylvania. Honorary LLD
1931 WILLIAM AND MARY COLLEGE, Virginia. Honorary LLD
1931 UNIVERSITY OF PUERTO RICO. Honorary LLD
1935 UNIVERSITY OF CALIFORNIA. Honorary LLD
1935 COLORADO SCHOOL OF MINES. Honorary Doctor of Engineering
1935 DRAKE UNIVERSITY, Iowa. Honorary LLD
1937 COLBY COLLEGE, Maine. Honorary LLD
1939 EARLHAM COLLEGE, Indiana. Honorary LLD
1939 LINCOLN MEMORIAL UNIVERSITY, Tennessee. Doctor of Humanities
1939 STEVENS INSTITUTE OF TECHNOLOGY, New Jersey. Honorary Doctor of Engineering
1940 UNIVERSITY OF PENNSYLVANIA. (2nd Honorary Degree). Doctor of Civil Law
1941 HAVERFORD COLLEGE, Pennsylvania. Honorary LLD
1941 PACIFIC COLLEGE, Oregon. Honorary Doctor of Humanitarian Science

1945 CLARKSON COLLEGE OF TECHNOLOGY, New York. Honorary Doctor of Engineering

1947 NEW YORK UNIVERSITY. Honorary LLD

1948 COE COLLEGE, Iowa. Honorary Doctor of Humanities

1949 AMERICAN UNIVERSITY, Washington, D. C. Honorary LLD

1949 OHIO WESLEYAN UNIVERSITY. Honorary Doctor of Humanities

1953 UNIVERSITY OF NEVADA. Honorary LLD

1954 STATE UNIVERSITY OF IOWA. Honorary LLD

1956 CARNEGIE INSTITUTE OF TECHNOLOGY, Pennsylvania. Honorary LLD

DEGREES FROM FOREIGN UNIVERSITIES

1918 UNIVERSITY OF BRUSSELS (Belgium). Honorary Doctor of Applied Sciences

1919 UNIVERSITY OF GHENT (Belgium). Honorary Doctor of Philosophy

1919 UNIVERSITY OF LIÈGE (Belgium). Honorary Doctor of Universal Medicine

1919 OXFORD UNIVERSITY (England). Honorary Doctor of Civil Law

1919 VICTORIA UNIVERSITY OF MANCHESTER (England). Honorary Doctor of Laws

1919 YAGELLONIAN UNIVERSITY OF CRACOW (Poland). Honorary Doctor of General Medicine

1921 TECHNICAL UNIVERSITY OF PRAGUE (Czechoslovakia). Honorary Doctor of Technical Science

1921 UNIVERSITY OF WARSAW (Poland). Honorary Juris Doctor

1922 JOHAN CASIMIR UNIVERSITY, Lemberg (Poland). Honorary Doctor of General Medicine

1922 UNIVERSITY OF LWOW (Poland). Honorary Doctor of General Medicine

1922 KARL FRANZ UNIVERSITY IN GRAZ (Austria). Honorary Membership in University

1922 NATIONAL UNIVERSITY OF TYROL (Austria). Honorary Member of University

1923 CATHOLIC UNIVERSITY OF LOUVAIN (Belgium). Honorary Doctor of Political and Social Science

1925 CHRISTIAN ALBERT UNIVERSITY AT KIEL (Germany). Honorary Doctor of Political Statesmanship

1928 ARGENTINE SCHOOL OF MUSIC AND DECLAMATION (Argentina). Honorary Diploma

1928 UNIVERSITY OF CHILE (Chile). Honorary Member of Faculty of Engineers and Architects

1928 UNIVERSITY OF RIO DE JANEIRO (Brazil). Honorary Doctor

1929 BADEN TECHNICAL INSTITUTE AT KARLSRUHE (Germany). Honorary Doctor of Engineering

1930 UNIVERSITY OF BRUSSELS (Belgium). Honorary Doctor of the University

1933 LEOBEN UNIVERSITY OF MINING AND METALLURGY (Austria). Honorary Doctor of Mining and Metallurgical Science

1938 CHARLES UNIVERSITY (Czechoslovakia). Honorary PhD.

1938 UNIVERSITY OF HELSINKI (Finland). Honorary PhD.

1938 UNIVERSITY OF LILLE (France). Honorary Doctorate of the University

1938 VIENNA TECHNICAL INSTITUTE (Austria). Honorary Doctor of Technical Science

1946 UNIVERSITY OF CAPO D'ISTRIA, Athens (Greece). Honorary Doctor of Science

1949 WIRTSCHAFTS-HOCHSCHULE, Mannheim (Germany). Honorary Doctor Rerum Politicarum

1954 EBERHARD KARL UNIVERSITY OF TUEBINGEN (Germany). Honorary Doctorate of the University

Honorary Degrees tendered but due to public duties not able to comply with requirement of personal appearance

1917 UNIVERSITY OF VERMONT

1917 UNIVERSITY OF WISCONSIN

1919 COLGATE UNIVERSITY (New York)

1924 UNIVERSITY OF CINCINNATI (Ohio)

1924 KENYON COLLEGE (Ohio)

1925 UNIVERSITY OF MISSOURI

1927 HAMLINE UNIVERSITY (Minnesota)

1927 ROLLINS COLLEGE (Florida)

1930 BEREA COLLEGE (Kentucky)

1938 MILLS COLLEGE (California)

1939 ST. ANDREWS UNIVERSITY (Scotland)

1943 DICKINSON COLLEGE (Pennsylvania). Honorary LLD

1945 NORWICH UNIVERSITY (Vermont). Honorary LLD

1949 WAYNESBURG COLLEGE (Pennsylvania)

1949 BAYLOR UNIVERSITY (Texas)

1949 WASHINGTON UNIVERSITY (Missouri)

1953 EUREKA COLLEGE (Illinois)

1956 PENNSYLVANIA COLLEGE FOR WOMEN

1956 CARNEGIE INSTITUTE OF TECHNOLOGY (Pennsylvania)

1956 WESLEYAN UNIVERSITY (Connecticut)

INDEX

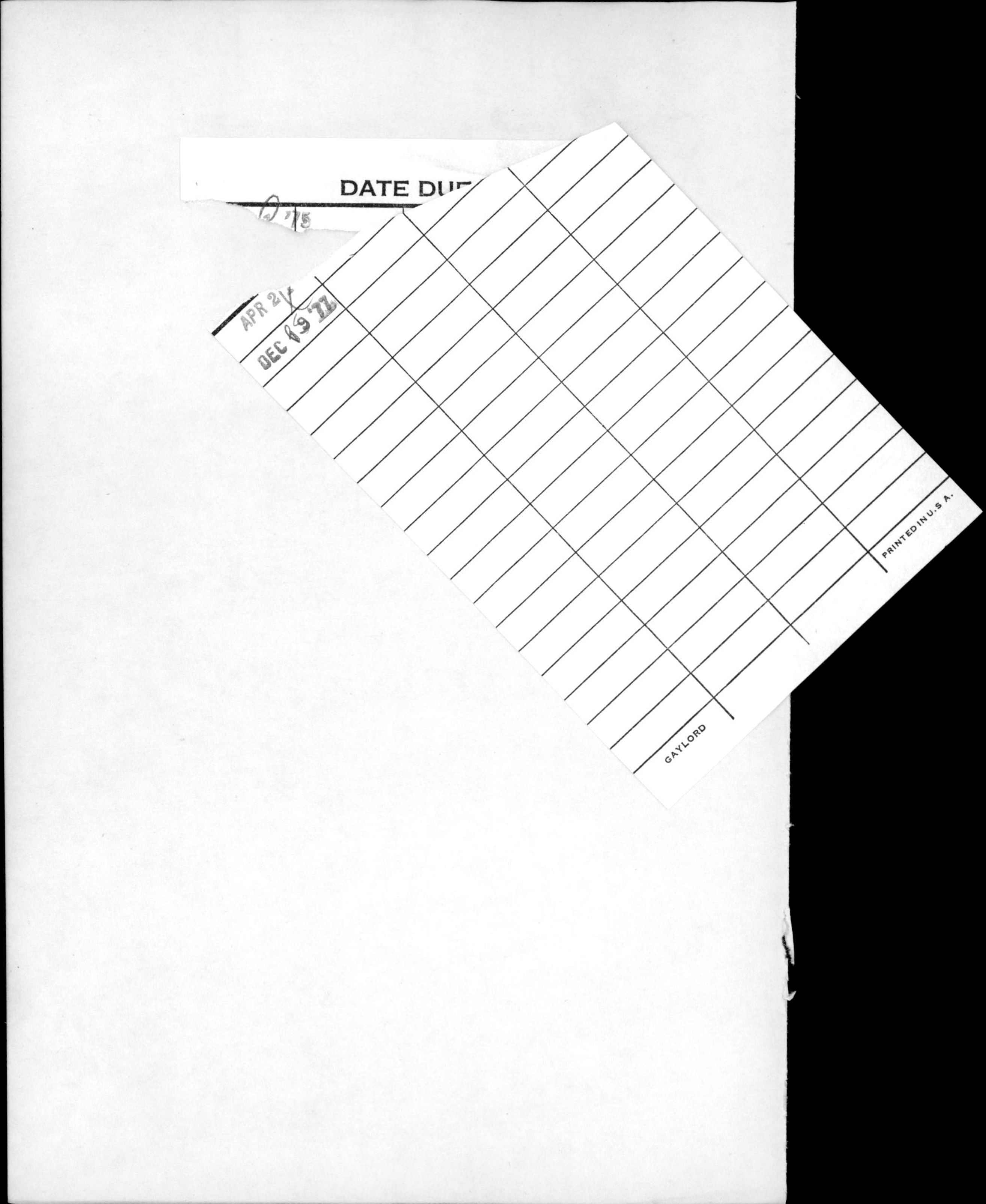

DATE DUE
APR 2
DEC 19 '77
GAYLORD
PRINTED IN U.S.A.